JOHN DEWEY AND
MORAL IMAGINATION

John Dewey and Moral Imagination

Pragmatism in Ethics

STEVEN FESMIRE

INDIANA
University Press

Bloomington & Indianapolis

Publication of this book is made possible in part with the assistance
of a Challenge Grant from the National Endowment for the
Humanities, a federal agency that supports research, education,
and public programming in the humanities.

This book is a publication of

Indiana University Press
601 North Morton Street
Bloomington, IN 47404-3797 USA

http://iupress.indiana.edu

Telephone orders   800-842-6796
Fax orders   812-855-7931
Orders by e-mail   iuporder@indiana.edu

The paper used in this publication meets the minimum requirements of
American National Standard for Information Sciences—Permanence of
Paper for Printed Library Materials, ANSI Z39.48-1984.

MANUFACTURED IN THE UNITED STATES OF AMERICA

Library of Congress Cataloging-in-Publication Data

Fesmire, Steven, date
John Dewey and moral imagination : pragmatism in ethics /
Steven Fesmire.
p. cm.
Includes bibliographical references and index.
ISBN 0-253-34233-3 (alk. paper) — ISBN 0-253-21598-6 (pbk. :
alk. paper)
1. Ethics. 2. Pragmatism. 3. Imagination (Philosophy)
4. Dewey, John, 1859–1952. I. Title.
BJ1031.F47 2003
171'.2—dc21
2002156520

1 2 3 4 5 08 07 06 05 04 03

For Heather

CONTENTS

ACKNOWLEDGMENTS

This book has been a long while in the making. Thomas Alexander (Southern Illinois University at Carbondale) and Mark Johnson (University of Oregon) inspired this project over a decade ago during my graduate education. I am profoundly grateful for their longstanding support, encouragement, and friendship.

I thank reviewers for Indiana University Press, particularly Douglas Browning (University of Texas-Austin), for irreplaceable assistance with both form and content. The project benefited substantially from the editorial attentiveness of Dee Mortensen, as well as the copyediting of Carol Kennedy.

Many of these ideas were initially presented at meetings of the Society for the Advancement of American Philosophy. Along with the annual Summer Institute in American Philosophy, SAAP continues to be a source for my rejuvenation. I am grateful to all members of the Society. Some who have assisted in one way or another with portions of this book include Charlene Haddock Seigfried, Vincent Colapietro, Larry Hickman, Michael Eldridge, John McDermott, Peter Hare, John Lachs, Gregory Pappas, Micah Hester, Casey Haskins, Lewis Hahn, Mary Magada-Ward, Todd Lekan, David Seiple, Joe Betz, Herman Saatkamp, Andrew Light, Erin McKenna, Shannon Sullivan, Phillip McReynolds, John Shook, and Randall Auxier. I am also grateful to the late Ralph Sleeper for his encouragement of my early work on James.

Much of Part II of this book was drafted during my year as a Visiting Scholar at Dartmouth College. I am especially grateful to James Moor and Bernard Gert for their generosity, and to the staff of Baker Library for their skilled assistance chasing down articles.

Many students and colleagues have been instrumental in honing this manuscript. I benefited enormously from the critical feedback and support of Ray Boisvert and Paul Santilli of Siena College, and I extend my thanks to Richard Gaffney, Jennifer McErlean, John Burkey, and Silvia Benso for their collegial support. Hugh Lafollette and John Hardwig offered helpful critiques of earlier incarnations of some chapters during my time at East Tennessee State University, where I also benefited from interactions with John Zavodny, Keith Green, Niall Shanks, Jeff Gold, Paul Tudico, Gail Stenstad, Jim Spence, and Marie Graves.

I extend my warm thanks to Ken Keith and Connie Keith for their friendship, inspiration, and assistance throughout this project. I am also very grateful to Ken Vos, Jon Jacobs, the late Lyle Eddy, the staff of the Center for Dewey Studies, and my parents Wayne Fesmire and Jayne Fesmire. For putting me on the scent of wisdom, I thank Rusty McIntire, Michael Mitias, Steven Smith, and Ted Ammon.

I am grateful to William Throop, Rebecca Purdom, Meriel Brooks, Philip Ackerman-Leist, Michael Blust, and many others for the growing friendships and intellectual vitality I have found in my new position at Green Mountain College. As poet David Budbill says of Vermont: "[T]here is solitude here and quiet, a kind of modesty in the landscape, an unassuming grandeur."

From Heather Keith I have learned what it means, both practically and theoretically, to identify my own good with that of another who reciprocates. I dedicate this book to her, my dearest friend and companion.

I also gratefully acknowledge permission to reprint, in substantially revised form, material from the following articles:

"Ecological Humanism: A Moral Image for Our Emotive Culture," *The Humanist* 61, no. 1 (2001): 27–30.
"Philosophy Disrobed: Lakoff and Johnson's Call for Empirically Responsible Philosophy," *The Journal of Speculative Philosophy* 14, no. 4 (2000): 300–305.
"Morality as Art: Dewey, Metaphor, and Moral Imagination," *Transactions of the Charles S. Peirce Society* 35, no. 3 (1999): 527–550.
"The Art of Moral Imagination," in *Dewey Reconfigured: Essays on Deweyan Pragmatism,* ed. Casey Haskins and David Seiple (Albany: SUNY Press, 1999), 133–150.
"Remaking the Modern Mind," *Southwest Philosophy Review* 14, no. 2 (1998): 65–81.
"The Social Basis of Character," in *Ethics in Practice,* ed. Hugh Lafollette (Oxford: Blackwell Press, 1997), 282–292.
"Dramatic Rehearsal and the Moral Artist: A Deweyan Theory of Moral Understanding," *Transactions of the Charles S. Peirce Society* 31, no. 3 (1995): 568–597.

ABBREVIATIONS

Citations of John Dewey's works are to the thirty-seven-volume critical edition published by Southern Illinois University Press under the editorship of Jo Ann Boydston. Citations give text abbreviation, series abbreviation, followed by volume number and page number.

SERIES ABBREVIATIONS FOR *THE COLLECTED WORKS*

EW   The Early Works (1882–1898)
MW   The Middle Works (1899–1924)
LW   The Later Works (1925–1953)

ABBREVIATIONS FOR SELECTED TEXTS

1908 E   *Ethics,* 1978 (1908), MW 5
DE   *Democracy and Education,* 1980 (1916), MW 9
EEL   Introduction to *Essays in Experimental Logic,* 1985 (1916), MW 10
RP   *Reconstruction in Philosophy,* 1982 (1920), MW 12
HNC   *Human Nature and Conduct,* 1983 (1922), MW 14
EN   *Experience and Nature,* 1981 (1925), LW 1
PP   *The Public and Its Problems,* 1984 (1927), LW 2
QC   *The Quest for Certainty,* 1984 (1929), LW 4
ION   *Individualism, Old and New,* 1984 (1929), LW 5
QT   "Qualitative Thought," 1984 (1930), LW 5
TIF   "Three Independent Factors in Morals," 1984 (1930), LW 5
1932 E   *Ethics,* 1985 (1932), LW 7
HWT   *How We Think,* 1986 (1933), LW 8
ACF   *A Common Faith,* 1986 (1933), LW 9
AE   *Art as Experience,* 1987 (1934), LW 10
LSA   *Liberalism and Social Action,* 1987 (1935), LW 11
LTI   *Logic: The Theory of Inquiry,* 1986 (1938), LW 12
EE   *Experience and Education,* 1988 (1938), LW 13
TV   *Theory of Valuation,* 1988 (1939), LW 13
FC   *Freedom and Culture,* 1988 (1939), LW 13
KK   *Knowing and the Known,* 1989 (1949), LW 16

Citations of William James's works are to the critical edition published by Harvard University Press under the editorship of Frederick H. Burkhardt, Fredson Bowers, and Ignas K. Skrupskelis. Harvard citations are followed by a page reference to a more widely accessible edition where this seemed helpful (the two-volume Dover edition of The Principles of Psychology, *the Hackett edition of* Pragmatism, *and John McDermott's* The Writings of William James *for the essays).*

SELECTED ABBREVIATIONS
AND DATES OF PUBLICATION FOR
THE WORKS OF WILLIAM JAMES

PP   *The Principles of Psychology,* 3 vols., 1981 (1890)
MPML   "The Moral Philosopher and the Moral Life" (1891)
SR   "The Sentiment of Rationality," 1979 (1897)
WB   "The Will to Believe," 1979 (1897)
VRE   *The Varieties of Religious Experience,* 1985 (1902)
PM   *Pragmatism,* 1975 (1907)
MT   *The Meaning of Truth,* 1975 (1909)
PU   *A Pluralistic Universe,* 1977 (1909)
ERE   *Essays in Radical Empiricism,* 1976 (1912)

JOHN DEWEY AND
MORAL IMAGINATION

Introduction: Revitalizing Ethics

The academic philosophers of ethics, had they possessed
virility enough to enter the field of real life, would have
realized . . . that the slavery to rigid formulas which they
preached was the death of all high moral responsibility. . . .
A clear-sighted eye, a many-sided sympathy, a fine daring,
an endless patience, are for ever necessary to all good
living. With such qualities alone may the artist in
life reach success; without them even the most
devoted slave to formulas can only meet disaster.

—Havelock Ellis, *The Dance of Life*

MORAL IMAGINATION
AND CLASSICAL AMERICAN PRAGMATISM

Debates about moral conduct remain at an impasse. Is it rule-governed or arbitrary, objective or subjective? Responding to this deadlock, numerous moral philosophers in the past two decades have rejected the Janus faces of absolutism and relativism and challenged the Enlightenment foundations of mainstream twentieth-century moral theory.[1] This has heightened attention to the ways human beings actually make sense of tangled circumstances and compose meaningful lives. As a result, we are witnessing an all too gradual shift in focus away from tedious polemics about ultimate moral criteria. Martha Nussbaum's reintroduction of Aristotelian practical wisdom, Alasdair MacIntyre's emphasis on narrative and character, Nel Noddings's highlighting of feminine caring, Bernard Williams's recognition of the role of moral luck, Charles Taylor's appreciation of the diversity of goods, Owen Flanagan's call for psychological realism, and Mark Johnson's studies of imagination and metaphor are good examples of this shift.[2]

But most of these theorists have ignored the highly articulated and distinctive American philosophical tradition. Classical American pragmatism, especially as developed by John Dewey, provides a rich yet still misunderstood and underappreciated framework for clarifying and extending achievements of contemporary moral philosophy. A resurgence of interest in classical pragmatism during the past two decades has been pronounced in epistemology with comparatively scant attention to implications for ethical theory. A thoroughgoing revitalization of moral theory (deliberately used in this book interchangeably with "ethical theory") would profit immensely from looking back to Dewey's theory of moral understanding, an understanding that is social, imaginative, and artful in character.

Traditionally, moral *philosophy* has been conceived as a non-empirical discipline. It professes to ascertain how we ought to deliberate and act, or it investigates the "metaethical" status of substantive moral theories and beliefs. Meanwhile, the *psychology* of moral behavior has, with some notable exceptions, been taken by philosophers to be of little or no direct relevance to value inquiry. We require a purified rational matrix for moral deliberation, it is claimed, precisely because our psychological propensities are such a muddle. Thus moral philosophy's question "How *ought* I to live?" is severed from moral psychology's question "How *do* human beings actually make sense of their moral experience?" Inattention to this latter question has shielded psychologically unrealistic theories from appropriate scrutiny. One consequence has been to ignore moral imagination.

This is in large measure why most philosophers since Kant have overlooked the importance of moral imagination—that is, until recently. According to the *Philosopher's Index*, over sixty books and articles in philosophy touched on the subject in the 1990s, compared to six in the 1960s. I would like to contribute to this budding awareness that imagination plays a vital role in moral judgments, and in so doing offer new insights into Dewey's philosophy. Although David Hume's and Immanuel Kant's theories of imagination have been the focus of careful study, Dewey's rich insights on the subject remain largely untapped. Remedying this requires going beyond much current Dewey scholarship, where the importance of imagination is often acknowledged but seldom examined, blunting appreciation of his robust theory of intelligence as indirect exploratory action (see QC, LW 4:178).[3]

THE NEED FOR
A NEW CENTER OF GRAVITY IN ETHICS

Mainstream ethics has yet to be fundamentally transformed by this increased interest in imagination and psychological realism. Despite sharp differences, the dominant contemporary moral philosophies in the United States and Britain share a quest for an irrecusable principle or system of rules regulating human conduct. This can be seen in the two most prominent examples in philosophical literature: utilitarianism, which bids us to act so as to maximize aggregate happiness, and Kantianism, the principle of which is to act in a way that you can logically will to become law. Behind surface differences, there lies a shared strategy: pursuit of a bedrock principle. Even the moral skeptic shares the monistic assumption that this pursuit is the irreplaceable foundation of philosophical ethics. If no supreme principle or unitary concept is ultimately justifiable, ethics is swept into the dustbin.

One underappreciated tradition avoids this strategy, and that tradition animates this book. For classical American pragmatism, overarching principles developed by the traditional quest for a moral bottom line, or rules derived from these principles (or derived from some "impartial" test), are valued and evaluated not as candidates for a commensurable moral concept but as instruments for ameliorating moral life. In opposition to anarchists, nihilists, or moral skeptics, pragmatists see, or ought to see, a baby in the bathwater of traditional ethical theorizing: the practical value of principles and rules. On a pragmatic view, principles and rules *supplement* philosophical ethics; they do not constitute it. They ideally play an orienting and economizing role in everyday decisions, so they must be conserved in some form. For ethics to be revitalized, what needs to be challenged is the belief that principles, rules, and the systems they comprise must constitute the tethering center of either ethical theory or practice. This dogma can obstruct experience rather than ameliorating it, yet it is tenaciously held to define ethics itself.

Rejecting this dogma is the first step toward properly understanding and liberating principles so that they can do the work for which they are suited. Moreover, such a rejection would emancipate moral philosophy from (1) the idolatrous worship of systematized rules and (2) the misguided quest for a grand "one size fits all" theory. The former diverts attention from situational exigencies. The latter assumes that manifold factors of moral life—such as good consequences (utilitarianism), duties and obligations (Kantianism), rights (libertarianism and welfare ethics), or virtues (virtue ethics)—are set in a winner-take-all opposition to one another.

The project I undertake in this book is the recovery of philosophical ethics from its monochromatic view of moral life, especially its view of deliberation. Bowing out of the quest for univocal principles and systematic rules is a preliminary step toward developing rich, textured accounts of ethical inquiry. My aim is to contribute to a richer account of moral experience, inquiry, and judgment. By urging a shift in the center of gravity of ethics from foundational principles to imagination, I also hope to contribute in some way to a more ambitious end. If growing tendencies in moral philosophy reach their logical culmination, the result will be a Copernican revolution in ethics.

Part One develops a classical pragmatist conception of character, belief, inquiry, and intelligence. Part Two presupposes the "pragmatic turn" in Part One as preliminary to developing an innovative account of ethical inquiry that de-centers the production of closed systems. This account shifts the focus—or perhaps better, rejects the demand for a single focus—to moral imagination. Together, the two parts point to a more nuanced view of moral experience than can be accommodated by piecemeal adjustments to traditional ethical theories.

I build a case for three interrelated theses: (1) Moral character, belief, and reasoning are inherently social, embodied, and historically situated; (2) Moral deliberation is fundamentally imaginative and takes the form of a dramatic rehearsal; (3) Moral conduct is helpfully conceived on the model of aesthetic perception and artistic creation. Since the first two theses are coherently elaborated and persuasively defended by Dewey, and the third inspired by him, I use Dewey's work as a platform. However, the scope is necessarily more modest than a fully comprehensive exposition of Dewey's moral philosophy.[4] Although I hope the emphasis on imagination and art contributes to a more robust understanding of Dewey's ethics than is currently extant, I draw from Dewey to develop theses that stand or fall independent of him.

"The place for an accurate definition of a subject," Dewey proposes, "is at the end of an inquiry rather than at the beginning" (1932 E, LW 7:9). But to clarify usage, *moral* deliberation is broadly conceived here as considered evaluation of incompatible alternatives when the choice of conduct bears on what sort of character and world is developing. Imagination is moral insofar as it enters into such choice, thus "moral imagination" as used here is value-neutral. It is redemptive only when joined to rigorous reflection about ideals and ends. Like the aesthetic, moral (i.e., ethical) as a term of judgment must be distinguished from the moral as a sphere of experience.

Ethics as a philosophical discipline is typically categorized into four approaches: descriptive ethics (neutral descriptions of moral thinking and behavior), metaethics (analysis of the central concepts of ethics), normative ethics (formulation and justification of basic moral values), and applied ethics (application of normative ethics to specific areas of activity). These lines are often drawn too sharply, severing theory from practice and prescriptions from facts. Yet they may also be taken as a practical division of labor. So taken, this book may be understood as an essay in metaethics that relies on a redescription of moral experience. Chapters 6 and 7 build on this analysis to justify appropriate norms and models for conduct.

Successive chapters build the case for moral imagination from its basis in social interaction to its culmination in artful conduct. The first thesis—

that moral character, beliefs, and intelligence are inherently social and historical—is established in Part I. We grow into a social milieu shot through with complex, stable, and often conflicting customs. These "social habits" structure public communication, but they also organize our inmost thoughts so that moral discernment is primarily a socialized capacity. In Chapter 1, I resurrect James Farrell's Dewey-inspired *Studs Lonigan* novels of the 1930s to illuminate the social basis of character and conduct. Because it is crucial to distinguish between socialized acts automated by rote habit on one hand and acts of reflective morality mediated by intelligence on the other, questions arise about the nature of human reason. If reason is an acultural, individualistic, ahistorical, or anesthetic affair detached from everyday problems, reflective morality must be conceived in like fashion. In drawing his own distinction between custom and intelligence, Dewey replaces obsolete notions of perspective-free rationality with flexible, rule-sensitive situational inquiry. This is the most psychologically realistic and philosophically defensible move. But if pragmatist ethics is to appear a plausible alternative to mainstream perspectives, inherited notions of belief, reason, and truth must be reconstructed. Chapters 2 and 3 elaborate and defend classical pragmatism's redescription of these concepts.

The second thesis—that moral deliberation is fundamentally imaginative—is defended in Chapters 4 and 5. Beginning with an analysis and defense of pragmatist ethics, these chapters explore the nature and function of imagination as it plays a role in moral conduct. I give special attention to the renascence of interest in moral imagination, including empirical research on metaphor that bolsters Dewey's claim that ethical deliberation—indeed all reasoning—is fundamentally imaginative. Central to this account of moral imagination is Dewey's theory of dramatic rehearsal in deliberation, which can be grasped only from the standpoint of the organic unity of his philosophy.

The third thesis is developed in Chapters 6 and 7, in which imaginative rehearsal is conceived on the model of aesthetic perception and artistic creation. Moral imagination as a cluster of psychological capacities is inherently neither good nor bad. In these chapters I argue prescriptively for a Deweyan ideal of moral valuation and elaborate it through an image of "moral artistry." The philosophical challenge here is to respect the uniqueness of imagination, artistry, the aesthetic, and the moral, while also disclosing their relations to one another. I argue that everyday moral decisions can be as richly developed as artistic productions. If moral philosophers are to aid this development and clarify worthy ideals for moral education, they must focus beyond sedimented moral criteria to moral perceptiveness, creativity, expressiveness, and skill.

Part I

CHARACTER, BELIEF, AND INTELLIGENCE IN CLASSICAL PRAGMATISM

ONE

Habit and Character

Individuals will always be the centre and consummation of
experience, but what an individual actually *is* in his life-experience
depends upon the nature and movement of associated life.
—John Dewey, "What I Believe"

THE SOCIAL BASIS OF CHARACTER

Moral character is taken to have a basis in will. Will is widely conceived as a function of mind, an inner space that does not depend for its structure on physical or social systems. The mythical encapsulated individual, powerfully criticized in recent years by communitarian thinkers emphasizing sociality, is contained by but not organically unified with the world. On this view, moral character essentially belongs to a rational ego, mind, or soul stuffed in the sack of an animalic body. Diverse moral philosophies uncritically assume the truth of this, like the contractarian: Since other egos must be reckoned with and private property protected, he or she makes strategic sacrifices for a social contract to govern individuals who are so insulated that other-regarding standards do not inhere in their interactions. If this is true, character and social environment are not tied to each other any more than a jelly bean is to its jar.

The self-world relationship is typically conceived through the metaphor of an item in a container. As John McDermott observes: "Traditionally, we think of ourselves as 'in the world,' as a button is in a box, a marble in a hole, a coin in a pocket, a spoon in a drawer."[1] For example, in some Christian traditions, to "be in the world but not of it" is taken to mean lives are properly oriented toward a spiritual realm more weighty and real than mere earthly interactions. On this view, we ultimately have our being and value independent of where we temporarily happen to be sheltered. John Calvin took this to one logical extreme: "If Heaven is our country, what is the Earth but a place of exile?—and if the departure out of this world is an entrance into life, what is the world but a sepulcher, and what is residence in it but immersion in death?"[2]

More accurately, we are in, of, and about the world. Mind is not an ontological space under the jurisdiction of free will; no pure solution of mind or soul would remain as a distillate if residual factors of identity were separated out. Instead, mind is a complex function of the doings and undergoings of encultured, embodied, historically situated organisms, continuous with physical systems. What is called mind and will are functions of nature and culture, with culture generally uppermost in a discussion of moral character.[3] We grow into social organizations that share complex sets of stable habits. These customs may take the form of simple moral beliefs, such as that life begins at conception or that stealing is wrong, but they also encompass symbol systems and practices that enable us to envision an indefinite future together.

Dewey helpfully uses the term "habit" broadly to encompass not only private behavioral patterns but also heritable interpretive structures such as symbol systems, stories, beliefs, myths, metaphors, virtues, gestures, prejudices, and the like. He discusses this usage:

> We need a word to express that kind of human activity which is influenced by prior activity and in that sense acquired; which contains within itself a certain ordering or systematization of minor elements of action; which is projective, dynamic in quality, ready for overt manifestation; and which is operative in some subdued subordinate form even when not obviously dominating activity. (HNC, MW 14:31)

"Social habits" are evolving customs that set the stage for personal habituation. They are the main objects *and* tools of philosophic interpretation and criticism. Maurice Merleau-Ponty similarly speaks in *The Phenomenology of Perception* of our "stable organs and pre-established circuits."[4] This concept is deliberately imprecise, covering an almost infinite variety of heritable cultural or subcultural structures for configuring experience. It sweepingly encompasses linguistic syntax and usage; conventions of dress; regional religious attitudes; capitalist consumer habits manufactured by commercial images that link love, friendship, and community to material commodities; and other factors. Pre-established social circuits range in value from the apex of civilization down to what Mary Pipher, a psychologist writing about anorexic and bulimic adolescent girls dying from the cultural obsession with the "perfect figure," aptly calls "junk values of mass culture."[5] Sedimented social habits set the scene for sublime arts. They establish conditions for ethnic hatred and genocide, acts of terrorism and retribution. Through them potential meanings are revealed and in greater proportion concealed. Dewey seized upon the moral import of this: "The community . . . in which we, together with those not born, are enmeshed . . . is the matrix within which our ideal aspirations are born and bred. It is the source of the values that the moral imagination projects as directive criteria and as shaping purposes" (ACF, LW 9:56). His is a neutral, descriptive statement.

The true logical opposite of a social self is radical autonomy; the practical opposite is a corpse. But even if a human baby could be imagined to have its physiological needs met without "the organized skill and art of adults, it would not amount to anything. It would be mere sound and fury." The level of meaning attained by this miraculous survivor, whether qualitative or semiotic, would be minimal. In short, the meaning of activities is acquired through "interaction with a matured social medium" (HNC, MW 14:65).[6] Language, verbal or gestural, from public communication to our innermost private thoughts, is the principal vehicle of this social medium. George Herbert Mead explains, "[T]he mechanism of thought, insofar as thought uses symbols which are used in social intercourse, is but an inner conversation."[7] In sum, the particular human environment(s) on which we depend, with its language(s), traditions, and institutions, penetrates thoughts, beliefs, and desires; channels impulses; and funds our aims and satisfactions (AE, LW 10:274–275). In a multicultural setting, especially for those living on a hyphen between cultures, the "inner conversation" may be penetrated by clashing social habits. The resulting arts and intellectual probing are fresh and intense where conditions permit, but they are in no sense nonsocial productions.

"It is not an ethical 'ought' that conduct *should* be social," Dewey says. "It *is* social, whether bad or good" (HNC, MW 14:16). As children inherit speech and customs they simultaneously inherit beliefs and ideals, then take them to be inevitable and uncontroversial. Child or adult, many ideas and ideals just seem naturally right, beautiful, or true.

For example, virtuous and vicious habits like courage and cowardice, honesty and deceit, love and malice, tolerance and bigotry are products of interaction between an individual and the social world. Virtues are not radically private possessions or ethereal saintly attainments, and vices do not merely result from weak wills or sinful natures. Adherence to virtues such as generosity, compassion, and gratefulness and avoidance of vices such as mean-spiritedness are socialized by approval and disapproval, as indeed is the conviction that these are virtues and vices.[8] Absent intellectual habits of reflective morality of some sort, valuation goes no further. The observation is sobering. Habits of democratic openness and those of authoritarian inflexibility, for example, equally carry the sentiment of psychological certainty. A cultural bell rings through synaptic pathways to guarantee individuals that the course being pursued is just, or holy.

Moral character, then, is interwoven with one's cultural horizon, a set of "symbol systems, values, beliefs, and histories which define a community."[9] A cultivated individuality is paramount for value-rich lives and healthy communities. Cultural reconstruction is, after all, initiated by individuals. But the presuppositions, prejudices, and confusions of one's cultural inheritance set the inescapable context for value inquiries. This holds equally if one is reacting *against* constrictive political, religious, moral, scientific, and aesthetic "truths" of one's day.

The opposition central to ethics is not so much between reasonable and customary action; it is between routine customs that possess and control us and intelligent ones whose worth we consciously judge (HNC, MW 14:55).[10] Customs possess us, but we are largely unaware of them. Forgetting their social histories, people "can be provincial in time, as well as place," Alfred North Whitehead wisely remarked.[11] Although a sort of provincialism is existentially inescapable, we can mature beyond arbitrary choices and submissive moral education. This is accomplished by owning and appraising social habits. Moral maturation is an ongoing process in which customs are evaluated and reconstructed in light of circumstances rather than championed in blind conformity or dismissed in reactionary defiance. "The choice," Dewey urges, "is not between a moral authority outside custom and one within it. It is between adopting more or less intelligent and significant customs" (HNC, MW 14:58).

STUDS LONIGAN: A STORY OF HABITS

In the 1930s novelist James T. Farrell wrote the *Studs Lonigan* trilogy, in which he consciously explored Dewey's theory of habit in narrative form. It is the story of a failure to mature morally. If Farrell's name rings familiar to American philosophers, it is as the writer who accompanied Dewey to Mexico for the Trotsky commission, or as the novelist in Corliss Lamont's *Dialogue on John Dewey*. It is little known that Farrell, recognized in American literature circles as a leading figure in American Realism, owes his greatest intellectual debt to Dewey. In a 1965 interview, he reflected on this influence:

> When I read book after book of John Dewey in the fall of 1929 and in 1930, I was permanently influenced. . . . I was concerned with how to conceive character. . . . James [and] Dewey on habit . . . influenced me, and Mead and Dewey and the social conception of self. . . . The book that . . . had most effect upon me in the writing of *Studs Lonigan* was *Human Nature and Conduct*.[12]

Farrell traces the life of an actual acquaintance from his youth in Chicago's South Side, from the eve of World War I through the early years of the Great Depression.[13] He writes from the premise that social habits must be foremost in a treatment of moral character. Telling in story form what Dewey declares in prose, Farrell renders abstractions about habituation concrete. Limiting the scope to features that contribute to the project of re-centering ethics on imagination, Dewey's abstract claims about habit can be reduced to four: (1) Habits are functions of organic interaction with natural and social environments, and they form our characters. (2) They comprise a horizon of possibilities for moral deliberation. (3) They are plastic and need to be flexible. (4) Habit-change demands a change in environment.

Habits of Character as Interactive

Farrell's trilogy shows that the social environment does not irrevocably determine Studs Lonigan's impoverished experience, but it does establish the conditions for it. In *Young Lonigan,* Studs chooses a way of life; in *The Young Manhood of Studs Lonigan* those habits coagulate; in *Judgment Day* he meets with the consequences of his choices. He *becomes* the kind of person who cannot grow, which for Dewey illustrates the most poignant human tragedy.

At fifteen, Studs is included in a practical joke, asked to fill a pipe with horse manure. Edgar Branch, in his biography of Farrell, observes "Studs feels good because he is stamped as an equal; ironically, he attains brotherhood through a sadistic action. . . . Here we see some of Studs's deepest feelings—his longing to count, to be alive. But we also see those feelings, basically admirable, becoming attached to corrupt objects, the idealism becoming distorted."[14] In William James's words, Studs is choosing by slowly cumulative strokes the self he wishes to become, and to this extent he is morally culpable for the self he is becoming. "We are doomed to choose," the pluralist Isaiah Berlin lamented, "and every choice may entail an irreparable loss."[15] Although capacities for love and understanding are not alien to Studs's constitution, these potentialities are wasted for want of practice and social support, and his eventual ruin symbolizes this waste for Farrell.[16]

In Studs's impoverished social setting, his peer ideals are to be tough, and not brainy or "goofy." Meanwhile, his family and church teach him to hate what is unfamiliar. Eventually Studs and the fifty-eighth street gang are marked only by "stereotyped thoughts, inflexible habits, and a potential for growth choked off at the roots." Derogatory social stereotypes for "non-white" races and ethnic groups become, for Studs, substitutes for inquiry. Kikes, niggers, jiggs, Polacks, sheenies, hunkies, and chinks are the scapegoat causes of life's difficulties. Eventually, as Branch observes, "Studs cannot conceive a communal heaven on earth, except as 'shines' and 'kikes' might be put in their place to make the world safe for white men."[17]

Quite clearly the epidermis does not define the self. In simple physical interactions, air, food, and ground are incorporated into habits of breathing, eating, and walking through interaction with lungs, stomach, and legs (HNC, MW 14:15; EN, LW 1:19).[18] All habits incorporate within themselves part of the environing world. So much the worse for Studs.

To illustrate, consider our use of conventionalized metaphors, conceived as linguistic habits. They are no more subjectively constituted than habits of walking or driving. With a different environment and different types of bodies, different shared metaphors would emerge: If we did not eat, ideas would not be food to be digested, devoured, or swallowed. Without sight and touch, I could not see your point or grasp an idea. If we did not take journeys, relationships would not be rocky or hit dead ends, and life would not be uphill. No wars, no attacking or defending positions. Such linguistic habits are products of interaction between the makeup of an individual and objective elements of the natural and social world. Since interaction is bidirectional, habits are nonsensical if viewed from a perspective that puts excessive weight on either the mental or the extra-mental, the internal or the external.

This emphasis on environment should not be confused with the Watsonian behaviorist view that habits are results of mechanical and thus precisely controllable stimulus-response events. John B. Watson defined the goal of psychology as "the ascertaining of such data and laws that, given the stimulus, psychology can predict what the response will be; or, given the response it can specify the nature of the effective stimulus."[19] Thus Fraser, in B. F. Skinner's utopian novel *Walden Two,* is presented with Watsonian tendencies toward hard determinism: "Give me the specifications, and I'll give you the man."[20] Skinner's own work on "operant behavior," versus respondent or reflexive behavior, holds that Watson's "botanizing of reflexes" is an "impracticable program."[21] Skinner's foray into philosophy, *Beyond Freedom and Dignity,* tainted appreciation of his work in philosophical circles, but his outlook should be distinguished from the Watsonian view he placed in the mouth of Fraser.

Dewey had toppled such views long before in his pivotal 1896 article, "The Reflex Arc Concept in Psychology." In contrast with mere stimulus-response reflexes, habits are continually reconstituted through coordinated activities. Thus they cannot be modeled as "a series of jerks, the origin of each jerk to be sought outside the process of experience itself" in an external, unidirectional "environmental" pressure (EW 5:99).

Habits form characters, which Dewey defines along Aristotle's lines as "the interpenetration of habits" (HNC, MW 14:29). Character makes someone a certain *kind* of person who acts, thinks, or feels according to a more or less stable, foreseeable, historically developed pattern of behavior. Socrates was the kind of person who would not break the laws of the polis. Martin Luther was the kind of person who at the Diet of Worms could "do no other."[22] Studs Lonigan was the kind of person who would not, and eventually could not, grow. In each case, habits operated as active means, projecting themselves into subsequent actions. If habits did not have this stability, experience would be a discontinuous sequence of isolated acts and people would have no developmental potential. Conduct could not even be morally significant, since no act could be "judged as an expression of character" (1932 E, LW 7:170). What is to be sought, on Dewey's view, is stability of character without stasis.

Habits and Possibilities

Largely due to pre-established social channels, Studs and the gang become insensitive, undiscerning, and imperceptive. Their capacity for moral judgment is stultified. Wandering in a park in search of something to allay perpetual boredom, they happen upon a soapbox speech by a Catholic bishop explaining evil as a result of the fall of Adam. An atheist has just countered this dogma, and the boys rise in defense of the cleric:

> "It would be worth going to jail to punch in your filthy blaspheming mouth."
>
> . . . The atheist slunk off. Red said it was the only way to talk with fellows like that. They had no brains, were ignorant and filthy-minded, and you couldn't argue with them.[23]

They saunter away in search of further entertainment. Farrell juxtaposes what follows with the self-righteousness paraded in the previous scene:

> When they got tired of hanging around . . . with nothing to do, they got drunk on Jamaica ginger. Their drunken attention was caught by a passing Negro hot-tamale-man. They slugged him and took the wagon. Red wheeled it and they marched down the street towards the park. They each had a hot tamale and debated what to do with the rest. Red caught a passing shine. They tossed him into the fountain by the curve in the boathouse path. He struggled to get out of the slippery fountain, and was shoved back, and pelted as long as they had hot tamales. Studs passed out. He was carried home, and they left him to sleep all night on the back porch.[24]

Habits that form characters, tolerant or xenophobic, egalitarian or racist, operate so automatically and efficiently that they typically go unnoticed. This is why, as Charles S. Peirce points out, the habits we betray are often more important than those we parade.[25] In *The Call of Stories*, Robert Coles similarly notes "the sad commonplace that ideas or ideals, however erudite and valuable, are by no means synonymous with behavior, that high-sounding abstractions do not necessarily translate into decent or commendable conduct."[26]

Whether or not we are conscious of their operations, habits—chiefly social habits—organize a horizon of possibilities for action beyond which we see dimly if at all. And they fund what is misleadingly called an "intuitive" sense of probable outcomes. Dewey clarifies: "Immediate, seemingly instinctive, feeling of the direction and end of various lines of behavior is in reality the feeling of habits working below direct consciousness" (HNC, MW 14:26).

In his discussion of customary conjunction in causal inferences, David Hume recognized something of the central role of habit. "When I see a billiard-ball moving towards another, my mind is immediately carry'd by habit to the usual effect, and anticipates my sight by conceiving the second ball in motion."[27] However, writing before the rise of social sciences, Hume did not fully grasp how individuals, along with the sympathetic capacities he esteemed, are shaped through social habits. Rather, he reversed this and sought to understand the diverse institutions of social life in terms of a universal and unalterable human nature (see HNC, MW 14:228–230).

Habits are, for better or worse, the fundamental instruments of conduct. Even more than the hammer for carpentry or the utensils for eating, the habits of hammering and utensil-using are instrumental. More fundamental than the kiss, for expressing affection, is perceiving when and how and why to kiss. This depends on one's stock of social habits. Lacking the relevant habits and thus the relevant "intuitions," conduct misses the mark. The results may be tragic, as with Studs, though they are frequently comic, as President Jimmy Carter belatedly realized in the late 1970s upon greeting England's Queen Mother with a kiss!

Plasticity and Flexibility

Studs's social milieu militates against flexible situational intelligence. Two conflicting systems of inflexible ideals—the street culture of tough-guy masculinity and the culture of 1920s conservative Irish Catholicism—married with an impoverished moral imagination are his sole guides in life.

Studs is impressed with a fiery sermon by Father Shannon on the subject of those "cheap little half-baked, second-rate anti-Christs" in the universities:

> "Recently, I conducted a mission in another part of the city, and a Catholic girl came to me and said: 'Father, what am I going to do? I'm given books [spouting the sin that man came from a monkey] to read in my courses, and

if I don't read them, I'll be flunked.' I told her what to do. I told her to take the books back to her professor and say that Father said she should tell him this: 'I am a Catholic. I will not read these books and endanger my holy faith. They are full of half-truths, paradoxes, lies, and the men who wrote them are either ignorant, or else they are liars. You must put a stop to this sort of thing.' That is what every Catholic student in a godless university should do."[28]

In effect, Father Shannon rails against the mutability of custom in favor of "enslavement to old ruts" (HNC, MW 14:48). Though perhaps a carica-ture, Father Shannon typifies a passive life shaped by convention. This in-flexibility inhabits Studs so that he learns neither to recognize his own ig-norance nor to skeptically appraise competing beliefs and values.

"Habits are arts," Dewey explains (HNC, MW 14:15). Just as an artist's medium (canvas, brushes, pigments, marble, etc.) has definite features that the good artist must perceive and work with, so our social environment is recalcitrant yet not wholly intransigent. It kicks back yet does not utterly refuse to be transformed. We must adjust to and reconstruct this environ-ment if it is to support us. If it changes, habits must do likewise. This is one reason sets of moral laws are maladaptive. Their operation requires a static, block universe of the sort endorsed by Father Shannon. Legalistic morality cannot otherwise keep up with the pace. Plato observes this in the *States-man,* when the Stranger says to young Socrates:

> The differences of human personality, the variety of men's activities, and the restless inconstancy of all human affairs make it impossible for any art whatsoever to issue unqualified rules holding good on all questions at all times. . . . [Law] is like a self-willed, ignorant man who lets no one do any-thing but what he has ordered and forbids all subsequent questioning of his orders even if the situation has shown some marked improvement on the one for which he originally legislated. . . . It is impossible, then, for some-thing invariable and unqualified to deal satisfactorily with what is never uni-form and constant. (294ac)[29]

The disparity between habits and the flux of environing conditions makes experience problematic, especially since there is no certainty that outcomes will satisfy expectations. There are "tendencies" or "probabilities in the long run," but a virtuous disposition is no guarantee of a good outcome since chance can "carry an act one side of its usual effect" (HNC, MW 14:37).

Because any equilibrium is precarious and we cannot "keep even with the whole environment all at once" (MW 10:9), temporality must be cen-tral to an account of moral experience. As a necessary condition of growth, habits must be flexible, nuanced, and open to intelligent reconstruction.

Insofar as intractable habits dominate us, they devolve into mechanisms for blind routine.

This is why James and Dewey underscore the plasticity of habit. Plasticity, as James explains it, "means the possession of a structure weak enough to yield to an influence, but strong enough not to yield all at once" (PP, I, 105). It is something distinct from the extreme pliability of wax or putty, signifying for Dewey "the ability to learn from experience; the power to retain from one experience something which is of avail in coping with the difficulties of a later situation" (DE, MW 9:49).

Settled dispositions enable us to learn but may also imprison. Habits are neural paths of least resistance, no more trustworthy because familiar. This fact will be critical to Dewey's theory of moral imagination. James lectures revealingly, if overzealously, on the potential horrors of concretized habits: "We are spinning our own fates, good or evil, and never to be undone" (PP, I, 127). "Spinning our *own* fates" pinpoints the difference between Dewey's social and James's individualistic theory of habit. "Surely," James argues, "the individual, the person in the singular number, is the more fundamental phenomenon, and the social institution of whatever grade, is but secondary and ministerial."[30]

Social institutions, as in Farrell's unfriendly portrayal of the Catholic Church in 1920s Chicago, tend to turn a deaf ear to the need for intelligent reworking. Past designs that may be ill-suited to managing current problems are dominant models for molding—a metaphor Dewey loathed—the young. By a perverse irony this is done in the name of inculcating responsibility and self-discipline. The liberating side of plasticity is ignored: children and youths may be empowered to overhaul prevailing ways.

It must be conceded that the force of habit "is a stronger and deeper part of human nature than is desire for change" (LW 11:133–134).[31] But the mere fact that a bundle of habits made a life virtuous in a past time or place does not entail that anyone should imitate that life, even if it be the imitation of Buddha or Christ. The true leader is not followed. Wisdom all too quickly settles into platitudes. Virtues of yesteryear may be stumbling blocks of this unprecedented moment if we simply repeat our conditioning. In most cases people respond to situations without much thought, and sometimes this may even be for the best. But being satisfied with past designs merely because once upon a time they were effective, in one's own experience or in that of some revered authority, is a way of being careless about managing problems of the insistent present (HNC, MW 14:48–49).

Habit-Change and Environment

Orthodox moralists cringe at the thought of collapsing the cherished distinction between the changing world of prudential problem-solving, where habit is important, and an unchanging moral realm of free will, where worldly habits are irrelevant and transcendental rationality or supernatural (i.e., priestly or customary) authority reigns. Dewey's theory of habit accommodates and clarifies what is practically relevant in traditional conceptions of will and choice, but rejects the dubious notion of a mental power of free will. In this he concurs with the Buddhist belief in conditioned genesis (*Patikka samuppada*): "If the whole of existence is relative, conditioned and interdependent," Buddhist monk Walpola Rahula asks, "How can will alone be free? Will, like any other thought, is conditioned."[32]

Farrell presents the doctrine of free will as a presumption that environment is subordinate to inner resolve when it comes to human behavior and its modification. Father Shannon exclaims: "When you meet someone defending birth-control, this must be said in answer: 'Birth control solves nothing. It is not Birth-Control that we need but Self-Control!'"[33] This popular belief in self-control independent of an altered social environment is in large part responsible for Studs's downfall. One cannot, no matter how zealous or penitent, simply will a change of character without support from objective conditions. Dewey pointedly observes:

> No one is deceived so readily as a person under strong emotion. . . . Generous impulses are aroused; there is a vague anticipation, a burning hope, of a marvelous future. Old things are to pass speedily away and a new heavens and earth are to come into existence. But impulse burns itself up. Emotion cannot be kept at its full tide. Obstacles are encountered upon which action dashes itself into ineffectual spray. Or if it achieves, by luck, a transitory success, it is intoxicated and plumes itself on victory while it is on the road to sudden defeat. (HNC, MW 14:175–176)

Studs wants to be a better person, to counter tendencies that are sapping his strength and killing friends. But the Church, the only belief system that competes with the culture of the South Side streets, presupposes that a powerful and generous resolve to sin no more will illuminate and propel one along a path of righteousness.

After escaping during a police raid on a "can house" the previous night, a twenty-year-old Studs repents at Christmas Mass: "Studs muttered the words of the Act of Contrition over and over again. He wished last night undone, like he had almost never wished for anything. He was lonesome, and contrite, and adoring."[34] Nevertheless, two years pass, and Studs's health continues unabated to decline from prohibition rot-gut gin, cigarettes, and unprotected sex. He has abundant good intentions on his road to a terrestrial hell. The death of a friend gives him pause:

He tossed aside the cigarette he was smoking. He thought of himself being cut off early. He slowly calmed his fears, because he was sure that it was not too late for him to start taking care of his health.

And he was going to stick to his determinations, fight not to break them. By God, he wouldn't! He shot his butt, realizing that he had determined to cut out smoking. Well, it hadn't been breaking his intentions, because he hadn't realized that he was smoking. He felt that he had will power, and will power was the main asset needed in every walk of life. He knew he was different from all the mopes in the poolroom, he was going to do different things and be more than they. It had made him learn his lesson in time, before he ruined himself like poor Paulie Haggerty had done.

[Red] came out of the poolroom [and] asked Studs about doing something. Studs shook his head, and felt superior to Red. It was the first exercise of his new will power.[35]

Studs predictably does not live happily ever after. Good intentions require support of altered circumstances, or reactive habits prevail. Studs modifies conditions a bit, exercising at a gym, going home earlier, hanging around the poolroom less. He meets with transitory success. For a while he is simply lucky. What he takes to be a sign of will power is mainly the absence of challenging circumstances, which inevitably present themselves. At a church event, Studs rallies to ask a woman to dance:

He ambled slowly towards her. With a forced effort of courage, he asked her if she'd like to dance. She thanked him but said that she was very tired. He walked away, sore. He tried to whistle.

After the dance, he thought that if he had danced with her, they would have talked, told their names, and he would have walked home with her.

It was all a goddamn pipe-dream. He was just filling himself full of the stuff.

"Jesus Christ, here comes the Fifty-eight Street Alky Squad," he said with a laugh as he met [the gang] at the corner of Fifty-eighth and Indiana. "We need another recruit," Slug said.

Studs chipped in with them. They bought paregoric in the drug store and drank it. They formed a drugged and stupefied line against the side of the drug store building. Studs was so helpless that Red Kelly had to take him home.[36]

He again vows to do better, but the pattern continues. This is partly fallout from his socialized conviction that he could simply will a change of habit. After staying in a "state of grace" for a few days, Studs and Red take communion and devote themselves afresh to their faith. That evening:

On Sunday evening, the boys gathered around the corner. Slug suggested a drink. They refused. They hung around, gassing, and smoking, looking at the drug store clock, wondering what the hell to do. Again they refused to drink with Slug. They hung around. Slug kept insisting that one beer wouldn't hurt them. They went down the street to Colisky's saloon and had a beer. They had another. Before they realized it, they were drinking gin. They got drunk and raised hell around the corner. They hung around until Slug talked them into going to a new can house. . . . They went and had the girlies, and gypped them out of their pay. It was a big night.[37]

Just as gestating organisms must be nourished to survive, a nurturing natural and social environment is required for human well-being. If substances are nutritious and not toxic, a healthy transaction can ensue. In a virulent environment, people become, in John McDermott's words, spiritually anorexic, starved of relations.[38] Left unaltered, it can be about as easy to avoid starvation or poisoning, physical or moral, as it is for a crack baby to avoid her mother's toxins.

Classical tragedies are of course characterized by a protagonist with some fatal character defect: Hamlet is indecisive, Lear is naïve, and so on. Many tragic flaws beset Studs: tough-guy ideals, unreflectiveness, racism and sexism, xenophobia and anti-Semitism, incapacity to empathize with others, his more general inability to grow. But the central and most fatal flaw of Farrell's protagonist is epic and universal: He was a live creature of habit and impulse interacting with a morally impoverished social world.

After a riotous New Year's Eve party in his late twenties, Studs contracts pneumonia and a sickliness from which he never recovers. Farrell offers a snapshot:

There was a drunken figure, huddled by the curb near the fireplug at Fifty-eighth and Prairie. . . . It was a young man with a broad face, the eyes puffed black, the nose swollen and bent . . . the suit and coat were bloody, dirty, odorous with vomit.

It was Studs Lonigan, who had once, as a boy, stood before Charley Bathcellar's poolroom thinking that some day, he would grow up to be strong, and tough, and the real stuff.[39]

Habits are coordinated with environing conditions, so they cannot magically be changed simply by will or coercion. Direct mental action cannot operate for an extended period in opposition to a habit any more than ordering a fire to stop burning will make it go out (HNC, MW 14:24–25). Dewey draws a favorite example from F. Matthias Alexander, developer of the "Alexander Technique": Try to change a habit of posture simply by willing it, and you discover the necessity for transformations reaching deep into somatic experience.[40]

This underscores the futility of puritanical condemnation and intimidation. Mead observes that self-righteously calling a prostitute a sinner does not alter the social conditions that give rise to her trade. We must "change the social conditions which have made her possible instead of merely scourging an abstract sin."[41] And we are inextricably part of these conditions. This helps to frame familiar insights in contemporary progressive political thought: "Getting tough on crime" by building more prisons to separate the "criminal element" from the morally pure diverts attention from the social and material conditions that give rise to crime; battling drugs with slogans such as "Just Say No" edifies shallow philanthropic sentiment without curbing the social problem of drug addiction; and so on. Geoffrey Canada, president of the Rheedlen Centers for Children and Families in New York City, similarly satirizes approaches to urban violence that fail to comprehend that violence is learned as a response to complex conditions:

> From this point of view, the cure for the current crisis is to get tough on crime—meaning more mandatory sentencing, longer jail terms, more arrests. It is assumed that this way the criminals will get the message, that in the criminal underworld the discussion will go like this: "You know Chuck? —he got caught robbing an old lady and got thirty years. And Charles, he got caught breaking into a house and they gave him twenty years. He'll be an old man when he gets out. They're catching everyone and giving them big time. I'm gonna stop robbing. I'm gonna put my gun up and start looking for work tomorrow. Crime just doesn't pay anymore!"[42]

NATURE AND CULTURE

Since Edward O. Wilson's controversial *Sociobiology* in 1975, genetics has held center stage of the nature-nurture debate. Genetic factors undeniably play a predisposing role in conduct far more powerful than Dewey could have envisaged in the first half of the twentieth century. There are, in novelist Barbara Kingsolver's words, "permanent rocks in the stream we're obliged to navigate." But since genes do not code for single functions, their role is not determinative. The fact that we must own up to our genetic inheritance does not mean people are born saints or sinners, contemporary sociobiology's equivalent of the Adamic myth. As with Studs Lonigan, habits of character take their distinctive forms through sociocultural interactions. They are not radically isolated attainments, on one hand, or strictly hardwired evolutionary products, on the other.

When Dewey was developing his theory of character in the 1920s and 1930s, raw instincts and drives, not genes, played the lead role representing nature. He presents his mature view in *Freedom and Culture:*

> It is at least as true that the state of culture determines the order and arrangement of native tendencies as that human nature produces any particular set or system of social phenomena so as to obtain satisfaction for itself. . . . These statements do not signify that biological heredity and native individual differences are of no importance. They signify that as they operate within a given social form, they are shaped and take effect *within* that particular form. (FC, LW 13:75–77)

Dewey's goal was to break down the barriers that separate nature from culture, to show that biological drives are transmuted by social life, that neither impulse nor culture simply trumps the other, and that culture lends itself as much to intelligent conservation and critical redirection as to transmission. There are deeply embedded prejudices against this sort of meliorism that must be briefly examined. From social contract theory such as that of Hobbes, Locke, and Rousseau to the reductionism of Freud, civilization has been thought to threaten individuality. There is, the story goes, something frighteningly unnatural about civilized life, something stifling and repressive to our raw, animal natures. We are, Nietzsche says, "forcibly confined to the oppressive narrowness and punctiliousness of custom."[43] This parallels claims made more recently by some sociobiologists, such as that fidelity contradicts male genetic programming to the degree that social expectations of loyalty are repressive to their natures.

It is a painful truth that much of "civilized" life is stifling. Of philosophical moment is the degree to which this is remediable. The deeper ethical truth Nietzsche points to is that superempirical claims of duty, such as Kant's, are unnatural and repressive. Taken pragmatically, duty is not an imposition of transcendental reason that constrains us come what may, nor is moral conduct necessarily unnatural and artificial. The truth in Kant's distinction between desire and duty is that a desire for sex, for revenge, for eating a veal cutlet may become almost uncontrollably inflamed when we dwell on its pleasures, but the dynamic power of desires is irrelevant to reflective judgment of their suitability as moral ends (see 1932 E, LW 7:194–195). However, parting with Kant, to judge the end unsuitable is to respond to demands of social interaction, not to obey the immutable dictates of universal reason.

Parting at the same time with Nietzsche and some sociobiologists, this is not simply civilized life irremediably oppressing animal nature. What Nietzsche misses in the *Genealogy of Morals,* a book he later criticized as too reductionistic, is that the desires at issue are already socially mediated products. Desires are always cooked, not raw like basic biological drives. Drives, despite sociobiology's credo, are so amorphous that redirection down alternative channels is generally possible without narrowing fulfillment. Of course stifling customs often block intelligent investigation of alternatives and limit fulfillments possible under other conditions. But this must be distinguished from the claim that oppression of native drives is universally engraved in the very nature of social existence. In sum, an unsatisfiable desire is not equivalent to an unfulfilled primal impulse. Conflating the two magnifies desires and belittles primal biological impulses.

The process by which a desire is judged unworthy of pursuing is distorted when it is conceived as custom defeating nature, superego subduing id, or reason reigning in appetite. This demeans both the capacity for judgment and the power and promise of organic impulses. Clearly moral judgments, along with the ideals, duties, and virtues that aid them at their best, are not primal constituents of human nature on a par with appetite for food and drink, sexual drives, or the like. But this does not imply that moral judgments are "unnatural" or that they shackle native impulses. Regardless of how we catalog their numbers (e.g., Are people biologically driven to want children, or is this a socialized desire?), primal tendencies are amorphous until canalized into definite desires. Just how they are socially channeled and fulfilled—as they demand to be—is almost infinitely variable, as witnessed by anthropology. Because of this variability, moral life has to do with intelligently transforming social arrangements, perceiving relationships, and envisioning alternative courses of action, not artificially reigning in a brute human nature.[44]

Non-pragmatic thinking about human nature and character runs deep. We have biological tendencies that, like genetic makeup, are temporally prior to organized individual behavior. What is less widely understood is that they are not the primary determinants of customs or conduct, although basic forces preceding forms of social organization are often treated as skeleton keys to explaining character and conduct. A tendency toward rivalry or even aggressiveness may, for instance, be part of our shared primate inheritance, but, as James urges in "The Moral Equivalent of War," this would not entail the inevitability of class systems or wars as the sole possible cultural configurations of these impulses.

In other examples, Freud, who agreed with James about diverting aggressive tendencies, nonetheless argues in *Totem and Taboo* and *Civilization and its Discontents* that civilization emanates from the Oedipal complex. And Nietzsche at times explains the growth of civilization, individuals, and even the growth of Nature itself in terms of the will-to-power.[45] More generally, it is a mistake, Dewey insists, "to make some one constituent of human nature *the* source of motivation of action; or at least to reduce all conduct to the action of a small number of alleged native 'forces'" (FC, LW 13:74). Marx's impulsion for economic security and Michel Foucault's concept of power are related examples of such reductionism.

Dewey scholarship is not immune to reading acquired social habits as artifacts of native impulses or fixed human nature. A recent example is James Gouinlock's *Rediscovering the Moral Life.* His account of character and conduct is representative of contemporary political conservatism, and it serves to set off Dewey's account.

Gouinlock echoes Dewey's paean that philosophers must turn away from manufactured pseudo-problems and toward pressing lessons and potentialities of mortal existence. The result is an engaging reading of contemporary moral philosophy. Yet in describing moral experience, he treats social phenomena, such as patriarchy, as manifestations of a relatively fixed human nature. In this, he follows the trend begun by Wilson. For example, he favorably cites *The Bell Curve* authors Richard Herrnstein and Charles Murray without reference to their critics, such as Leon J. Kamin and Stephen Jay Gould, who observed that the work repeatedly confuses correlation with causation. Murray purportedly shows that welfare cultivates irresponsibility because it is designed to "rescue individuals from the consequences of their acts." Thomas Fleming shows that a real family is a traditional nuclear family. Michael Levin offers "substantial scientific evidence" about "innate gender or racial [intellectual] differences." Steven Goldberg supports the plausibility "that male dominance is both universal and inevitable" so that laws demanding equality of representation are lamentable.[46]

Gouinlock opposes welfare programs because they reward rather than punish people for not working, so people learn not to work. This presupposes that human behavior is motivated primarily through expectation of reward or fear of punishment, the stick and carrot. Welfare programs, on his view, block the road to responsibility by "excusing weak behavior" and "rewarding the most self-defeating conduct."[47] Philosophic difficulties aside, these psychological assumptions are problematic. Far from cultivating self-reliance and self-discipline, punitive enforcement of strict rules tends to make children dependent on external control.[48] Moreover, it is a commonplace in psychology that punishment is like cutting off a hydra's head; worse forms of behavior tend to replace the previous one, calling forth increasingly painful punitive measures.[49]

Coupled with this is Gouinlock's belief in an innate and inviolable Lockean demand for individual desert. With Melvin Lerner he claims that "the universal motivation of human beings is to get what they deserve." Due to an inborn impulse for desert, programs such as affirmative action go against a "natural imperative," a "law organic to human nature."[50] Rewards must therefore be distributed on the basis of radically individual desert. The psychological assumptions are again suspect. How could even the simplest behavior be learned? Do we forego reinforcing a child's failed attempts to walk because the child is not yet deserving? How, then, will the child ever become deserving? In child rearing as in politics, to wait to reinforce only those who have reached sanctioned ends is to wait forever.

Because Dewey does not recognize this innate demand to get what we deserve, Gouinlock criticizes his social philosophy as that of an unconstrained utopian whose progressivism "is based more on ideology and wishful thinking than candid thought and observation." In Gouinlock's provocative portrayal, Dewey conceives culture as omnipotent over nature so that "moral life is an empty canvas to be painted by the educator, upon whom our nature places no limitation."[51]

Dewey's writings are not free of such tendencies,[52] but the claim that he regarded nurture as omnipotent is itself rooted in the dualism he fervently criticized between culture and nature. Moreover, Gouinlock commits a fallacy of reification, taking human characteristics as we may find them and treating them as invariable. In Dewey's words, he mistakes "social products for psychological originals" (HNC, MW 14:99). This was Aristotle's assumption when he claimed some people are born with slavish natures fulfilled only through subservience. A push to abolish the institution of slavery would have been disdained by Aristotle as a utopian affront to human nature. Similarly, conservatives have long claimed grounding for their commitments in unreformable human nature. Dewey puts it succinctly:

> Wary, experienced men of the world have always been sceptical of schemes of unlimited improvement. . . . This type of conservative has thought to find in the doctrine of native instincts a scientific support for asserting the practical unalterability of human nature. . . . Heredity is more potent than environment, and human heredity is untouched by human intent. Effort for the serious alteration of human institutions is utopian. As things have been so they will be. The more they change the more they remain the same. (HNC, MW 14:76)

Just as plants are not independent of interactions within biotic communities requiring soil, water, air, and sun, people are born into communities and traditions that cannot be detached from their individual characters. Without the inheritance of established habits from adult forerunners, death is inevitable. Yet without intelligent reformation of these habits, successors may be little better off. Thus Dewey's central message to the classic moral tradition: moral conduct is not an issuing in of moral laws from the cocoon of autonomous transcendental reason. Individuals must be replanted in their social soil.

TWO

The Pragmatic Turn

Have we done any harm by making him perplexed and
numb as the stingray does? . . . Indeed, we have probably
achieved something relevant to finding out how matters
stand, for now, as he [realizes] he does not know, he
would be glad to find out. . . . Would he have tried to find
anything out before he fell into perplexity and realized
he did not know and longed to know?

—Plato, *Meno*

By asking *why* one should act one way rather than another, or whether one should stay the course in perpetuating a prized good, reflective morality properly sits in judgment of customary morality. This attempt to make socially habituated moral discernment more intelligent marks a pivotal transition from customary morals automated by habits to reflective morals mediated by intelligence. Since the eighteenth century, this transition has been widely conceived to entail that ethics relies at least as a norm or ideal on transcendental reason, a nonsocial, emotion-free view from nowhere.

In contemporary ethics, the ideal of perfect, unbiased moral reasoning lives on in the quest for idealized starting points for insuring impartiality. The most elegant and influential is the "original position" proposed in John Rawls's *A Theory of Justice*.[1] Rawls offers a non-foundationalist reconstruction of Kant, a "Kantian Constructivism" that is culturally and historically contextual with regard to first principles. These first principles and their corollaries, deductively derived as in a geometric proof, must be followed without consulting the multitudinous contingencies of personal situations. For the sake of perfect impartiality, these contingencies must be hidden behind a "veil of ignorance." The material particularities of a situation are scrutinized only to discover what collectively preapproved formal principle applies.

Rawls's thought experiment and analysis of fairness was a monumental contribution to social and political philosophy, but pragmatism rejects his geometric paradigm inasmuch as idealized matrices for moral reasoning oversimplify the richness and complexity of moral experience *as lived.* Without downplaying the practical need to rein in biases and prejudices, pragmatist ethics urges that moral reflection must begin where all genuine inquiry begins: *in medias res,* with the tangles of lived experience. Dewey in particular argued that moral deliberation is not disembodied cerebration deciding which action is derivable from ultimate principles, but is a form of engaged inquiry touched off by an uncertain situation.

Classical pragmatism situates reason within the broad context of the whole person in action. It replaces beliefs-as-intellectual-abstractions with beliefs-as-tendencies-to-act, pure reason with practical inquiry, and objectivist rationality with imaginative situational intelligence. In contradistinction from orthodox moralists, *all* reasoning is in some sense prudential. There is no refuge to be found in a pure and universal "Reason itself" lurking mysteriously behind concrete acts of thinking.

These moves mark a pragmatic turn that appears a dead end to anyone who conceives reasoning as acultural, ahistorical, radically autonomous (yet impersonal), disembodied, or anesthetic. If a pragmatist ethics centered on imaginative deliberation is to appear a compelling alternative to mainstream ethics centered on bedrock principles and rules, some preliminary reconstructive work on the nature of belief, inquiry, and reason is essential. The remainder of Part 1 is devoted to a selective overview and defense of this pragmatic reconstruction. Of necessity, this includes material already familiar to specialists in American pragmatism. The aim is to establish a working frame for Part 2, a revitalized account of ethical inquiry.

Philosophers have traditionally sought unchanging, universal ways to organize their experiences, hoping thereby to escape the precarious indeterminacy of existence. The quest for an ahistorical moral bedrock is one instance of this "escape from peril." The "real" world, for many empiricists, or our way of apprehending the world, for many idealists, is thought to have a fixed structure. Rationality aims at an ahistorical (objective) representation—a god's-eye-view—of this permanent structure.[2]

Philosophers and other intellectuals still betray, even if they less frequently parade, a cluster of habits of conceiving reason (moral or otherwise) as: separable from any cultural conditioning, transcending time and not historically conditioned, at its best when detached from a community of co-investigators, substantially separated from the limitations of physical life, and able to be cleaved from feelings and bodily inclinations. Reason is in a word *pure,* structured and operating independently of the practical pressures of living. The goal of moral philosophy, according to Kant, was to show that such purified reason *can,* despite Hume's opposing assertion, be practical. His account of pure practical reason as the grounding of morality exemplifies all of the aforementioned traits. Contemporary moral theories typically exhibit one or more.

Daniel Kahneman's theory of rational action, awarded the 2002 Nobel Prize in Economics (with Vernon L. Smith), is a troubling case in point.[3] As the mainstay of "Decision Theory," this classic model of rationality in information-age garb has become influential in the field of analytic ethics. The rational-actor model conceives rational choice mathematically as cost-benefit analysis, which is "literal, logical, disembodied, dispassionate, and consciously calculable." A version of game theory, it aspires to be descriptive of probabilistic reasoning, seemingly unaware that the mathematics requires metaphorical interpretation, via the "Nash equilibrium," to be relevant to human choice. The Nash equilibrium is "the set of strategies, such that each strategy is the best reply for all the actors. That is, it is the overall set of strategies that will allow all to maximize their payoffs."[4] Moral education is reduced to training in cost-benefit calculations of self-interested actors striving to maximize their individual satisfactions. Any role for imagination is utterly missing. The account is descriptively inadequate and prescriptively bankrupt.

In spite of the strictly *descriptive* pretensions of its adherents, the rational-actor model plays a significant *prescriptive,* or normative, role today in education, economics, international relations, and environmental policy. It is becoming the philosophy of the emerging global free market. Increasingly markets are tailored to the model. Since cultures, nonhuman animals, ecosystems, and landscapes do not count as autonomous rational actors striving to maximize payoffs, consequences include unraveling of ecological diversity and the disintegration of whole cultures. The model also contributes to an educational paradigm in the United States in which knowledge is conceived as a commodity to be bought and sold in privatized, consumer-based institutions.

On other fronts, the past few decades have witnessed a growing concern to reveal the futility, as well as the inevitable destructiveness, of this quest for perfect, emotion-free rationality. Appearing in its place are less arrogant, more cognitively realistic accounts of reason not at odds with our humanness. Such accounts would be genuinely practical because not given over to the autocratic tendency to mold moral and social life in an allegedly pure and disinterested image. Philosophers engaged in this project must mediate between the ineptness of theories complicit in the quest for static truth and the anemia of perspectives fabricated in isolation from refined traditions.

What follows brings the American pragmatic tradition as a whole into focus in order to contrast the thick working psychology of pragmatist ethics with the thin intellectualism of much mainstream ethics. This is accomplished by introducing pragmatism's theories of belief and inquiry as an essential preliminary to developing an account of imaginative situational moral intelligence.

Moral beliefs have been variously conceived, for example, as direct Cartesian intuitions of goodness (intuitionism), ventings of emotion (emotivism), determinations of a Reason-ruled Will (Kantianism), and indissoluble associations of ideas (Mill's utilitarianism). According to classical pragmatism, each relegates the practical function of moral thinking, which is to deal with troubled or ambiguous situations. Each has immediate implications for an account of moral imagination. For example, if Kant's intellectualized view is correct, imagination would distract us from forming and appraising moral beliefs. If emotivism is correct, moral imagination would simply be pointless.

Beginning with Peirce's pivotal 1877 article "The Fixation of Belief," the classical pragmatists, inspired at least in part by the Scottish philosopher and psychologist Alexander Bain, contended that thinking stems from the necessity for adapting to discordances in experience.[5] Past adjustments often falter when challenged to meet the divergences of a changing environment, and thought ensues as a process of adaptation. To conceive beliefs, moral or otherwise, as intellectual abstractions ignores the most important thing about them: they are the consequences of and materials for the struggle to establish stability.

BAIN

In his 1859 *The Emotions and the Will*,[6] Bain makes a case against intellectualized theories of belief. A belief, he says, is "an attitude or disposition of preparedness to act" that re-establishes a composed state of expectation following a period of doubt. To believe something is to be ready to act one way rather than another when an occasion is presented, even if the appeal to action is only tacit. This readiness makes belief more than mere caprice.[7]

Belief's logical opposite is disbelief, but its psychological opposite is "not disbelief, but *doubt*, uncertainty."[8] To doubt P is not to assert not-P. It is wanting to know what to believe. The upshot of this deceptively simple insight was left to the pragmatists to develop. It meant abandonment of the assumption that beliefs either decisively do or do not abstractly correspond with a brute given (in science) or with the dictates of unitary principles and rules (in morality).[9] Whether a moral belief coincides with an abstract principle is secondary to its value in ameliorating circumstances.

The chief factor of belief, according to Bain, is *primitive credulity*, "the natural trust that we have in the continuance of the present state of things, or the disposition to go on acting as we have once begun."[10] As any teacher of philosophy will attest, questioning is elicited by the Socratic gadfly of doubt. The discomfort and aggravation of inquiry can come at the price of a comfortable tone of mind. Beliefs have a familiar inertial force. In James's words: "Any object which remains uncontradicted is *ipso facto* believed and posited as absolute reality" (PP, II, 289). Yet consciousness is punctuated by worldly surprises and demands that discompose expectations and check credulity.[11]

Bain's theory played a role in the development of Peirce's and James's pragmatism. Peirce even maintains that his pragmatism is "scarce more than a corollary" to Bain.[12] This is overstated and perhaps even misattributed, but the truth in it becomes clear when the evolution of Bain's idea among the pragmatists is sketched. Its moral implications were most thoroughly developed by Dewey, whose grasp of the basic idea came primarily from William James and Jane Addams in the 1890s.

PEIRCE

In a 1907 letter to the editor of *The Nation,* Peirce suggests that Bain influenced pragmatism through the lawyer Nicholas St. John Green, in the setting of the "Metaphysical Club" at Cambridge in the early 1870s. Because of this influence, Peirce calls Green the "grandfather of pragmatism," claiming paternity for himself.[13] The extent of Bain's influence is controverted. But it should not be overlooked, as by Louis Menand in his recent and otherwise excellent *The Metaphysical Club.*[14]

Peirce's early writings locate doubt as a principal concept. In his 1868 onslaught on Cartesianism, "Some Consequences of Four Incapacities," he rooted out the notion that it is possible simply to step out of history and will to doubt. Doubt is contextual. We *come* to doubt something because we have "a positive reason for it, and not on account of the Cartesian maxim. Let us not pretend to doubt in philosophy what we do not doubt in our hearts."[15]

Bain's influence is conspicuous in Peirce's seminal essays of 1877–78, "The Fixation of Belief" and "How to Make Our Ideas Clear."[16] He recasts Bain's "tendency to action" in terms of an organism's habits. To have a belief means a habit has been established that will determine action. "Doubt never has such an effect."[17] Belief, says Peirce, is "the demi-cadence which closes a musical phrase in the symphony of our intellectual life." He terms the struggle to attain belief *inquiry,* though he admits that terms such as inquiry, doubt, and belief are sometimes not apt. Even when these are awkward terms, as when deciding which pocket change to use to pay a fare, "I am excited to such small mental activity as may be necessary to deciding how I shall act."[18]

Ideally, inquiry struggles to attain not just any belief, but one that will "truly guide our actions so as to satisfy our desires." But the cessation of doubt is accompanied by the cessation of inquiry, even if cut short before eventuating in a trustworthy reorganization. Inquiry does not wait to arrive at an accurate map of mind-independent reality (in science) or the mythical single "right thing to do" (in morality) before coming to a close. It waits on establishment of a firm belief-habit that will determine action.[19]

Given this unseemly predicament, Peirce examines and appraises four ways interrogatives are replaced by declaratives. One popular approach is to dismiss reason and avoid doubt altogether: "When an ostrich buries its head in the sand as danger approaches, it very likely takes the happiest course. It hides the danger, and then calmly says there is no danger. . . . A man may go through life, systematically keeping out of view all that might cause a change in his opinions." Those who follow this "method of tenacity" do not survey the alternatives before them, but "fastening like lightning upon whatever alternative comes first, they hold to it to the end, whatever happens, without an instant's irresolution."[20]

A second approach is to hold beliefs because institutionalized authority declares them to be true, come what may in the way of discovery. Those who took a literalist view of scripture were infuriated by Copernicus's *On the Revolution of Heavenly Bodies*. Martin Luther quoted Joshua 10:12–14, in which Joshua commands the sun to stand still: "The sun stayed in the midst of heaven, and did not hasten to go down for about a whole day." If the sun stood still, then it must have been moving. Therefore, the sun is in motion rather than the earth. John Calvin chimed in by proving the immobility of the world, quoting Psalms 93:1: "Yea, the world is established; it shall never be moved." On the basis of scriptural authority, Copernicus was thus refuted, and human beings could for a few more years believe they were the literal center of the cosmos. Peirce evaluates this "method of authority" with biting sarcasm: "If it is their highest impulse to be intellectual slaves, then slaves they ought to remain."[21]

The problem with those who follow the method of authority, Kant famously declared in "What Is Enlightenment?" is not "lack of intelligence, but lack of determination and courage to use that intelligence without another's guidance. *Sapere aude!* Dare to know! Have the courage to use your own intelligence."[22] The a priori method, Peirce says, is far more intellectually respectable, but "its failure has been the most manifest." Its autonomous armchair reasonings form a deductive chain as weak as the weakest link, whereas communal scientific scrutiny forms a cable with "numerous and intimately connected" fibers.

The sole rule of reason, according to Peirce, is that you "not be satisfied with what you already incline to think." His famous corollary follows: *"Do not block the way of inquiry.*" The a priori approach of rationalism commits an unpardonable offence: it "barricades the road of further advance toward the truth." Unlike the method of science, which joins with a community of co-inquirers to put beliefs to the test in the world, systems such as those of Descartes or Kant are cloistered and individualistic. And they are ultimately self-deceptive: They "have been chiefly adopted because their fundamental propositions seemed 'agreeable to reason.' This is an apt expression; it does not mean that which agrees with experience, but that which we find ourselves inclined to believe."[23]

Peirce turns to science for his model of patient, experimental, communal, error-correcting inquiry. He stands alone among the classical pragmatists for conceiving his experimentalism as ultimately transcending the contingencies of what Martin Heidegger called our being-in-the-world. Inquiry carried "sufficiently far" provides the objective, universal meaning of a belief. This convergence to a "final opinion" of the scientific community is what is meant by Truth. It is reachable only in principle, never in fact. The object of inquiry, says Peirce, is an objective reality that transcends "the vagaries of me and you."[24]

Both James and Dewey reject Peirce's position on the object of inquiry. Nonetheless, in concert with Peirce, Dewey applauds the distinctive *morale* of an experimental method. This morale is a keynote of pragmatism, though it is with Dewey that it is carried to fruition in moral philosophy:

> Some of its obvious elements are willingness to hold belief in suspense, ability to doubt until evidence is obtained; willingness to go where evidence points instead of putting first a personally preferred conclusion; ability to hold ideas in solution and use them as hypotheses to be tested instead of as dogmas to be asserted; and (possibly the most distinctive of all) enjoyment of new fields for inquiry and of new problems. (FC, LW 13:166)[25]

JAMES

In *The Principles of Psychology,* James celebrates the "wonderful stream of our consciousness":

> Like a bird's life, it seems to be made of an alternation of flights and perchings. . . . Let us call the resting-places the "substantive parts," and the places of flight the "transitive parts," of the stream of thought. It then appears that the main end of our thinking is at all times the attainment of some other substantive part than the one from which we have just been dislodged. (PP, I, 243)[26]

Inquiry ceases when a substantive conclusion is reached, imbuing belief with an emotional quality of fancied security (PP, II, 283). Any theory of

belief as purely intellectual and abstract slights this quality. In "The Sentiment of Rationality," James explains that beliefs have a *felt* mark of "unim-
peded mental functioning" (SR, 65; 324). If expectations about the future
are jostled, an "uneasiness takes possession of the mind" and motivates a
readjustment.

The troubling subjective tone of James's assertions is taken up in the
next chapter. It suffices here to observe that inquiry is kindled by ardor for
equilibrium, yet the idea of perpetual equilibrium would horrify James because of its paucity of real possibilities. This metaphysics of indeterminacy
led Charles M. Bakewell to preface, tongue in cheek, his 1907 criticisms of
James's *Pragmatism:*

> It reads like the philosophy of a "new world" with a large frontier and, be-
> yond, the enticing unexplored lands where one may still expect the unex-
> pected. It appeals to one's sporting blood and one's *amour du risque,* for it is
> hospitable to chance. It is a philosophy in which one can take a gamble, for
> it holds that the dice of experience are not loaded.[27]

James likely appreciated this characterization. A perfectly congenial world
with no unsettled spots would signal flatness and mediocrity, a world without inventiveness and moral growth. The foreseeable future would merely
repeat the past so that expectations, far from being baffled, would be fully
determined. Like Odysseus at the island of Calypso, there would be no
risks to make life deeply significant.[28]

There is something of the masculine conquering spirit in James's remarks that calls to mind Charlotte Perkins Gilman's criticism in her utopian novel *Herland* of the odd notion that we need something "to oppose, to
struggle with, to conquer." But the truth of the pragmatist insight into
what is required for growth is equally well stated by Gilman: "The pressure
of life upon the environment develops in the human mind its inventive reactions, regardless of sex."[29] Precipitousness activates inquiry. If an ideal
moral universe could be created a priori by philosophers, it would be a
world in which goods did not have to compete. The goods of family life,
for example, would not have to compete with those of one's career. But in
our universe, James observes, a good can hardly be imagined that does not
compete for "the same bit of space and time with some other imagined
good" (MPML, 202). We live in a world that is not complete and ready-
made, in which situations emerge that force choices between real incompatibles. These situations unsettle and incite exertions. Such intensified activity is, for James, the locus of meaning. Peirce's insight on the role of doubt
in science is complemented by this humanistic temperament of James.
Both temperaments are fused in Dewey.

DEWEY

The life of an organism, Dewey echoes, is marked by "the rhythm of loss of integration with environment and recovery of union" (AE, LW 10:20–21; cf. HNC, MW 14:125).[30] Reflective thought, as distinguished from the general stream of consciousness, random chains of so-called thought, and prejudicial beliefs, is occasioned by situations that are "disturbed, troubled, ambiguous, confused, full of conflicting tendencies, obscure, etc." (LTI, LW 12:109).

Dewey employs ordinary English words in technical ways, so it is important to explain (or eschew) his usage of words such as *experience* and *situation*. The term *experience* designates not the subject side of an encounter with the world, but experiencing and experimenting as a transactive whole. *Situation* is similarly a double-barreled word. It allows him to "refer peremptorily to what is indicated by such terms as 'organism' and 'environment,' 'subject' and 'object,' 'persons' and 'things,' 'mind' and 'nature,' and so on" (EEL, MW 10:324). It is the transactive scene of any action (Greek *pragma*) or event (Latin *res*). *Situation* refers to any experience at hand, from its tensive focus—brilliant, conspicuous, and apparent—to its qualitative field or background, the obscured, concealed, reserved, enveloping context (EEL, MW 10:323). Finally, given the subjectivistic sense of the word *belief* and the infallibilistic sense of the word *knowledge*, Dewey came to prefer "warranted assertibility" to designate the terminus of inquiry (LTI, LW 12:15–16).

Thinking is provoked by a hitch in the workings of a habit. The habit operates unconsciously so long as it is in sync with the environment (HNC, MW 14:125). A toddler who wants you to pick her up might be stumped about how to convey this if her habit of crying falls short. If she has reached an appropriate developmental level, she imagines ways that might do the trick and then tries one that seems best. Perhaps remembering a previous stray success, she raises her arms to you and looks up with pleading eyes. If she is hoisted into your arms, and if this is braced by a personal realization of the relation between act and consequence, then she has learned something.

We can generalize from such an ordinary early learning event. The appearance of incompatible factors engages us emotionally and stimulates a readjustment from old habits to new ones. A problem is encountered, alternatives suggest themselves and are tested in thought as we *imaginatively* envision them carried out, and this "goes on till some suggested solution meets all the conditions of the case and does not run counter to any discoverable feature of it" (HWT, LW 8:197). In this way, active intelligence occupies an "intermediate and reconstructive position" between an unstable situation and a controlled one, the latter having "a richness of meaning" (EEL, MW 10:331). Thus elaborated, pragmatism's theory of belief and inquiry becomes the heart of Dewey's theory of deliberation. He labels this imaginative process *dramatic rehearsal.*

Critics and admirers alike sometimes take Dewey as reducing all reflection to simple means-end engineering. Moreover, while it is true that Dewey is at times unduly anthropocentric (e.g., QC, LW 4:80–82), some have mistakenly relegated him to obsolescence, accusing him of contributing to unchecked consumption in pursuit of control and technological "progress." This is partly attributable to his use of the word *problem,* a word that usually signifies a set task, to characterize the impetus to inquiry. As a result, some conclude that what Dewey once called his "instrumentalism" is a master plan for ready-made, preselected problems. But Dewey means the opposite. Most thinking is *not* like changing a flat tire.[31] This conception would put blinders on inquiry instead of facilitating observation and reflection on the emerging situation as it presents itself (see LTI, LW 12:112). Moreover, ends fixed in advance, such as Bentham's goal in ethics of maximizing pleasures, can impoverish the *art* of inquiry.[32] Larry Hickman clarifies that Dewey's pragmatism "was never the vulgar sort that valorizes bald expediency. Nor was his instrumentalism the 'straight-line' variety that works toward fixed goals, heedless of the collateral problems and opportunities that arise during the thick of deliberation."[33] Consequently, Dewey's philosophy squares with contemporary critiques of narrow instrumentalism in ethics. For example, to disregard life or biotic systems for the sake of control and progress is to sacrifice the goods this "progress" is defensibly a means toward.

The life of a perplexity often goes through what James calls a "subconscious incubation" or "fermentation" process. Originating in life experiences, they mature and ripen, until finally "the results hatch out, or burst into flower" (VRE, 174; 186). Incubating perplexities in myriad stages of maturity, perhaps only loosely coordinated, constitute much of one's sense of self.

Perplexities may be as momentous as career choices and moral dilemmas or as trivial as a decision about which road to take home. No philosophical difficulty would arise if there were not, as Peirce demonstrated, competing methods for dealing with perplexities. Conclusions that mature through fallibilistic experimental methods are truer, in the Old English sense of *treowth,* trustworthiness. Because they arise through interactively engaged inquiry, we can better trust them. When acted upon, they can be relied on not to go wide of the mark, as when an arrow is *true* to its target. Taking the pragmatic turn to an experimental method in conduct as in science, I cease asking to what creed should I commit myself irrevocably and begin asking which belief-habits are trustworthy instrumentalities.

In ethics, the pragmatic experimentalist is a fallibilist who inspects beliefs for their value as directive hypotheses. In contrast, the rationalist in ethics is like a spider, to appropriate Francis Bacon's image of scholasticism's "cobwebs of learning," who spins beautiful and intricate webs from her own innards. If there is a single lesson of the sciences, for Dewey it is that beliefs that mature through ongoing interactive engagement with the world are truer to the mark.

Suspense is endured gladly in films, novels, and magic. It is not always welcomed in matters of belief. This explains the prevalence of formalistic methods, such as Descartes's. A pragmatic turn, particularly in ethical inquiry, would spell an end to the dogmatism and fanaticism that mark the idea that beliefs can be true "independent of what they lead to when used as directive principles" (QC, LW 4:221). In *The Quest for Certainty,* Dewey describes the bearing of this on all beliefs: "Any belief as such is tentative, hypothetical. . . . When it is apprehended as a tool and only a tool, an instrumentality of direction, the same scrupulous attention will go to its formation as now goes into the making of instruments of precision in technical fields" (QC, LW 4:221–222). It is this experimental, fallibilist morale, not any alleged purity of moral reason, that warrants subordination of customary morality to reflective morality.

The classical pragmatists recaptured the humanness of reflective beliefs as the closing phase of encultured, historical, communal, engaged inquiry. The lesson Dewey drew from this foreshortens his philosophy: The education of disciplined yet flexible experimental intelligence, in moral life as much as in science, must be given the highest priority.

THREE

Pragmatism's Reconstruction of Reason

> We must find a theory that will *work;* and that means
> something extremely difficult; . . . Our theories are
> wedged and controlled as nothing else is.
> —William James, *Pragmatism*

Critics and admirers alike have misrepresented James and Dewey as unconstrained subjectivists and relativists in matters of reason and truth. This has postponed a fair hearing for pragmatist ethics. If this prejudice were justified, it would be sensible to believe classical pragmatism has nothing significant to say about ethics. Yet perhaps it is not pragmatism but much mainstream ethics that is riddled with unwarranted assumptions about reason and truth. As Alasdair MacIntyre points out, theories of moral understanding and theories of rationality necessarily co-evolve within a single tradition. By implication, an account of ethical inquiry premised on a dubious theory of reason will, and rightly should, be treated with deep suspicion. It implies, moreover, that accounts of moral inquiry and of reason must be reconstructed in tandem.

Ongoing scholarship is correcting groundless prejudices about classical American pragmatism's purported subjectivism and relativism. Yet familiarity with the scholarly reassessment of James and Dewey cannot be presupposed in a sustained argument, directed at more than a choir of specialists, to place ethics on a pragmatic footing. So an overview is preliminary to developing in Part 2 a defensible account of imaginative moral reasoning.

The prototypical idea of reason as dispassionate and transcendent, along with the impacted Augustinian notion that reason is the Divine spark within us, goaded Dewey altogether away from the concept of rationality. He speaks instead of *intelligence* as the mediation of problematic situations and of truth as warranted assertability. He dismissed the longing of traditional epistemology to exactly align the inner with the outer and of moral philosophy for a universal matrix. The scale of this dismissal was so revolutionary that approaching philosophy through Dewey, rather than detouring around him, signals the end of much traditional epistemology, metaphysics, aesthetics, and ethics. It concurrently promotes a recovery of philosophical engagement with human problems of knowing, experience, art, and moral life.

As with their conceptions of belief and experimental method, to comprehend the classical pragmatist's reconstruction of reason requires familiarity with Dewey's predecessors, particularly James. James's intellectual and personal struggles gave rise to distinctive, newly forged tools, but he was hesitant to go as far as Dewey did in accepting the radical implications of pragmatism. He was uncomfortable with the vertigo of a world in flux, without absolute foundations and ultimate meaning. In Charlene Haddock Seigfried's words, he felt "adrift in a world with no guarantees."[1] Dewey was comparatively at home because he had James's reconstructive work to build upon. James is in this respect a transitional figure, to the American tradition as Nietzsche to the German. To present the pragmatic turn from transcendental reason to engaged intelligence in a way that emphasizes the magnitude of this break with the philosophic tradition while correcting standing prejudices, we must turn the spotlight on James. In steering between the Scylla of hand-waving toward others' scholarship and the Charybdis of an all-inclusive treatment, perhaps the best approach is to sketch several interrelated claims about James's notions of reason and truth: Reason is embodied, evolving, and practical, and as such it is subject to physical, conceptual, and historical constraints. Further, reasoning is contingent upon perspectives and is characterized by an educated aesthetic response that can emerge from trust in a situation's potentialities.

REALISM AND TRUTH

> Woe to him whose beliefs play fast and loose with the
> order which realities follow in his experience.
> (PM, 99; 94)

James's brand of "realism" has appeared convoluted to many philosophers. As in Bertrand Russell's caricature of James's "will to believe" as "the will to make-believe," James is accused of having thrown our "compass overboard" and of adopting "caprice as our pilot" (VRE, 263; 257). This is largely because he rejects the model of the disengaged spectator who rationally assents or dissents to propositional claims about mind-independent objects or states of affairs. E. M. Adams, for example, declares that James gives us a picture "of a culture gone wild, cut loose from epistemic accountability to the real world."[2] Yet for each of the pragmatists, reason is physically, conceptually, and historically constrained. "Our ideas," James asserts, "must agree with realities . . . under penalty of endless inconsistency and frustration" (PM, 101; 96).

James's infamous "will to believe" hypothesis is often targeted to support the claim that pragmatism is subjectivistic. There is "a certain kind of truth" (WB, 28; 24) that can emerge from a sort of faith because faith—for James, readiness to act even though doubt remains plausible—is the origin of personal contribution. Trusting in a situation's potentialities, one acts as if something were true, and experience *may* continue to confirm it. This notion has applications well beyond James's controversial defense of theism. In fact, James's attempt in "The Will to Believe" to carve a niche for theism might, as Dewey surmised, be sifted out by pragmatism's own threshing machine.[3]

In "The Sentiment of Rationality," James uses a formula, "Mx," to discuss faith, where M stands for mundane phenomena, "the entire world *minus* the reaction of the thinker upon it," and x stands for personal contribution as vitalized by faith (SR, 81; 338). M has countless possibilities that x can actualize. For example, for a pessimistic temperament, "M + x expresses a state of things totally bad. The man's belief supplied all that was lacking to make it so, and now that it is made so the belief was right" (SR, 83; 339).

In an indeterminate world in which life exceeds logic (PU, 148; 323), the self-fulfilling prophecy is the lifeblood of personal and social growth. Scarcity of melioristic confidence is what makes inaction of the "my participation won't make a difference" variety the most prevalent type of action. This confidence, then, must be admitted "as an ultimate ethical factor" (SR, 82; 339). According to James's "will to believe" hypothesis, one may "run the risk of acting as if" (WB, 31; 27) something were true in cases where "faith in a fact can help create the fact" (WB, 29; 25).

Nonetheless, faith is checked at every turn by the push and pull of interactions. Faith does not move mountains, nor can it predispose us to act without a mainspring in established habit and temperament. "We can make ourselves more faithful to a belief of which we have the rudiments, but we cannot create a belief out of whole cloth when our perception actively assures us of its opposite" (VRE, 174; 173).

James's realism is similar to Dewey's. They both acknowledge "that certain brute existences, detected or laid bare by thinking but in no way constituted out of thought or any mental process, set every problem for reflection and hence serve to test its otherwise merely speculative results" (EEL, MW 10:341). This serves to distinguish classical pragmatists from both idealists and objectivists. Contrary to idealists, they do not "start with a power, an entity or substance or activity which is ready-made thought or reason and which as such constitutes the world" (EEL, MW 10:338). Contrary to analytic realists or objectivists, they deny that "even though it [experimentalism] were essential in *getting* knowledge (or in learning), it has nothing to do with knowledge itself, and hence nothing to do with the known object: that it makes a change in the knower, not in what is to be known" (EEL, MW 10:339).[4]

"World" derives from *werald*, a Germanic word meaning man-era. This is more than an etymological curiosity. To speak of a world implies a human interpreter. It has become commonplace in physics, for instance, that inquirers get at the world only through interpretation, which in turn alters what is interpreted. Unless one wishes to resurrect the doctrine of Malebranche, that minds match the world through Divine fiat, it is best to settle for the more humble view of his critics, from Locke to Kant, that we cannot perceive a world-in-itself. This fact does *not* entail the absence of structural factors independent of immediate human perception. But we need not play the games of Locke and Kant, taking refuge in a subjectivity that draws its content from an external source about which we "know not what" and takes its form miraculously, independent of interactions in what phenomenologists helpfully call the *Lebenswelt,* or lifeworld. As traditionally conceived, neither realism nor idealism can accommodate these insights.

James is often accused of neglecting the role, in our best reasonings, of external objects. He attributes this misunderstanding to the predominance of subjective language in his writings (MT, 130). This language is used to counter the supposition that the truth-seeker is irrelevant to a definition of truth. As an example, consider his sculpting metaphor for the selective (or intentional) character of human consciousness: "Other sculptors, other statues from the same stone!" (PP, 277; I, 289).[5] His metaphor has been justly criticized for highlighting the contribution of the individual while downplaying the way an impinging world sets situations. Nonetheless, the sculptor cannot express herself through the medium without, so to speak, allowing the medium to express itself through her. It resists being given just any sort of form. The good sculptor, like the good reasoner, is one whose habits are coordinated with these resistant features.

Analogously, we confront a common world that answers to experimental inquiry. The world-in-the-making is not wholly predictable as to exactly how it will bite back from one situation to the next. But there is stability. This is Jamesian realism: If reason is aimless, then surroundings destroy us rather than sustain us. The structure of mind and reason is not ghostly coincidence. With a different range of organism-environment interactions, the necessity for adaptation would produce a different human reason. James's account situates us in the environments from which rational capacities emerged and in response to which these capacities evolve. Only in this way do we elude E. M. Adams's supposed hell of being "cut loose from epistemic accountability to the real world."[6]

In *Pragmatism*, James offers as a generic definition of truth: "agreement with reality." This statement has fueled misguided debate on whether James's theory of truth is reducible to the traditional correspondence theory.[7] But he argues that the correspondence theorist says this and nothing more. D. M. Armstrong, for example, writes: "Beliefs . . . are structures in the mind of the believer which represent or 'map' reality. . . . The *truth* of propositions, and so the truth of what is believed, is determined by the correspondence of actual or possible belief-states, thoughts or assertions to reality."[8] For James, truth as correspondence is an empty abstraction if it is not pragmatically grounded. Dewey, with more than a touch of sarcasm, points out that in an operational and behavioral sense of correspondence the pragmatist alone is a correspondence theorist if taken in the sense

> of *answering,* as a key answers to conditions imposed by a lock, or as two correspondents "answer" to each other; or, in general, as a reply is an adequate answer to a question or a criticism—as, in short, a *solution* answers the requirements of a *problem*. On this view, both partners in "correspondence" are open and above board, instead of one of them being forever out of experience and the other in it by way of a "percept" or whatever. (LW 14:179)[9]

Truths are those transactive understandings we can trustingly act upon. To put the same point in James's popular yet misleadingly simplistic terms, the only *meaning* of agreement with reality lies in whether a belief—scientific, moral, or otherwise—*works*.

Classical pragmatist theories of truth have been misrepresented by adherents of Richard Rorty's neopragmatism. For instance, in a work on moral imagination, Edward Tivnan treats truth as "simply the way a particular society—our society—describes how it justifies certain ways of doing things, how it determines what is right."[10] In contrast, for James scientifically or humanistically "workable" beliefs are those that reliably help us to get along in a way that fits our lives to the world's facts. They are insofar true.

The colloquial meaning of "pragmatist" can thwart comprehension of this notion of workability, which is especially troublesome in an ethical context. In common parlance, the cold-eyed pragmatist is opportunistic, calculating, morally indifferent.[11] For example, journalist Eric Schlosser characterizes McDonald's corporate founder Ray Kroc: "Promoting Mc-Donald's to children was a clever, pragmatic decision. 'A child who loves our TV commercials,' Kroc explained, 'and brings her grandparents to a McDonald's gives us two more customers.'"[12] This feeds the current European perception that pragmatism is the American "businessman's philosophy," and among Hispanic philosophers James's idea of truth as an idea's "cash value" is taken to be the philosophical wing of American imperialism and shallow "industrial-utilitarianism."[13] The pragmatic theory of truth is commonly criticized in a similarly narrow way. Thus in 1911 Paul Carus wrote in *Truth on Trial*, his polemical response to James's *Pragmatism:*

> Was not the night of Bartholomew a success? . . . Was not the Reformation suppressed by foul means in Bohemia, when at the time of the Hussite movement it seemed to be lost to the Church? Must we be reconciled to a pragmatic policy of this kind because it works within certain limits? It certainly paid those who acted upon this pragmatic conception of truth.[14]

To the chagrin of philosophical pragmatists, Carus's idea of the pragmatic test was reinforced for many in Europe and America by Benito Mussolini in a 1926 interview: "The pragmatism of William James was of great use to me in my political career. James taught me that an action should be judged rather by its results than by its doctrinary basis." Mussolini apparently hoped this comment would win support for fascism among Americans, and for him this end justified misrepresentation of James.[15] But pragmatism is not pragmatic in this opportunistic sense, driven by results regardless of reflection and a wide scope of consequences.

What does James mean by the "reality" that constrains or gives direction to reasoning? He makes a three-fold distinction.[16] Implicitly modifying Hume, he divides reality into, first, matters of phenomenal, concrete *fact*, and second, "flagrantly man-made" relations of ideas. Neither of these classes is "without the human touch," despite the fact that James, in his hesitancy to embrace the logical implications of his own pragmatism, sometimes contradicts himself by positing an eternal conceptual world.[17] As Hilary Putnam likes to quote *Pragmatism:* "The trail of the human serpent is over all."[18]

Reality also consists of, third, a dynamic, prefigured body of "funded truths," a background of previous dealings with facts and ideas. This "humanized mass" of beliefs (PM, 119; 112), which Dewey treats as habits, tethers reasonings and keeps them from roving haphazardly. James's notion in the *Principles of Psychology* of the "horizon," "penumbra," or "fringe," which was a principal influence on Edmund Husserl's phenomenology and

Hans-Georg Gadamer's hermeneutics, includes these evolving circuits for meaningful interaction.[19]

In sum, to avoid entanglement, beliefs must deal productively with concrete facts, abstract principles, and prefigured truths. The pragmatist, James exclaims, is pent in "between the whole body of funded truths squeezed from the past and the coercions of the world of sense about him" (PM, 111–112; 104).

As a truism, there are existences outside of and including our optic nerves. But propositions or beliefs do not have the magical ability to "refer" on their own to brute entities. Pragmatically, we can speak meaningfully of reality-for-us and indeed of reality-for-*others*, but not of a hidden reality-in-itself, "metaphysical reality, reality for God" (PP, 924; II, 295). We cannot just "look and see" what a world-in-itself is like independent of relations to it. In fact, the world beyond sense organs cannot even provoke investigation except insofar as it touches experience: recall with Peirce that we must *come* to doubt. Still, it is *reality* for us, and not a fiction.

The human touch cannot be bracketed out to gain neutral access to a world-as-it-is—an insight forcefully articulated today in the phenomenological, genealogical, and hermeneutic traditions of Continental philosophy. Kant recognized this, but he did so at the expense of both petrifying the human touch and severing thinking from feeling. Contemporary phenomenologists begin with this insight, though some mistakenly conclude with poststructuralists and against Merleau-Ponty that it implies an indictment of rather than an aid to scientific method.

Contemporary cognitive science also reveals this intertwining of self and world. To take one generalizable example, studies of perceiver-dependence show that color concepts such as blue emerge from complex interactions of retinal cones, neural makeup, local light conditions, and wavelength reflectances. The assertion "That is blue" is warranted interactively, not objectively or subjectively. Unfortunately, cognitive scientists tend to make these pronouncements with an ironclad certainty that does little to allay suspicion that they regard their own minds as neutral instruments.[20]

Reflected-upon beliefs are not inherently fabricated by the play of linguistic signifiers, as some French poststructuralists would have it, nor are they anchored in a foundational or transcendent ahistorical matrix, as posited from Descartes to Kant. Beliefs are not grounded by an idea-fact correspondence or solely by a harmonious cohesion of funded truths. But they *are* in a sense grounded and constrained, experientially, by their trustworthiness. And a belief or theory works reliably only if it is reflexively guided by existential circumstances.[21]

EMBODIMENT, EVOLUTIONARY INTELLIGENCE, AND THE PHILOSOPHER'S FALLACY

> [C]lassification and conception are purely teleological
> weapons of the mind. The essence of a thing is that
> of its properties . . . so *important for my interests*
> that in comparison with it I may neglect the rest.
> (PP, 961; II, 335)

James sees philosophy as having fled from a thick, robust concern with human existence. He retrieves rationality from its angelic elevations in a supposedly pure formal realm and returns it to the lifeworld. (In a significant contrast with Dewey, however, his individualism led him to downplay sociocultural interactions.)

A view has prevailed that embodiment (used here in Merleau-Ponty's helpful dual sense enveloping the experiential and biological) is of little relevance to conceptual structures. A variation of this asomatic standpoint is manifest today in the dominant computer metaphor for mind, in which neurons are mental hardware. Computer hardware is required for software to operate, and it sets minimal parameters that programs must comply with to be compatible. Thus the mind needs the brain to operate as software needs hardware. Most of a computer's formal operations are supplied by software programs exchangeable from machine to machine, so concepts, reason, and the mind have only the loosest relationship with embodiment. Up-down bodily orientation and shape, kinesthetic activities, physical differences (sex, disability, etc.), and environments are cognitively irrelevant. The result is a mitigated Cartesian notion of reason, and thus of moral reasoning, as disembodied, transcendent, and universal. In contrast, James's "corpus" is shot through with awareness that bodily life is fundamental to cognitive structures. He frequently alludes, for example, to the way somatic sensations pervade conscious activity, forming a felt horizon that orients us in the world.[22]

The belief in disembodied concepts became a trademark of the logical positivist movement in the 1920s through 1950s. Logical positivists assumed that the categories through which we have a world, when properly translated into a logical symbol system purified of linguistic distortions (provided by Whitehead and Russell's *Principia Mathematica*), correspond in a one-to-one fashion with objective entities or states of affairs that have fixed properties and stand in determinate relations to one another. But as Wittgenstein recognized in his theory of "family resemblances," things are not naturally contained in these categories wholly independent of our putting them there. Cognitive scientists such as Eleanor Rosch are further elaborating this insight.[23] This is not to say, with some idealists, that ready-made minds have molded a formless reality. Categories have evolved as an ordered response to the world's dynamic structure, which is in turn altered —though almost invariably with insufficient care and sensitivity—by our categories.

On the standard view, knowledge is a correct description of mind-independent reality. The knower is incidental to this. If the knower can be separated from the known, the final word on a subject may, in principle, be catalogued. One problem with this is that, unlike the pragmatic theory of knowing, it renders any notion of moral or aesthetic knowledge incoherent. Another problem is that it is incompatible with a lesson of evolutionary biology, namely that what is fixed and finished does not precede what is coming-to-be.[24] There just is no essential nature of things to catalogue; there are no Platonic Forms or Aristotelian fixed species. Why, then, slight the human context of categorization in favor of threadbare essences?

James the psychologist answers: We name categories after what stands out most distinctively in a situation (given purposes, for better or worse) and filter out what seems unessential. Dewey explains: "The term 'essence' is highly equivocal. In common speech it denotes the *gist* of a thing; we boil down a series of conversations or of complicated transactions and the result is what is essential. We eliminate irrelevancies and retain what is indispensable" (AE, LW 10:298). We may be mistaken about what is the heart of the matter, and in such cases purposes may be frustrated. The difficulty is intransigent because selection is inherent in all inquiry. This is painfully true of ethical inquiry, and its effects are exacerbated by system-building around generic essences of morality. By simplifying we *will* slight potentially significant features of situations. This partiality is an unavoidable side effect of living. Far better that our theories not contribute to the problem in the zeal to solve it.

Yet there *is* a remediable problem here. It stems from a failure to treat essences experientially and experimentally, conceiving them instead as self-existing. This occurs, for example, when people mistake names for things, as when we ignore the warnings of Franz Boas, Alain Locke, and contemporary geneticists and treat racial and ethnic groups as biological kinds rather than as complex social phenomena. Or in ethics we may come to believe in the objective existence of the Good and Right, Duty and Virtue, Rights and Rules.

As Irwin Edman remarks in *Philosopher's Quest,* we get "taken in by our own clarities." Duped by what James dubs the "psychologist's fallacy," we take thin abstractions and reify them as fixed verities, like Greek and medieval *Forms,* British empiricism's *ideas,* or pre-Darwinian *species.* Dewey will observe that the historic quest for a foundational ethical principle follows the same pattern. James's self-styled "radical empiricism" (versus *British* empiricism, which ignores direct experience of continuities and relations) is distinctive for awareness that abstractions originate in practical purposes. Our proclivity for drinking of the river of Lethe, and not of the stream of interactive life, is dubbed by Dewey *the* philosophic fallacy. It occurs when we forget that the world comes in a "relational mosaic."[25]

This fallacy is exemplified by the subject-object dichotomy that drives the "epistemology industry" castigated by Dewey. The development of science, of *technai,* was aided by the evolution of a knower-known distinction between spectator and spectacle. So, for adaptive purposes, we speak of thought and thing, mental and physical, internal and external, idea and sensation. We split experience from nature, signifier from signified, representation from represented, word from object. Then we mistakenly conclude that these binaries correspond to independently existing entities or states of affairs, like Descartes's *res cogitantes* and *res extensa.*

What James calls the categories of "common sense"—for example, things, kinds, minds, bodies, subjects and attributes, and the like (PM, 85; 80)—are rooted in this tendency to turn teleological distinctions of convenience (abstractions for the sake of) into ontological ones (disjunctions in the nature of things). Failure to attend to the genealogy of philosophic categories has petrified intellectual tools that might otherwise be of service. For example, consciousness is presumed separable from matter just as the pigment of oil paint is separable from its base. But a "paleontologist of truth" exposes this as a chimera.[26]

In this context, James sums up his goal as "the reinstatement of the vague and inarticulate to its proper place in our mental life."[27] This has recently been fruitfully explored as the keynote of radical empiricism—James's brand of therapy for relation deprivation, as John McDermott puts it—by William Gavin, Eugene Fontinell, and others. According to Fontinell:

> James's desire to reinstate the "vague and inarticulate" is . . . not a defense of obfuscation or romantic cloudiness. Paradoxically, it is an effort to describe our experience as rigorously as possible and to avoid any procrustean cutting of experience so as to fit neatly into what can be named or conceptualized. . . . This in no way denies the legitimacy and even necessity of extrapolating from or speculating upon our personal experiences. It does, however, caution against explaining away that which is present in our immediate experience.[28]

It is readily apparent that this phenomenology of consciousness challenges some tendencies in contemporary Anglo-American philosophy. For example, even Putnam's recognition that there can be no one correct linguistic description of reality is not freed from the legacy of correspondence theories. For Putnam, philosophical inquiry begins and ends with language, not with organism-environment *interaction*. How language non-propositionally represents extra-conceptual traits is still taken to be the essential problem of philosophy.

PERSPECTIVISM AND PLURALISM

> For what a contradictory array of opinions have objective
> evidence and absolute certitude been claimed! . . .
> [T]here is indeed nothing which some one has not
> thought absolutely true, while his neighbor
> deemed it absolutely false. (WB, 23; 16)

No perspective has a monopoly on truth, so with James the *effects* of taking things one way rather than another become paramount. What does it *mean* to look at things this or that way? What follows from acclaiming one ordering principle over another? Recalling Bain's idea that a belief is a tendency to act, an outlook's meaning for James is in what it *does*.

Even if the world *were* metaphysically fixed, finished, and absolutely determined, it could not be apprehended as such. In opposition to the rationalist's hypothesis, there exists no universal human reason that, rightly cultivated, will even in principle enable all rational agents to reach precisely the same conclusions. (James's opposition here has been investigated more recently by W. V. O. Quine in his work on the underdetermination of statements).[29] Furthermore, habits are filters. It is impossible to precipitate habit out of an experience and be left with a purified glimpse of the world. The filter of habit, Dewey observes, is not "chemically pure. It is a reagent which adds new qualities and rearranges what is received" (HNC, MW 14:26).

The absence of bedrock does not entail radical moral, aesthetic, or scientific relativism. The truth-experience remains what it has always been independent of theories about it: the continuous confirmation and falsification of hypotheses. James goes beyond grudging tolerance to embrace competing perspectives as potentially complementary; each may compensate for something concealed by the other. There is, he claims, "nothing improbable in the supposition that an analysis of the world may yield a number of formulae, all consistent with the facts" (SR, 66; 325). Nietzsche observes contemporaneously with James: "There is *only* a perspective seeing, *only* a perspective 'knowing'; and the *more* affects we allow to speak about one thing, the *more* eyes, different eyes, we can use to observe one thing, the more complete will our 'concept' of this thing, our 'objectivity,' be." "An eye turned in no particular direction," Nietzsche adds, is "completely unthinkable."[30] Instead of our setting out individually to construct a foundational, perspective-independent truth, in science or morals, communal dialogue between diverse perspectives allows us to develop flexible, well-tested points of view.

THE AESTHETICS OF INTELLIGENCE

> Although all men will insist on being spoken to by
> the universe in some way, few will insist on being
> spoken to in just the same way. (SR, 74; 332)

In *Descartes' Error* and *The Feeling of What Happens,* the neuroscientist Antonio Damasio explains that damage to prefrontal cortices of the brain induces disaffection, leaving people emotionally numb, so that topics and activities that once stirred emotions evoke only a cold-blooded response. The brain's prefrontal cortices are not critical for language and motor functions, but they are essential for basic decision making, means-end reasoning, socially appropriate behavior, and empathy.[31] It follows from this that the neurobiological equivalent of Kant's demand for moral reasoning to be purified of emotion is, in fact, moral incompetence. It is true that conduct may be warped by emotional biases; it is equally true that conduct will be warped by absence of emotion.

This confirms James's claim that educated emotions are invaluable guides, not impediments, for negotiating life's twists and turns. Martha Nussbaum argues exhaustively for this in her recent work, though she unfortunately fails to appreciate contributions of the classical pragmatists.[32] Compare to Dewey: "The gist of the matter is that the immediate existence of quality, and of dominant and pervasive quality, is the background, the point of departure, and the regulative principle of all thinking" (QT, LW 5:262). Damasio's work contributes to concretely understanding the qualitative nature of thought, which Dewey vaguely attributes to "some physiological process, not exactly understood at present but to which the name 'habit' is given" (QT, LW 5:261).

In his watershed essay of 1879, "The Sentiment of Rationality,"[33] James implies that philosophers have missed the whole point of rationality: the restoration of manageability to doubtful circumstances. Because this restoration culminates an uneasy process, it is marked by "a strong feeling of ease, peace, rest." He dubs this state of resolution the rational sentiment, a telltale sign that fluid interaction has been restored.

James proposes that a belief's rationality is recognized by these psychological marks, so reason walks hand in hand with emotion. (This may be distinguished from the famous James-Lange theory that bodily changes are interposed as the cause of all emotions [PP, 1058–1097; II, 442–485].) James's proposal does not intimate an insouciant disregard for objective traits of the world—a view proliferated by Rorty.[34] Since the world answers to acts, a merely subjective sentiment could lay no claim to interactive workability.

This seemingly oxymoronic "rational sentiment" is not to be equated with truth. For pragmatism, to discern the truth of a belief requires investigating what follows from acting on it. How will the world answer back? Meanwhile, the rational sentiment is felt *whenever* doubt is replaced with substantive belief. One of the greatest challenges of liberal education is to provoke inquiry by shaking up this credulous sentiment.

Beliefs are of course often formed with little or no regard for their trustworthiness. This is especially true of values, but is well illustrated by myriad claims of pseudoscientific certainty: The world was created in 4004 B.C. The alignment of stars and planets dictates fortunes. Millions have been abducted by extraterrestrials. Past-life regression therapy helps to recover repressed memories.[35] These cherished certainties spring from "limited and private" intuition, wishful thinking, hallucinations, or indoctrination rather than the "open and public" method of naturalistic empiricism (ACF, LW 9:27). They are *subjective* products of questioning cut short rather than *transactive* products of cooperative, sustained, fallibilistic inquiry. Experimental method eventuates in a consummatory emotion that is an interactive product. Thus it provides the most reliable model for inquiry in science and, particularly for Dewey and Mead, in morals. As Peirce observed, it prolongs inquiry in cooperation with others despite an almost irresistible urge for quick settlement.

What is perhaps most revolutionary is that James treats even the most subtle and sophisticated forms of symbol-mediated inquiry as aesthetic activities. In this way, he simultaneously de-subjectivizes the aesthetic and de-objectivizes understanding. A person feels a re-establishment of relatively fluent activity, funded by the whole of personal and sociocultural life, when she hits upon a reliable way of meshing past experience with future expectations.

Very briefly, what is involved in this aesthetic continuity? As lived, inquiry is story-structured. It concludes with resolution of discordance, not objective correspondence. "Things tell a story," James writes. Events fall "into a dramatic form [an "aesthetic union"], with a start, a middle, and a finish" (PM, 70; 67). Experience is composed just as the composer of music configures a tone with a heightened sense for the dying echo of the prefigured flow of tones and a dawning sense of the future flow (see PP, I, 246; 255). Stephen Pepper helpfully calls this the "spread" of an event.[36] The present is funded by the past and inclines toward "the next day's funding operations" (PM, 107; 101). Reasoning, then, is a story-structured, aesthetically funded capacity. In Paul Ricoeur's and Alasdair MacIntyre's terms, it has a narrative structure.[37]

Unfortunately, James, ever a sexist, equates feeling with "the feminine method of direct intuition" (PP, II, 369).[38] In his chapter on "Reasoning" in the *Principles of Psychology*, James writes:

> The very lack of preappointed trains of thought is the ground on which general principles and heads of classification grow up; and the masculine brain deals with new and complex matter indirectly by means of these, in a manner which the feminine method of direct intuition, admirably and rapidly as it performs within its limits, can vainly hope to cope with. (PP, II, 369)

Coupled with limitations of late-nineteenth-century neurobiology, this chauvinism kept James from fully developing his insights on the pervasive role of emotion in cognition. Still, he made revolutionary contributions by recognizing there is no translucent Reason to be revealed by distilling "wish and will and sentimental preference" from experience (see WB, 18; 8). Perhaps Hume would have concluded this had he not been trapped by a dualistic psychology into concluding, "Reason is, and ought only to be the slave of the passions."[39] Emotional engagement is essential to being rational animals; it cannot be separated out like oil from water through a Cartesian training of the will. James was ahead of his time in recognizing that such an attempt is "ideally as inept as it is actually impossible" (SR, 77; 335).

Emotional engagement differs from person to person in accord with temperament, which James calls "the potentest of all our premises" (PM, 11; 9). One aspect of temperament for James is a quasi-religious sensibility for how affairs ultimately hang together (see VRE, 36–37; 45). But his discussion in *A Pluralistic Universe* is richer. We each have "visions, modes of feeling the whole push, and seeing the whole drift of life, forced on one by one's total character and experience" (PU, 20–31).[40] This suggests temperament is a function of habituated character (see PP, I, 104–128). This socialized setup of possibilities is, for good or ill, a primary determinant of what will appear reasonable to us. Temperament is not always a reliable guide, but it is no more subjective than habits of driving a car or throwing a ball, since our "common-sense prejudices and instincts are themselves the fruit of an empirical evolution" (VRE, 264; 257).

Temperament also makes the world uniquely mine or yours. On James's view, we weave individual tapestries from the shared strands of an otherwise inexpressive chaos. Or to change the metaphor, we read different worlds from the same facts (cf. PM, 118; 111).

Temperament educates expectations yet has a blinding effect. If something contradicts my perspective, it holds little interest, so I may not attend to it. Selective attention explains why novelties that would jar prior commitments usually escape notice. If one *must* modify old opinions, the transitions are smoothed over with "a minimum of jolt and a maximum of continuity" (PM, 35; 31). Marrying new perceptions with pre-existing tendencies contributes to the aesthetic continuity of experience.[41]

Classical pragmatism remakes the intellectual architecture of modernity, toppling the traditional assumption that reasonings and actions can be measured by an ahistorical standard. In its place it offers a new model, which recognizes reason's ineliminatively temporal, aesthetic, evolving, embodied, practical, and contextual character. Rejecting both foundationalism and subjectivism, the classical pragmatists transferred the burdens of reflective life to situated, emotionally engaged intelligence. It remains to develop this general account of reasoning into a defensible theory of imaginative moral inquiry.

Part II

MORAL IMAGINATION

FOUR

Imagination in Pragmatist Ethics

A man, to be greatly good, must imagine intensely and
comprehensively; he must put himself in the place of
another and of many others. . . . The great instrument
of moral good is the imagination.
—Percy Bysshe Shelley, *Defense of Poetry*

PRAGMATIST ETHICS

There is a central dogma of ethical theory, namely that it rests on revealing or constructing a moral bedrock that tells us the right way to think about moral problems. Moral skeptics accept this dogma, plausibly reject that such a foundation can be discovered or erected, and hear the bell toll for ethics. Many self-described normative ethicists hear no such bell. They argue, or uncritically assume, that the fundamental fact of morality is the capacity to set aside our patchwork of customary beliefs and then to discern and apply moral laws or rules derived from one or more foundational principles. This is indeed an ineliminable assumption of ethics, moral skeptics rejoin, but sadly we all lack such a capacity.

The resulting diversity of proffered objective moral foundations is fascinating, and endless: universal laws of reason, the principle of respect for persons, natural rights, timeless moral intuitions, divine commands, natural laws, the doctrine of agape, to name a few. Ethicists also establish bedrocks by procedures whereby a person: discerns real duties among conflicting prima facie duties, impartially constructs socially contractual principles and rules from behind a "veil of ignorance," maximizes aggregate happiness by giving weight to the ends or preferences of others equal to that we give to our own, renders rules of common morality consistent, or the like. Debates rage within and between each camp over which is exclusively entitled to be hailed "the right way to reason about moral questions."[1] Such debate is synonymous with "doing ethical theory." Normative ethicists hope these principles and procedures will tell us what we should do, or at least specify precise limits on what we can and cannot do.

Virtue theory, with its pragmatic emphasis on habits and character, offers one way out. Alasdair MacIntyre, for example, turns back to Plato and Aristotle and rejects modern rule-governed ethics as great mistakes of the eighteenth-century Enlightenment. Yet MacIntyre still locates a moral bedrock in the human telos, implying a catalog of character traits uniquely suited to actualizing this end-for-humanity. Others, including classical pragmatists such as Dewey and, to a degree, feminist ethicists like Nel Noddings, favor a radically reconstructed conception of ethics that entreats people "to attend more fully to the concrete elements entering into the situations in which they have to act" (TIF, LW 5:288). What is needed, Dewey urged, is to reject the quest for "a single, fixed and final good" and "transfer the weight and burden of morality to intelligence" (RP, MW 12:172–173) with the aim of ameliorating the muddles of moral life.

In "Three Independent Factors in Morals," Dewey argues that ethical theorists should cease asking which principle is the ultimate and unitary one and attempt instead to reconcile inherent conflicts between irreducible forces that characterize all situations of moral uncertainty. He identifies three such forces that need to be coordinated: individual ends (the origin of consequentialist ethics), the demands of communal life (the origin of theories of duty and justice in deontological ethics), and social approbation (the principal factor in virtue theories) (LW 5:279–288).

The preference for three primary factors may be an aesthetic one for Dewey, and he knowingly exaggerates differences among the three (TIF, LW 5:503). What is more interesting is his idea that moral philosophers have abstracted one or another factor of moral life as the central one and then treated this as a foundational source of moral justification to which *all* morality is reducible. Other factors are encompassed within this nexus of commensurability. Hence, ethical theories are categorized according to their chosen bottom line. In addition to Kantianism and utilitarianism, some contemporary examples include A. I. Meldon's exclusive focus on welfare rights (Act so as not to violate others' unalienable rights to pursue their legitimate interests.) and MacIntyre's call to cultivate the virtues, which he has most recently described as traits of character that bring about the distinctive flourishing of one's species.[2] Additionally, hybrid views abound, such as R. M. Hare's Kantian-utilitarian principle that we should weigh others' preferences equally with our own.

The mainstream ethicist develops a theory on which to base moral arguments by distilling very sensible principles like these into the one judged to accommodate whatever is valued in the rest. Mission accomplished, she can apply the theory to cases and make adjustments to it in light of counterexamples. Yet when facing the ambiguities and conflicts of real situations, much of her labor is to no avail. For example, what responsibilities do children have to their aging parents? Should couples in industrialized countries voluntarily limit their reproduction to reduce environmental impact? Should an employee blow the whistle on illegal corporate practices? Should a soldier shoot upon command? Plainly, seeing any of these situations solely through the lens of one factor—as a matter of duty not virtue, of rights not consequences, and so on—relegates other factors that require coordination.

The pragmatic pluralist refuses to play the winner-take-all game. Take a taxonomy of current perspectives on hunting as an illustration. Because most ethical theories treat all but one of the following questions as secondary, they cannot on their own do justice to the ambiguity and complexity of the situation. The ecocentrist helpfully asks: Is therapeutic culling of "management species" (especially ungulates such as deer or elk) ecologically obligatory, regardless of whether anyone would prefer to pull the trigger?[3] The virtue theorist wonders: What traits of character are cultivated by sport and trophy hunting, and do these contribute to the good life? Do these traits carry over to treatment of humans? The deontological rights theorist inquires: Do other animals have rights; that is, might their interests as we perceive them override any direct benefits to humans? The feminist ethicist of care asks: Does hunting affect our ability to care for animals; indeed, are we genuinely capable of caring about beings with whom we have no sustained relationship? The utilitarian questions: Should all animals' preferences or interests as we perceive them, including our own, have equal weight when evaluating consequences?

To spotlight only one of these questions risks bringing inquiry to a premature close. Tunneled perception inhibits deliberation at least as much as it helpfully focuses it. To invoke James, much ethical theorizing is "a monstrous abridgement of life. . . . This is why so few human beings truly care for philosophy" (SR, 61; 320–321). In contrast, on the view that there are *plural* primary factors in moral situations, the role of moral philosophy shifts. It functions not to provide a moral bedrock, but to clarify, interpret, evaluate, and redirect our natural and social interactions. Philosophers such as Locke, Kant, Mill, and Aristotle serve ethical theory and practice best if we resist, in Emerson's image, becoming satellites orbiting their systems as libertarians, Kantians, utilitarians, or virtue theorists.

There is a siren lure to the hyper-rationalist's quest for the grand theory or metaethical principle that will systematically unify, without sacrificing robustness, competing ethical theories. It entices the same enchantment Leibniz must have felt in showing how Catholics and Protestants could preserve their doctrines if only they would adopt *his* metaphysics.

It would nonetheless be preposterous to deny a role in moral judgment for the guidance of general principles, or a role in moral theory for critical reflection on rules. Not only do we need their aid in troublingly ambiguous situations of moral conflict; we need all the help we can get to make judgment more reasonable, less biased by what Dewey correctly calls "the twisting, exaggerating and slighting tendency of passion and habit" (HNC, MW 14:169). Thus the demand in ethics, vocally championed by John Rawls, for consistency and impartiality.

But ethical theories too often favor adherence to codes to the neglect of wisdom and intelligence. This is not true of all ethics based on foundational principles. It is, however, especially marked in rule theories, regardless of whether the rules are taken to be absolute. Moreover, all systematizing in morals risks myopia, even those that advocate contextual reasoning, forswear absolutism, and forego the attempt to provide definitive answers to genuine moral dilemmas.

Alan Donagan's *The Theory of Morality* provides a helpful foil. He writes: "The theory of morality is a theory of a system of laws or precepts, binding upon rational creatures as such, the content of which is ascertainable by human reason."[4] He derives a system of specificatory premises and precepts from the fundamental principle that we should always act so as to respect others as persons (i.e., as autonomous rational agents). The derived precepts act as laws or rules to govern the permissibility or impermissibility of specified kinds of actions. Ethical deliberation amounts to applying these laws to particular cases.

Pragmatist ethics turns away from such rigid abstractions and returns to the ordinary life-experiences of inherently social, embodied, and historically situated beings. In addition to interminable dealings with incompatible moral demands, we all daily and hourly encounter situations too unique— *unique,* not just complicated—for reflection to be exhausted merely by subordinating what is before us as an instance of an already sedimented classification (HNC, MW 14:167–168). Plainly you cannot put your foot in the same river twice. It is equally true that you cannot *unproblematically* apply a rule to the same situation twice. Situations do not come in duplicates. Yet imagination thankfully finds circumstances relevantly analogous, so that general principles are often indispensable as improvable tools to experimentally develop a situation's individualized meanings. Any system that pretends to determine once and for all the limits and conditions of moral action is out of step with the existential world as encountered: "uncertain, unpredictable, uncontrollable, and hazardous" (EN, LW 1:43).[5] It is false to the texture of moral life and is therefore not capable of meeting the daily challenges of existence.

Ethics has literally come to be defined by its idolatrous worship of rules, as that "branch of philosophy that seeks to understand the nature, purposes, justification and founding principles of moral rules and the systems they comprise."[6] As a record of past moral experimentation, conscious principles and rules are indispensable for "economizing effort in foresight" (HNC, MW 14:167). The problem is *not* with attempts to "find general principles which shall direct and justify" conduct (1932 E, 173). It is with academic philosophers' and the public's misconception of the nature of principles and rules. Rules, whether products of common morality or of systematic theory, are generalizations. It is of course true (in the sense of trustworthy-to-act-upon) that one generally should not lie or steal or break promises. It is equally true that generalizations, no matter how warranted, cannot replace personal decision making by determining what someone ought to do. In applied sciences such as medicine, Dewey observes, this is called quackery. And it serves little better in ethics.

Anthropologist T. O. Beidelman perceptively notes that real life "is too diverse and manifold to be sustained by any entirely consistent system."[7] If so, it follows that no system can supply in advance a *definitive* procedure for determining what conditions justify violating a rule (except a priori, internal to the system), as Bernard Gert attempts. If an impartial person could "publicly allow" killing, cheating, causing pain, breaking the law, or the like, then Gert concludes the violation is permissible; otherwise, moral life is simply a matter of not violating the ten rules he defends: Keep your promises, obey the law, and do your duty, but do not kill, cause pain, disable, deprive of freedom, deprive of pleasure, deceive, or cheat.[8] Similar formalistic difficulties attend W. D. Ross's procedure for ranking prima facie duties to determine one's actual duty.

Rules, along with their superordinate first principles, overstep their pivotal function as idealized summaries of moral wisdom when they pretend to be more than guiding hypotheses that help open situations to inquiry. They are properly conceived experimentally, as "intellectual instruments to be tested and confirmed—and altered—through consequences effected by acting upon them" (QC, LW 4:221). Dewey spells this out:

> A moral principle, such as that of chastity, of justice, of the Golden Rule, gives the agent a basis for looking at and examining a particular question that comes up. It holds before him certain possible aspects of the act; it warns him against taking a short or partial view of the act. It economizes his thinking by supplying him with the main heads by reference to which to consider the bearings of his desires and purposes; it guides him in his thinking by suggesting to him the important considerations for which he should be on the lookout. (1932 E, LW 7:280)

Despite the best intentions, the quest for a more prestigious role for principles and rules gags intelligence and rings too hollow to engage the whole
person.

Admittedly, Dewey's ethics requires some tolerance for moral vertigo.
He urges us to abandon the *governance* of principles in favor of their *guidance*. Nonetheless, pragmatism does not suggest all proffered foundations
are created equal. Debates between competing perspectives can be deeply
significant and illuminating. For example, the near universal rejection
among ethicists of Ayn Rand's egoistic first principle to pursue one's own
selfish interests is a sign of the untenability of her position, not merely
proof of widespread monistic thinking.

Dewey's idea, in *Reconstruction in Philosophy,* that the quest for a moral
bottom line must be surrendered is overstated. This search has pragmatic
worth, manifest for instance in the "Discourse Ethics" of Jürgen Habermas.[9] But is its worth disproportionate to its monopolizing place at the
center of ethics? If there *must* be a central focus in ethical theorizing, as
convention dictates, we should consider imagination for this role, and not
merely as a minor supplement to a theory of rules. To be precise, however,
there is no one central component. Even a "Copernican revolution" in ethics would be incomplete. A fixed center is implied. As Raymond Boisvert
explains of Dewey's empirical naturalism, it "disallows any absolute centers.
It admits that the component elements of a situation reciprocally influence
each other."[10]

The point here is *not* that it is high time to abandon insights of traditional ethical theories. To the contrary, it is time to return to these traditions with an eye to reconstructing their troublesome elements. To deny the
categorical imperative, utilitarian maxim, or the like the status of irrecusable principles is not to deny, all or nothing, their pragmatic worth as distinctive emphases and fruitful tensions in ethical theory. Their genuine
service to moral life would, ironically, be *furthered* by a Copernican shift in
ethics from foundational principles to imagination. Consider Kant's moral
image of a kingdom of ends, which some contemporary Kantians interpret
as respect for the inherent worth of the subjectivity of others. Kant's
protests aside, not only is the ideal itself a product of imagination (no matter how it is interpreted), but understanding the subjective life of another is
the province of empathetic imagination. Or consider utilitarian conse-
quentialism. The utilitarian metaphor of deliberation as calculation hides
the fact that any wide survey of consequences is imaginative.

So, among its virtues, Dewey's ethics provides a matrix for pragmatically interpreting extant theories. But it is not simply parasitic upon these
theories, or consigned to a diplomatic role enhancing rapport between en-
trenched systems. This would imply that prevailing theories, laid side by
side, complete a panoramic scene of whatever is worthy of general theo-

retic reflection in moral life and that Dewey merely took on the role of commentator. To the contrary, he was deeply dissatisfied with traditional descriptions of moral experience, and his redescriptions laid bare undeveloped dimensions of moral inquiry. Chief among these is imagination.

THE RENASCENCE OF IMAGINATION

James urges in *The Principles of Psychology,* "There are imaginations, not 'the Imagination,' and they must be studied in detail" (PP, II, 50). His meaning was fairly simplistic: for some people visual imagery is uppermost in their thinking, whereas for others auditory or motor images may be predominant (PP, II, 57). But he rightly implies that there is no essential definition of the term, in contrast with no less an authority than Mary Warnock.[11]

The question What is the imagination? is loaded with the implication that there *is* such a ready-made thing. Imagination is thus conceived as an autonomous mental power—a primitive force instead of a function—whose task is to do specifiable things such as form images. Such reification flowered in the faculty psychology of the eighteenth century. Imagination's job, the dominant story ran, is to synthesize sensations from Perception into reproducible images (Kant's reproductive imagination) and relate them to the Understanding, which classifies and schematizes the images (what Kant called productive imagination) as instances of universal concepts (a process of judgment).[12] Understanding then passes these on to Reason, which decides, perhaps consulting Memory, what to do about the matter. Reason orders Will to attend to it, hopeful that Will is strong enough to subdue the disruptions of Feeling.

Imagination, on this view, is usually a trusty crafter of images but is given to mischief. Thus Kant's suspicion. Imagination as free reflective play is essential to aesthetic judgment, for Kant, but in morals it is too self-indulgent. It may sap moral strength, usurping Reason and yielding victory to Feeling. If a person "surrenders authority over himself, his imagination has free play," Kant claims. "He cannot discipline himself, but his imagination carries him away by the laws of association; he yields willingly to his senses, and, unable to curb them, he becomes their toy."[13] Doing one's duty, on Kant's view, requires little imagination; therefore "its cultivation is at best a luxury, at worst a danger."[14]

Despite eulogizing of imagination by Adam Smith and David Hume,[15] Enlightenment faculty psychology, following the lead of Plato's low estimation of imagination in the *Republic* and *Ion,* is responsible for imagination's being ignored even by those who urge that moral theories must be psychologically plausible. As a limited capacity prone to frivolous fancy and opposed to reason, imagination has little relevance to practical issues. So it can be dismissed altogether as a prescientific relic or, transfigured by Romanticism, admired on a pedestal as a "godlike power that enters into the world on the wings of intuition, free of the taint of contingency and history."[16] In contemporary philosophy of mind, our flickering imaginations are thought at best merely to form a pre-intentional (i.e., not directed beyond itself) "background" for rational thought, as John Searle proposes.[17] It is unfortunate that the mainstream of European thought ignored Giambattista Vico's elevation of the creative imagination as civilization's source of renewal and direction.

No theory could be fully adequate to imagination. But there is a budding awareness among philosophers that it plays a vital role in moral judgments such that, in Warnock's words, "in education we have a duty to educate the imagination above all else."[18] "No longer is it necessary," Yi-Fu Tuan remarks hopefully, "to contrast a moral but dour person with an imaginative but flamboyant and irresponsible one."[19]

Still, in this promising renascence there is a tendency to retain an unhelpful residual split between self-contained faculties, whereby reason without imagination is empty, imagination without rule-governed reason blind. Imagination is thus given a limited role that does not intervene widely in conduct. Charles Larmore, for example, explores moral imagination as a supplement to moral rules, needed to take up the slack of a limited objective rationality. It is "our ability to elaborate and appraise different courses of action which are only partially determined by the given content of moral rules, in order to learn what in a particular situation is the morally best thing to do."[20] This relegation of imagination to a subsidiary role is often repeated, as in R. M. Hare's *Freedom and Reason,* which argues for a "sentimental education" of sympathetic imagination that adds finesse when applying rules.[21] Despite Larmore's and Hare's strides beyond previous rule theories, imagination here merely supervenes *upon* conduct; it does not intervene *in* conduct (ACF, LW 9:13).

Similar examples in the recent literature abound, with the unfortunate result that imagination, in Dewey's words, is conceived as "limited and partial. It does not extend far; it does not permeate deeply and widely" (ACF, LW 9:14). For example, according to Oliver Williams in *The Moral Imagination,* imagination is essential to responsible morality. It attunes us to the Good in a way codes of conduct or commandments cannot, enabling us, as a form of Aristotelian practical wisdom, to "more astutely *recognize* obligation and wrongdoing." Meanwhile, following the Thomist tradition, the process of *justification* is carried out by human reason with reference to universal moral rules and principles.[22] There is an antecedently established Good and Right, in no way constituted through imaginative engagement, and imagination schools us to see this Good truthfully and "desire rightly." Imagination's circumscribed task is to aid our ability to do what universal reason, which must be carefully demarcated from imagination, demands.

In her excellent study of management decision making inspired by Mark Johnson's *Moral Imagination,* Patricia Werhane agrees that imagination is essential to moral judgment. "Moral imagination," she says, "is the ability in particular circumstances to discover and evaluate possibilities not merely determined by that circumstance, or limited by its operative mental models, or merely framed by a set of rules or rule-governed concerns." Through imagination one can project novel ways to frame situations and thus "broaden, evaluate, and even change one's moral point of view." However, echoing suspicions of imagination cut loose from rule-governed reason, she questions the thesis that moral understanding is *fundamentally* imaginative and argues that "Without moral reasoning one may slip into moral fantasy."[23]

Edward Tivnan takes the opposite route by following Rorty's neopragmatic dismissal of all attempts at moral justification. Assuming the lack of any substantive moral knowledge, when values clash we must learn to keep the peace, unstable as this peace must be in a democracy, by developing the empathetic ability to "imagine the world from the other side of the barricade." Tivnan reduces moral imagination to the peacekeeping function of empathetic leaps, a democratic substitute for a Hobbesian Leviathan that serves to stay our hands from throttling each other. Thus, says Tivnan, "by developing your moral imagination, you will be less likely to burn your adversary at the stake for fear that no matter how strongly you feel that the death penalty is right, say, or that affirmative action is unjust, you may actually be wrong."[24] Again, imagination plays a partial role; it does not penetrate deeply into moral life.

Thomas McCollough, in *The Moral Imagination and Public Life,* offers a more expansive view of imagination than Tivnan, closer to the theory of Dewey, whom he overlooks. He writes: "The moral imagination may be understood as a capacity to empathize with others and to discern creative possibilities for ethical action. The moral imagination considers an issue in the light of the whole. . . . [It] broadens and deepens the context of decision making."[25] Unlike Werhane, McCollough does not ultimately attempt to restrict imagination's role in conduct.

John Kekes, in *The Morality of Pluralism,* helpfully identifies moral imagination with "mental exploration of what it would be like to realize particular possibilities." He contrasts this with imagination as image formation, problem solving, and fantasizing. Moral imagination has two simultaneous functions, exploratory and corrective. As exploratory, it gives breadth to forward-looking reflection. By enlarging our field of possibilities beyond provisions of tradition, especially through "exposure to other traditions—usually through history, ethnography, and literature," moral imagination provides "a basis for contrast and comparison" that lets us "view critically the possibilities with which we start."[26] Setting aside Kekes's conservative treatment of limits (which serve to restrict imagination), this accords with Lionel Trilling's *The Liberal Imagination:* "[T]he moral imagination . . . reveals to us the complexity, the difficulty, and the interest of life in society, and best instructs us in our human variety. . . . [I]t is the human activity which takes the fullest and most precise account of variousness, complexity, difficulty—and possibility."[27]

In its corrective function, according to Kekes, moral imagination gives depth to retroactive assessment of past mistakes in evaluating possibilities. By imaginatively re-creating past choices and identifying sources of error such as narrow-mindedness, sluggishness, fantasy, misplaced hopes and fears, and self-deception, we can more realistically estimate how "we can guard against their recurrence in situations we presently face." Through these functions moral imagination makes us freer, says Kekes, though not free, by increasing control over possibilities.[28]

DEWEY'S THEORY OF IMAGINATION

These are promising developments by philosophers grappling with how to make moral judgments wiser. Nevertheless, this renascence of imagination has proceeded more or less in ignorance of Dewey's fecund insights. This is partly due to the fact that he never explicitly developed this key concept of his philosophy into a coherent theory. Some blame may also be laid on the odd stereotype of pragmatism as obsessed with bald expediency: Why would a pragmatist have anything to say about imagination? Yet even Dewey scholarship seldom appreciates the import of imagination, despite the fact that it is a prerequisite to grasping his theory of intelligence as indirect exploratory action: "Thought is, as it were, conduct turned in upon itself and examining its purpose and its conditions, its resources, aids, and difficulties and obstacles" (HWT, LW 8:201; cf. QC, LW 4:178).

On Dewey's view "imagination is as much a normal and integral part of human activity as is muscular movement" (DE, MW 9:245). Peirce observed likewise that imagination is as inherent in humans as dam building is for beavers or nest building is for birds: "the whole business of ratiocination, and all that makes us intellectual beings, is performed in imagination."[29] This extends well beyond Vico's argument for the dominance of poetic imagination over logical intellect, and beyond the conventional dualism, echoed uncritically by Stuart Hampshire in his influential *Innocence and Experience,* that imagination "leaps and swerves" while rational intellect advances "by rule-guided steps."[30]

We can, of course, distinguish reason and imagination. Dewey's distinction is an operational or functional one between phases of undifferentiated experience, not between restrictive and liberating mental powers. All active intellectual life, poetic or theoretical, is imaginative *to the degree* that it "supplements and deepens observation" by affording "clear insight into the remote, the absent, the obscure" (HWT, LW 8:351).

Acknowledging the "verbal difficulties owing to our frequent use of the word 'imagination' to denote fantasy and doubtful reality" (ACF, LW 9:30), Dewey cautions against the custom of identifying the *imaginative*, which is interactively engaged and rooted in problematic conditions, with the *imaginary*, which is subjective. Neither the imaginative nor the imaginary occurs ex nihilo, independent of a bio-cultural matrix, but only the imaginative necessitates courage to engage the present and stretch.

Two "imaginations" recur as themes in Dewey's writings, each concerned only indirectly with the prototypical notion of imagination as the formation of familiar and unfamiliar mental images. They are:

1. *Empathetic projection.* As a form of direct responsiveness, empathy is "the animating mold of moral judgment" (1932 E, LW 7:270). Taking the attitudes of others stirs us beyond numbness so we pause to sort through others' aspirations, interests, and worries as our own. This should be distinguished from the common misguided habit of projecting our own values and intentions onto others without respect for differences. Empathy, for Dewey, is necessary but not sufficient for moral judgment (1932 E, LW 7:268–269).

2. *Creatively tapping a situation's possibilities.* This is Dewey's central meaning, as when he cites Shelley's statement that "Imagination [not established morals] is the chief instrument of the good" (AE, LW 10:350).[31] In contrast to imaginative experience, the inertia of habit may override adjustment of past and present, yielding uniformity and routine. Imagination in this cognitive, concrete, contextualized sense, when wed to makings, results in expressive objects.[32] A variant is highlighted in Peirce's theory of "abductive inference."

Imagination in Dewey's central sense is the capacity to concretely perceive what is before us in light of what could be. Its opposite is experience narrowed by acclimation to standardized meanings. Mechanical and unimaginative experience is on the level of "savages" and "animals," Dewey says to the raised eyebrows of contemporary readers (e.g., EW 5:364–365, MW 6:13, MW 14:74, LW 17:257–258). The salvageable point here is that well-trod pathways may seem the only ones available. On one interpretation of a pivotal scene in the *Iliad*, Achilles, in his role as warrior, could see Hector only as a vanquished foe. Priam's pleas for the return of his son's body were futile so long as Achilles' perceptions were contracted and his emotions numbed by his habituated role. At this point, before Priam's kiss evokes a perceptual shift, Achilles fails to see "in terms of possibilities, . . . old things in new relations" (ACF, LW 9:34).[33]

This is why imaginative products, in science, industry, art, philosophy, religion, or morality, are at first condemned. Recall the skepticism that greeted the first personal computers, or the cautionary voices that provoked Martin Luther King Jr.'s "Letter from a Birmingham Jail." "It is not merely in religion," Dewey declares, "that the prophet is at first stoned (metaphorically at least) while later generations build the commemorative monument" (AE, LW 10:274). Imaginative experience ventures beyond restatements of convention to grasp undisclosed opportunities and to generate new ideals and ends.

Whether in art, industry, or moral conduct, imagination reaches deep into the "hard stuff of the world of physical and social experience" and seizes upon possible new relations for thought and action. New aims and ideals emerge to guide behavior, "generated through imagination. But they are not made out of imaginary stuff" (ACF, LW 9:33). Far from a euphemism for frivolousness or caprice, the imaginative is "a warm and intimate taking in of the full scope of a situation" (DE, MW 9:244). It is imbued with sociocultural meanings and rooted in problematic conditions, whereas imaginary flights of "mind-wandering and wayward fancy are nothing but the unsuppressible imagination cut loose from concern with what is done" (DE, MW 9:245).

In fanciful experience (Dewey does not seem to be referring to expressive forms of play-activity that may go by the name of fantasy), as when someone sees a ghost, is abducted by an alien, trips on a hallucinogenic drug, or is mentally poisoned with paranoia, "mind and material do not squarely meet and interpenetrate. Mind stays aloof and toys with material rather than boldly grasping it. The material . . . does not offer enough resistance, and so mind plays with it capriciously" (AE, LW 10:272).

Imagination amplifies perception beyond the immediate environment. It "constitutes an extension of the environment to which we respond."[34] This is true of imagination both as empathy and as the creative tapping of possibilities. Dewey discusses empathy as "sympathy," a subcategory of what Mead describes in neutral terms as taking the attitude of another. It is defined as "entering by imagination into the situations of others" (1908 E, MW 5:150). Sympathy names a type of immediate responsiveness and sensitivity without which not only would we be callous and indifferent, but there would not even be "an inducement to deliberate or material with which to deliberate" (1932 E, LW 7:269).[35]

In contrast, for Kant absence of sympathetic responsiveness, or even coldness and indifference to others' sufferings, best demarcates (at least for the sake of theoretical exposition) acts of the highest moral worth. Empathy is on his view morally, though not prudentially, worthless since it infuses feeling into motives for action instead of subjecting oneself to the command of reason alone.[36] In defense of Kant's disparagement of empathy, it is true that, in the absence of a wide survey of the situation, sympathetic inclination may prejudice one in favor of what or who is near and dear, to the point of not caring for others affected. Dewey, like Hume, grappled with this problem. In opposition to Kant's extreme view that sympathy is unnecessary, even subversive, they each concluded that it is essential to all moral judgment, while not on its own sufficient. Recent evidence from neuroscience, such as Antonio Damasio's *Descartes' Error* and *The Feeling of What Happens,* favors Dewey, Hume, and much recent work in feminist ethics: disaffective behavior is cold-blooded and morally warped.

On Dewey's view, direct valuing such as empathy is complemented and expanded in deliberate, practical reflection, which requires tapping possibilities for action—especially through communication and dialogue—and forecasting the consequences of acting on them (1932 E, LW 7:271). Both aspects of imagination, empathy and creative tapping of possibilities, operate simultaneously. This focuses deliberation concretely on the present yet expands attention beyond what is immediately experienced so that the lessons of the past, embodied in habits, and as-yet-unrealized potentialities "come home to us and have power to stir us" (ACF, LW 9:30).

Alexander defines imagination along these lines, as a capacity "to see the actual in light of the possible." He explains:

> It is a phase of activity . . . in which possible activities are envisaged in relation to our own situations, thereby amplifying the meaning of the present and creating the context from which present values may be criticized, thus liberating the course of action itself. . . . Imagination is temporally complex, an operation in the present, establishing continuity with the past, anticipating the future, so that a continuous process of activity may unfold in the most meaningful and value-rich way possible.[37]

As a capacity to engage the present with an eye to what is not immediately at hand, imagination is more than a niche for fictional embellishments, as when someone has an "over-active imagination" or is "imagining things." Nor is it the exclusive possession of fine artists. It is integrated with everyday life and learning.

The implications for ethics are far-reaching. Moral imagination is not limited to the declawed life Oliver Williams envisions for it, schooling us to recognize pre-existing obligations filled in super-empirically by an authoritative faith tradition or by transcendental reason. On the standard model of moral knowledge, imagination at most follows on the heels of principled ethical reflection as a means of bringing circumstances in accord with the determinations of cool reason. The utilitarian ethicist, for example, rationally determines that causing unnecessary suffering detracts from the greater good, identifies resistance to euthanasia as a vast source of needless suffering, and only then invokes empathy—feeling oneself "in the place of the victim," in Peter Singer's words. It is engaged ad hoc to rally people to do the right thing.[38]

However, if Dewey is right, "only imaginative vision elicits the possibilities that are interwoven within the texture of the actual" (AE, LW 10:348). If so, imagination intervenes deeply in moral life. It is at the foreground of deliberation and so must be central, not merely supplementary, to moral judgment and knowledge. Piecemeal adjustment to contemporary moral philosophies cannot accommodate this. At most, such adjustment would consign imagination to a fenced-off role attuning us to do Reason's bidding. Yet a Copernican shift centering ethics on imagination *can* accommodate what is of pragmatic worth in these philosophies.

FIVE

Dramatic Rehearsal

Deliberation is a dramatic rehearsal (in imagination) of
various competing possible lines of action. . . . [It] is an
experiment in finding out what the various lines of
possible action are really like. . . . Thought runs ahead
and foresees outcomes, and thereby avoids having
to await the instruction of actual failure and disaster.
An act overtly tried out is irrevocable, its consequences
cannot be blotted out. An act tried out in imagination
is not final or fatal. It is retrievable.
—John Dewey, *Human Nature and Conduct*

IMAGINATION IN DELIBERATION

Dewey's work on the psychology of moral deliberation—which he calls
dramatic rehearsal—is his most protracted attempt to highlight the
pivotal function of imagination as a "vicarious, anticipatory way of acting"
(LW 8:200).[1] This theory has been underemphasized in the philosophical
literature, and where it has been discussed it has often been misrepresented.

In Jennifer Welchman's otherwise laudable *Dewey's Ethical Thought* and
Charles Stevenson's introduction to the critical edition of Dewey and Tuft's
1908 *Ethics* (MW 5), dramatic rehearsal is treated as yet another "method"
or "procedure"—differentiated by being "scientific" and thus more warranted—competing with other procedures for a winner-take-all prescrip-
tion about how people *should* deliberate.[2] Stevenson and Welchman thereby place dramatic rehearsal on a logical par with Bentham's calculating units
of pleasure and pain, W. D. Ross's ranking *prima facie* duties, or the like.
Dewey's is instead an experimentally testable theory about the psychology
of deliberation. His idea is that if we get clear about traits of prototypically
"normal" deliberation, then the potential of everyday reflection may be
more fully realized. Dramatic rehearsal is not a procedure, woven whole

cloth from Dewey's cerebrations, to replace or make rationally consistent our normal cognitive processes and cultural milieu. It has no parallel in the categorical imperative or utilitarian maxim.

The focus of most college courses in ethics is to cultivate respect for "giving reasons." This is indispensable in moral reflection. Far from relegating the importance of reason giving in ethics, a theory of imaginative inquiry helps to explain its crucial role rather than simply reciting the moral philosophers' mantra of "reason over feeling." Its role is to contribute to an expansion of imagination.

What Dewey had in mind can be grasped only from the standpoint of the organic unity of his philosophy, particularly his pragmatic theories of habit and the social self, belief and inquiry, experimental intelligence, and imagination. In deliberation (moral, scientific, artistic), we singly or collectively hunt for ways to settle difficulties and ambiguities by scoping out alternatives and picturing ourselves taking part in them. Imagination continues until we are stimulated to act by a course that appears to harmonize pressing interests, needs, and other factors of the situation. A "complete" moral deliberation takes into consideration factors highlighted by traditional ethical theories, such as duties and contractual obligations, short and long-term consequences, traits of character to be affected, and rights. So ideally, the relative and usually tenuous harmony effected is not at the expense of careful appraisal of the worth of competing factors claiming attention.[3] The point is to look *and* evaluate before leaping.

In his ethical writings, especially *Human Nature and Conduct* and the two editions of *Ethics*,[4] Dewey has confused commentators by his carelessness regarding a distinction about deliberation otherwise made clear in his logical works. Dramatic rehearsal is one phase or function of the deliberative process. It is not the sum of this process. But this function of *crystallizing possibilities and transforming them into directive hypotheses* is so essential that it lends its name to the whole process. This is why in his ethical writings Dewey treats dramatic rehearsal and deliberation synonymously.

Rehearsal illuminates, opens up a situation so it is perceived in a new way. This should not be confused with the prevalent view of deliberation as a private soliloquy. For example, a family pondering whether to buy a particular house imagines day-to-day life in and around the house, mortgage payments, repair costs, and other aspects. They must consider these in relation to their careers, economic circumstances, long-term goals, and moral-social-political priorities. This is more than an armchair affair. Moreover, it is not a matter of prancing arbitrarily in one's mind from one imagined scenario to another. The process is neither slapdash nor rigid, but somewhat ordered. Effective imagination about this requires visits to the house, research, consultation with specialists, and most importantly, since democratic colloquy is more trustworthy than cloistered soliloquy, a great deal of communication with each other. Much deliberation is more private than this example, but the process is seldom as cloistered as mainstream ethical theorists pretend. And far better that it not be. To borrow a word coined by Boisvert for the tendency to equate thinking with disembodied heads, Dewey's theory of deliberation is not "cephalocentric."

Returning to the toddler who wishes to be picked up, her repertoire included a mastery of crying techniques and pleading gazes. A novel situation provoked her to explore other ways of communicating. This illustrates that, in addition to a state of doubt, reflective thinking involves "an act of searching, hunting, inquiring, to find material that will resolve the doubt, settle and dispose of the perplexity" (HWT, LW 8:120–121). Conflicting factors kindle a search for ways to make circumstances manageable, and possible ways of settling the perplexity are pursued. In this search, the actual consequences of past activities "become possible future consequences of acts still to be performed" (HNC, MW 14:155).

Imagination, like all thought, is kindled by such perplexities. "Any imagination is a sign that impulse is impeded and is groping for utterance" (HNC, MW 14:113). Dramatic rehearsal is a reflective phase of this groping. As in a game of chess or a jazz quintet, the more refined one's imagination (a function of relevant habits), the richer the fund of germane possibilities and the more reliable one's valuations.

This tidy picture should be qualified: An accurate psychology of deliberation cannot pretend people are on the whole serene models of Buddhist detachment when it comes to decisions. We worry, revel, recoil, and dwell monotonously. Much of this is at least peripherally part of deliberation. A student may correctly identify fretting as an undesirable element in her studies. Still, fretting over a paper or exam may take on something of the form of dramatic rehearsal, whether or not the student set out with the intention of thinking a matter through.

In the eighty years since *Human Nature and Conduct* appeared, Dewey's theory of deliberation has been bolstered by empirical discoveries, some of which will be explored in this chapter. It is a unique strength, not a liability, that Dewey's theory is self-consciously fallible and revisable. As a result it is amenable to ongoing adjustment in light of studies of mind and culture. Moreover, it allows attention to and respect for psychological and cultural differences.

For example, work by neuroscientists on morally educable people who are not prototypically "normal" calls for adjustment to Dewey's de-emphasis on rules. Consider a high-functioning autistic person (with Asperger's syndrome) whose brain inhibits normal empathy. To assist perceptions, she compensates by relying more strictly on learned—yet not emotionally fathomed—formal social rules, codes of behavior, and intervention by others. To flourish, she also needs special assistance with imaginative rehearsal and evaluation of consequences. If morality were *reducible* to following rules or codes, high-functioning autism would be the moral ideal. Meanwhile, a moral philosophy centered on imagination offers an empirically responsible and sensitive resource for working with autism. A person with moderate mental retardation may likewise rely more on governance by rules without intellectual assent. As is quite common, she may have enhanced empathetic capacities to guide social interactions, and people who note this will value her moral perceptions. Contrary to the view of intellectualists in ethics, she is a moral agent, not simply a moral patient. But there will be an increased need for direct communal intervention and support. This helps to compensate for her challenged capacity for imaginative rehearsal of possibilities and consequences.[5]

Dramatic rehearsal is not uppermost in some decisions. Faced with a difficulty, some may seek a divine sign, consult astrology charts, throw dice, clutch crystals. It is fatiguing for minds not habituated to inquiry to go down unusual paths. A novel by Clyde Edgerton provides a nice illustration. A well-intentioned seventy-eight-year-old Appalachian woman, Mattie, must decide whether to take a juvenile delinquent, Wesley, into her home. She begins rehearsing, but quickly gives this up:

> Mattie looked across the den into the kitchen, dark except for the light from the lamp beside her. What if Wesley was sitting over there right now doing something he ought not to be doing: eating hard candy, or worse still, drinking beer. What would she say? She'd talk to him and explain. Maybe take more time to explain than she used to take with Robert and Elaine.
>
> She closed her eyes. Now was the time. How could she do it? Well, it had to be some sort of instant decision, something quick. There was just no way she could *figure* it out. It would have to come in a flash.
>
> She had an idea. She pictured herself standing in the pulpit looking out into the church sanctuary. The church was empty except for three little . . . little ghostlike figures, sitting in the middle of the auditorium on her right, and three in the middle on her left. Mattie spoke to the three on her right. "If I am to keep Wesley, you three stand up—when the time comes," she said. She looked at the three on her left. "If I am *not* to keep Wesley, you three stand up when the time comes. All of you take your time. Don't move until you have to. Now. Do what you have to do." She stood before them, watching and waiting.
>
> Together, the three on the right stood. Mattie opened her eyes.
>
> That was that.[6]

In prior scenes Mattie subconsciously rehearses alternatives for Wesley, so her decision is less arbitrary than this snapshot suggests. There is much to admire in Mattie's deliberation. She is guided primarily by her empathy with Wesley. Empathy is essential to the content and quality of all deliberation, and in this case it appears to guide her well. Yet empathy is most trustworthy when it operates seamlessly with rehearsal of consequences. Reading the passage in isolation as a sign of Mattie's deliberative habits, there is cause to worry that her rehearsals go unconsummated and that this makes her choices less reliable than they could otherwise be.

In a similar yet less charming instance, a southern woman told her professor how she labored over a marriage proposal from a man who opposed higher education for women. As she rehearsed this possible future her doubts intensified. Instead of following through, she cut deliberation short, let her *Bible* fall open, and randomly placed her finger on a verse. "Honor all men," said Peter, and she announced her engagement.

Ideally, possible avenues for acting are rehearsed before trying them out. Intelligence is abdicated when this process is cut short. This idea is readily grasped. It is as familiar as "look before you leap" and other proverbs. What is needed is to reconstruct the elements of an experimentally defensible theory of moral imagination, using Dewey's scattered discussions of dramatic rehearsal as a template.

DEWEY ON DRAMATIC REHEARSAL

Descriptions of deliberation in Dewey's early writings and lectures underscore themes not as well elaborated in his middle and later work, yet essential to full appreciation of the theory. He was deeply influenced by reading and teaching James's *Principles of Psychology* in 1890. James presents deliberation as constituted by two battling impulses: "the impatience of the deliberative state" (i.e., the desire to re-establish equilibrium and continue acting) and "the dread of the irrevocable" (i.e., the hesitancy of carrying an imagined alternative into manifest action). These two motives retard decisions so that a situation may be reasonably negotiated. A great part of this negotiation "consists in the turning over of all the possible modes of *conceiving* the doing or not doing of the act in point" (PP, 1138–1139; II, 531).

Dewey gradually clarified his own theory of deliberation from the mid-1890s on.[7] In his 1894 *The Study of Ethics: A Syllabus* (EW 4), he proposes that ethical intentions or ends ("what an agent *means* to do") are constituted by mediation of impulses through reflection. This process is beset by difficulties. The perceived satisfaction of following the original impulse may vie with the satisfaction of following the mediating course (a struggle traditionally dubbed "desire versus duty"). Or the various aims may conflict so that one must either eliminate some or "discover a still more comprehensive aim in which the claims of the conflicting intentions shall be adjusted" (EW 4:251). This is the onset of deliberation, concerning which Dewey writes: "We are apt to describe this process as if it were a coldly intellectual one. As matter of fact, it is a process of tentative action; we 'try on' one or other of the ends, imagining ourselves actually doing them, going, indeed, in this make-believe action just as far as we can without actually doing them" (EW 4:251).

This deliberative process can easily lead one astray. An impulsive idea may have such a hold on us that it is overtly acted upon while it is "tried on," even though we do not consciously intend the action.[8] The proper outcome of deliberation, however, is "decision, *resolution,* the definitely formed plan." And a deliberate intention, end, or aim is ethically justifiable only if it gives "attention to all the bearings which could be foreseen by an agent who had a proper interest in knowing what he is about" (EW 4:251–252). This can be especially difficult since, as Kekes points out, hopes and fears may "lead us to ignore, overlook, or forget about other facts that are just as salient but whose salience is obscured by the feelings we have allowed to rule us."[9] But the mere fact that deliberation is difficult does not justify a flight from contingency to foundational principles.

In his 1900–1901 lectures on ethics at the University of Chicago, Dewey distinguishes four of the ways in which people deliberate, then explores the generic pattern: (1) "Some people deliberate by dialogue." (2) "Others visualize certain results." (3) "Others rather take the motor imagery and imagine themselves doing a thing." (4) "Others imagine a thing done and then imagine someone else commenting upon it."[10] What unifies this diversity is that deliberation "represents the process of rehearsing activity in idea when that overt act is postponed. It is, so to speak, trying an act on before it is tried out in the objective, obvious, space and time world." Following Peirce's belief-doubt-inquiry continuum, opposed tendencies create a tension, evoking an affective phase in which emotions come to the fore. This tension spurs deliberation. To escape the tension requires "an objective survey of the situation." The deliberative phase is marked by inhibition of activity and involves "turning back, as distinct from the projective or going-forward attitude."[11] Prior experience is analyzed in order to find a way to direct current activities.

Deliberation tells one "what experiences he would get . . . if he were to follow out a given tendency or act upon a particular desire." Hume recognized this capacity, but his separation of reason from emotion led him to minimize the role of intelligence in moral choice. In contrast, Dewey warns against separating the three phases, which must not be conceived as "a mere sequence because everything is going back and forth all the time like a shuttle." Each is diffused through the whole process. Emotions climax as a choice is made that reabsorbs the emotional and deliberative phases back into the active.[12] This emotional penumbra, richly developed in terms of the aesthetic in Dewey's later work, gives the experience its distinctive quality.

This qualitative dimension of deliberation has been missed by some commentators. In his introduction to the critical edition of the 1908 *Ethics* (MW 5), the emotivist C. L. Stevenson condescendingly proposes to clear up Dewey's "analytical clumsiness." The result is a barren analysis of deliberation without regard for the dramatic and qualitative aspects of thinking, an emphasis of Dewey's that Stevenson elsewhere dubs "needless and clumsy."[13] Stevenson reduces dramatic rehearsal to a quest for "scientifically true propositions." These propositions are literally the outcome of appeal to already established scientific knowledge, and they determine the rightness of a proposed act. All valuations are reduced to fact finding, oddly committing Dewey to G. E. Moore's infamous "naturalistic fallacy." A "speaker," Stevenson claims, must "carry out completely" this quest for scientific truths—"established by psychology, . . . economics, biology, physics, and so on—if he or she is to assent to the proposition that an action is right" (MW 5:xxii). In *Dewey's Ethical Thought,* Welchman appears to accept this scientistic and reductionistic account of dramatic rehearsal.[14]

Victor Kestenbaum points out that such an interpretation diminishes dramatic rehearsal to a mere prelude to the *real* work of moral evaluation, likely some form of moral accounting or rule following.[15] The truth in Stevenson's analysis is that the tentative solutions arrived at in deliberation must be testable in the world. As the world answers back, imagination is refined in its projection of scenarios and consequences. Stevenson misses that this testing is intelligible only as the close of inquiry. Dewey does see the sciences as a resource, and the patient, fallibilistic morale of science as a model for all experimental inquiry. In *Theory of Valuation* (LW 13), published in the late 1930s at the time Stevenson's views crystallized, Dewey even longs for a "science" of moral valuation. But it stretches credulity to infer on this basis that the physical sciences play the role of a moral bedrock, particularly given that there is for Dewey no single right way to reason about moral questions. Despite pretenders for such a method, there is no antecedent procedure that, rigorously adhered to, can be *trusted* to determine right behavior.

Such misinterpretations of Dewey at any rate spot that there is more to the theory of dramatic rehearsal than can be captured in proverbs such as "A stitch in time saves nine" or "Act in haste, repent in leisure" (TV, LW 13:219). What, then, are the nuances of the theory, and how, specifically, does it operate within Dewey's theory of inquiry?

First compare to utilitarianism. The absence of a supreme governing principle or procedure marks one crucial difference between Dewey's pragmatic pluralism and utilitarianism. Yet their theories of moral judgment are often conflated. In *Human Nature and Conduct,* Dewey sharply criticizes utilitarianism for separating means from ends and privileging cold calculation over imagination. During the industrial revolution, Dewey contends, pleasure and pain came to be identified with financial profit and loss while, carrying over the Christian doctrine of our fallen state, human nature was thought an inherently lazy thing put to work only through briberies and threats. The summum bonum was conceived as "a maximum net gain of pleasures on the basis of analogy with business conducted for pecuniary profit." Enter Jeremy Bentham with a hedonistic calculus of hedons or utils of pleasure; for him a theory of moral deliberation could serve "only to enlighten the search for good or gain by instituting a more exact calculus of profit and loss" (HNC, MW 14:147–149). Since there was no role in morality for any "faculty" believed to threaten impartial calculation, utilitarians up to the present have followed a model of calculative rationality in which imagination has little or no relevance.

Dewey esteems utilitarianism's naturalism and respect for social consequences, but he decries the attempt—regarded today as inessential by some prominent utilitarians—to reduce all moral judgments to calculating future profit and loss of an antecedently fixed end, generally conceived as pleasure. Not only does this universalize a historical cultural phenomenon, the profit motive, but it also reduces moral theory to a science of accounting relevant only to those cases in which ends are predetermined. The exclusive focus of moral education is thus calculative reason. Moral imagination is at best irrelevant. "It resembles the case in which a man has already made his final decision, say to take a walk, and deliberates only upon what walk to take. His end-in-view already exists; it is not questioned. The question is as to comparative advantages of this tramp or that" (HNC, MW 14:149).

Conceiving deliberation as calculation inhibits imagination by forsaking the present. Ironically, it is calculation, not imagination, that distorts moral reflection by impeding our ability to see the near in terms of the remote. It locks in a course of action before we even discover what the situation is about, what it portends and promises. What is most at stake in moral life is not some quantifiable pleasure or pain, but "what kind of person one is to become" and what kind of world is to develop (HNC, MW 14:150). These questions are explored in imagination.

According to pragmatism's theory of inquiry, impulsion toward action persists even when disturbing circumstances arrest overt action. Echoing Peirce's concept of abductive inference (i.e., educated hunches), Dewey observes that the tendency to act is diverted and reconfigured as an idea or "suggestion" that acts as "a substitute for direct action" (HWT, LW 8:200). These investigative guides "just spring up, flash upon us, occur to us" (LTI, LW 12:113–114).[16] Deliberation is not cold calculation of advantage and disadvantage; it is habit and impulse driving us forward. He explains: "We do not act *from* reasoning; but reasoning puts before us objects which are not directly or sensibly present, so that we may then react directly to these objects, . . . precisely as we would to the same objects if they were physically present" (HNC, MW 14:139). (The "stretch" of inference is a function of imagination, for Dewey, but it is not identical to imagination [see HWT, LW 8:190ff; EN, LW 1:13].)

In *How We Think,* Dewey argues that deliberation is an indirect mode of acting: It is "a kind of dramatic rehearsal. Were there only one suggestion popping up, we should undoubtedly adopt it at once." But when alternatives contend with one another as we forecast their probable outcomes, the ensuing tension or suspense sustains inquiry (HWT, LW 8:200; cf. LW 8:187ff.). In this way bearings are foreseen. "An act overtly tried out is irrevocable, its consequences cannot be blotted out," Dewey says in his most extensive discussion of dramatic rehearsal. "An act tried out in imagination is not final or fatal. It is retrievable" (HNC, MW 14:132–133).

Of more than historical interest is Dewey's insistence that this capacity is the exclusive purview of humans. Other animals, he contends, do not deliberate; their actions are "fully geared to extero-ceptor and muscular activities" and hence immediately translate into overt rather than indirect imaginative behavior (EN, LW 1:221; cf. MW 10:282). Only with humans are "means-consequences tried out in advance without the organism getting irretrievably involved in physical consequences." Contemporary research on animal intelligence has made such sweeping claims obsolete.[17] Still, these claims throw Dewey's idea of dramatic rehearsal into relief.

Homer's Penelope weaves and unweaves Laertes's shroud, and we weave and unweave in imagination possible narratives for action. We project ourselves into alternative futures and imagine possible actions carried through, always with the option of undoing the still revocable outcome. "We give way, *in our mind,* to some impulse; we try, *in our mind,* some plan. Following its career through various steps, we find ourselves in imagination in the presence of the consequences that would follow" (1908 E, MW 5:293 and 1932 E, LW 7:275).[18]

This statement occurs in the context of a discussion of moral intuition, otherwise called "prizing," "direct sensing," or "appreciation" (TV, LW 13:195; 1932 E, LW 7:275). Intuitions appear as part of an "imaginative dramatic performance of various deeds carrying to their appropriate issues the various tendencies we feel stirring within us" (1908 E, MW 5:292). A felt sense that a prospective action may best harmonize factors in a situation could plausibly be termed an intuition if one means a naturally conditioned, educated sense of probable outcomes of behavior. This opposes G. E. Moore's intuitionism, which leaves inquiry irrelevant to establishing goodness. According to Moore: "If I am asked 'what is good?' my answer is that good is good and that is the end of the matter. Or if I am asked 'How is good to be defined?' my answer is that it cannot be defined, and that is all I have to say about it."[19] Pragmatically understood, intuition is a "direct sense of value" (1908 E, MW 5:293) provoked by a suggested stimulus to action. But it is always *mediated* immediacy, in Hegel's phrasing. It is not apprehension of a timeless essence that bestows a certificate of certitude. Consequently, prizings and appraisals must be entertained subject to revision and correction by ongoing observation and questioning (1932 E, LW 7:273).[20]

Intuitions have a mainspring in established habits, as has been discussed. They are nurtured for good or ill in the same way that a gestating organism is nurtured or poisoned by its uterine environment, and their reliability depends upon the flexibility or intractability of habits. In Dewey's words: "The more numerous our habits the wider the field of possible observation and foretelling. The more flexible they are, the more refined is perception in its discrimination and the more delicate the presentation evoked by imagination" (HNC, MW 14:123).

Dramatic rehearsal is the reflective phase of the process of reconstructing frustrated habits. For example, in a close relationship another's objective presence has been woven into the fabric of one's habits. Loss of the relationship throws these habits out of equilibrium with changed surroundings. The prior habits cannot just be willed to change; rather, they ground, motivate, and structure ensuing readjustments, as when an unmet need for companionship provokes imagination of viable prospects for reestablishing stability: say, strengthening old friendships or actively pursuing new ones. These imaginings are not "pale bloodless abstractions." Rather, they are "charged with the motor urgent force of habit" (HNC, MW 14:39). New habits emerge from formerly satisfying ones, and they incorporate the altered structures of the new environment.

Imagination, as Alexander explains, is "a *creative* exploration of *structures* inherited from past experience which thereby allow[s] the future . . . to guide and interpret the present."[21] Imaginative rehearsal is *dramatic* because the options before us are intelligible only in the context of larger life narratives. To deliberate is to co-author a dramatic story with environing conditions in community with others. As dramatic, rehearsal is both immediately meaningful and instrumentally valuable. Application of universal rules to particular instances, or pseudo-mathematical calculation of means to already coagulated ends, may play substantial roles *within* dramatic rehearsal.

Labeling deliberation dramatic underscores that it is story-structured and that its imaginative phase is not limited to supplementing rule-guided conduct. A dramatist configures a present line or verse with a rich aesthetic sense for possible meanings within a maturing, multidimensional scene.

She develops conflicts and contrasts among characters and contingent events until these instabilities are resolved. The good dramatist's imagination is neither rapturous nor reserved; neither effusive nor formal. Moral imagination is analogous. Through imagination, an expansive field of possible behaviors can be disclosed and conflicts brought to successful issue. Just as a character in a drama acts "in character" and those acts make no sense if taken out of context, moral behavior is intelligible only in the setting of a life-narrative, which of course interplays with other life-narratives. A possible course of action, Dewey observes, would be "as meaningless in isolation as would be the drama of Hamlet were it confined to a single line or word with no context" (AE, LW 10:29).

Recent work in pragmatist bioethics supports these claims. As Micah Hester explains, a "sociology of bioethical practice" reveals "a method of narrative construction and reconstruction of situations and experiences of actual persons (patients, physicians, etc.) in order to understand a given situation and to project into the future where we see these stories 'going from here.'"[22] An experience of deliberation is not a simple, detached episode. It is continuous with an individual's developmental history, which is in turn situated within the developmental histories of others. Hence MacIntyre observes, "I can only answer the question 'What am I to do?' if I can answer the prior question 'Of what story or stories do I find myself a part?'"[23] This is diametrically opposed to Kant, for whom attention to traits of human experience is relevant to prudential reasoning (*Pragmatisch*) but not to what is ironically called practical reasoning (*Praktisch*). Morality, for Kant, is strictly concerned with the latter. Kant explains the moral irrelevance of individuals and their developmental circumstances in *Lectures on Ethics:* "Moral laws must never take human weakness into account, but must be enunciated in their perfect holiness, purity, and morality, without any regard to man's actual constitution."[24] Deliberation that has moral worth follows a universal form purified of material, factual content.

For another perspective on what, in opposition to Kant, is story-structured about deliberation, take the "journey" language in Paul Ricoeur's description of stories: "To *follow* a story is to *move forward* in the midst of contingencies and peripeteia under the *guidance* of an expectation that finds its fulfillment in the 'conclusion' of the story. . . . It gives the story an *'end point.'* . . . To understand the story is to understand how and why the successive episodes *led* to the conclusion."[25] To say that deliberation is dramatic or story-structured means that it follows the form of any experience transformed toward consummation: it has a beginning, middle, and conclusion just as journeys have starting points, paths traversed, and end points or destinations. Each phase is qualitatively distinct, though not disconnected, as events are *conducted* to fulfillment (cf. 1932 E, LW 7:168).

"We compare life to a traveler faring forth" (HNC, MW 14:127). As seen in Part One, the beginning or starting point is for Dewey an active phase of stable habits setting a dominant tonal quality of relative equilibrium. This distinctive quality guides the situation as it develops and gives it its specific identity as *this* experience. The middle or path traversed is characterized by disrupted habit, disharmony, imbalance, loss of adaptation to surroundings, and competition and disunity among habits and desires. The troubled situation becomes increasingly organized as a reflective phase of rehearsal is provoked. The conclusion or destination is a consummatory phase of recovered action and stability felt to answer and give closure to the problem. It is characterized by relative equilibrium and reunification of desires.

Dewey balances this "temporally dynamic" source-path-goal scheme with a center-periphery image of experience as a field event. As Alexander explains, experience is "a total *field* of action which has a complex structure at each and every moment and different degrees of focus, clarity, obscurity, and organization. . . . [E]xperience for Dewey is *both* process and field—a 'field-process,' if you will."[26]

The role of these schemas in pragmatist philosophy merits more careful study, as do Dewey's key metaphors of organic growth, balance, evolutionary adaptation, scientific experimentation, and the arts. As a model for understanding processes and products, the teleological journey metaphor—inescapable though it is—tends to separate the process from the product, the "means whereby" from the "goal sought." The end is prototypically thought of as a preset destination "down the road," the very separation of means from ends to which Dewey objected. This sheds light on why the pragmatic conception of means and ends is so often misinterpreted.

All metaphors emphasize some features of experience and de-emphasize or hide others. The metaphor of dramatic rehearsal highlights active consolidation and imaginative remaking. But the conventional stage drama calls up misleading associations, and Dewey's failure to qualify the metaphor is partly to blame for misinterpretations of his theory of deliberation. The moral production is not a dress rehearsal for a ready-made play, as it appears to be in many rule theories. Dewey's moral stage is atypical. Scenes are actively *co-authored* with others and with a precarious environment. The acting is improvisational, the performances open-ended. The drama is experimental, not scripted.

Two dimensions of the notion of co-authorship deserve scrutiny. A prevailing view among those in correspondence with Dewey and Arthur Bentley in the 1940s was that the distinction of "interaction" from "transaction" in *Knowing and the Known* (LW 16) marked a shift away from Dewey's earlier mentalistic view of deliberation toward a far more thoroughgoing organic-environmental approach.[27] But such a view neglects that, from the mid-1890s on, Dewey conceived deliberation as a *phase* of an overall action. This phase or function can be isolated for philosophical analysis without implying that deliberation proceeds within the confines of inner mental space. The chief work of tentative rehearsals is to reflect on consequences of actions *before* they "affect physical facts outside the body" (HNC, MW 14:133). This comment should not be misconstrued as reifying an inner-outer dualism, as though all existentially disturbed situations are subjective disorders curable by mental rearrangement. Dewey did not downplay the role of tactile activity or physical coordination in inquiry. The erotic interplay of sexual expressiveness, for example, reminds us that intertwining bodies engage in the reflexive process of moral deliberation. Or consider somatic intelligence in everyday problem solving: if you are deliberating on how to drive a stick shift, it will do little good merely to sit and ponder the matter. You must physically manipulate the objects in your immediate environment (clutch, brake, gear shift, etc.). In both cases, deliberation is part of the overall undifferentiated action. It is the action in its intelligently directed aspect.

A more substantive yet related criticism is that Dewey occasionally slips into cephalocentric language about deliberation. This tendency, which needs a corrective, is especially pronounced in *Human Nature and Conduct*. C. L. Stevenson may have had this in mind in pretending he had "corrected and supplemented" Dewey's emphasis on personal rather than interpersonal decisions.[28] Without exonerating Dewey, this should be considered in the context of his corpus. For Dewey as for Mead, imagination begins with communicative social interaction.[29] This is essential to Dewey's naturalistic empiricism. Alexander emphasizes this:

> [C]ontrary to Dewey's language at this point, subjective speculation is secondary to the primary power of social deliberation. We debate with ourselves because we have debated with others. Discussion of how to deal with a problem in a social context, for Mead as well as Dewey, is what teaches us to deliberate privately. On a more elementary level, we are *taught* to be mindful and thoughtful. Mind is social and situational, and our efforts at "working" the immediate problematic phase involve organizing dramatic, dynamic habits of action and meaning into a coherent field.[30]

This highlights that imagination is a result of social action that is internalized, a theme painstakingly explored in Mead's work and echoed by Dewey in *Experience and Nature*:

> Soliloquy is the product and reflex of converse with others; social communication not an effect of soliloquy. If we had not talked with others and they

with us, we should never talk to and with ourselves. Through speech a person dramatically identifies himself with potential acts and deeds; he plays many roles, not in successive stages of life but in a contemporaneously enacted drama. Thus mind emerges. (EN, LW 1:135)

Deliberation is social not only in the sense that we must take consequences for others into consideration but also in the sense that conversation with others provides the means for reflection.

Moreover, deliberation requires more than cloistered speculations about what others *might* think, need, or feel. What Alexander helpfully describes as Dewey's "democratic imagination" is, at its best, consultative. As Gouinlock observes, the best way "to adjust and reconcile human conflicts and bring welcome ends into existence" is to consult with others rather than approaching deliberations solipsistically.[31] We must rely on pooled, social intelligence. This stands in stark contrast with Kant's disparaging of interpersonal moral discourse: "Inexperienced in the course of the world, incapable of being prepared for all its contingencies, I ask *myself* only: Can I will that my maxim become a universal law?"[32]

METAPHOR AND MORAL IMAGINATION

As experimental, pragmatist ethics must continually be revised in light of empirical discoveries. Recent research in cognitive science, particularly in the field of cognitive semantics,[33] bolsters and expands Dewey's claims that ethical deliberation—indeed all reasoning—is fundamentally imaginative and that imagination is not internal and subjective. This work offers sustained treatments of the social nature of imagination, meaning, and reason.[34]

George Lakoff and Mark Johnson in *Philosophy in the Flesh* explore some work in cognitive science relevant to more concretely developing Dewey's insights on moral imagination. "The question is clear," they say. "Do you choose empirical responsibility or *a priori* philosophical assumptions? Most of what you believe about philosophy and much of what you believe about life will depend on your answer." Choosing the path of empirical responsibility, we are primed to consider three central findings about the mind and language that have emerged from "second generation" cognitive science (i.e., freed of the assumptions of Anglo-American analytic philosophy):

1. *The Cognitive Unconscious.* Conscious awareness is the tip of the iceberg of thought. Thus there exists a sort of "cognitive unconscious," cognitive defined very broadly to include all "mental operations concerned with conceptual systems, meaning, inference, and language." Their claim is not that thought is repressed and its structures unknowable à la Freud; it just

works too quickly and automatically for us to catch it in the act, and it is not directly accessible via Cartesian introspection. Among the key constituents of the cognitive unconscious are metaphors, metonymies, folk theories, image schemas, basic-level categories, and prototypes. These are part of our cultural heritage, and since they are "embodied in our synapses," they resist change.[35] Along with more conscious imaginative structures such as trans-generational myths, stories, and cosmological world-pictures, not discussed by Lakoff and Johnson, these are part of an often contradictory and continually changing horizon of social habits.

By disclosing our use of these structures, cognitive science affords limited freedom from "cognitive slavery," that is, "uncritical dependence on our unconscious metaphors." The history of philosophy has been marked by such slavery, Lakoff and Johnson contend, since "the conceptual systems of philosophers are no more consciously accessible than those of anyone else."[36] This supplements Dewey, who restricts imagination to conscious experience. "All *conscious* experience," he writes, "has of necessity some degree of imaginative quality. . . .The conscious adjustment of the new and the old *is* imagination" (AE, LW 10:276). Dewey thus highlights imaginative experience as "a venture into the unknown" (AE, LW 10:276), but he does not explore cognitive habits that are products of imagination.

2. The Embodiment of Mind. Concepts and the mind in general are embodied, though not in the trifling computational sense in which independently structured mental software can run on any compatible neural hardware. Kant recognized that the mind is empty without the body; he did not grasp that it is also formless. The body is in the mind. That is, conceptual structures ride piggyback on and evolved from basic sensory and motor systems.

The most pervasive instance of this is metaphorical thought, which is more than a mere matter of words. It involves the projection in our brains of "activation patterns from sensorimotor areas to higher cortical areas." Due to the central role of this sort of embodied metaphor, reason is fundamentally imaginative rather than disembodied, universal, transcendental, and literal. This is supported by convergent evidence from multiple methodologies, including linguistic analysis, psychological experiments, etymology, gesture studies, language acquisition studies, and studies of American Sign Language. That conceiving minds fit the world is no mystery. Minds "have evolved from our sensorimotor systems, which have in turn evolved to allow us to function well in our physical environment."[37]

3. Metaphorical Thought. Metaphors are unavoidable and indispensable. Lakoff and Johnson are concerned with conventional metaphors that operate as habits, in Dewey's sense. They are not primarily concerned with idiomatic expressions, isolated remarks such as "Richard is a gorilla," or poetic novelties such as "Juliet is the sun." On their rather unorthodox sense of the word, metaphors are not limited to mere elliptical similes or rhetorical flourishes. They are conceptual mappings that project knowledge and inference patterns from one domain to another. Typically, the logic of a concrete, "physical" source is ferried over (Gr. *meta-pherein*, to carry across) to a more abstract, often "mental," target. Thus, metaphors "are a consequence of the nature of our brains, our bodies, and the world we inhabit."[38]

They locate the experiential basis for metaphors in Dewey-esque primary experiences in which source and target domains are conflated. Dewey pointed to this phenomenon, in which the body is in the mind: "Every thought and meaning has its substratum in some organic act. . . . It roots in some definite act of biological behavior; physical names for mental acts like seeing, grasping, searching, affirming, acquiescing, spurning, comprehending, affection, emotion are not just 'metaphors' [i.e., they are not mere elliptical similes]" (EN, LW 1:221).

For example, the everyday experience of getting information through vision gives rise to, without universally determining, a conception of abstract knowing in terms of seeing, if you see what I mean. This motivates common expressions such as "I see what you're saying," "It looks different from my point of view," "Let me point something out to you."[39] We also obtain information in more tactile ways, motivating utterances such as "Do you grasp what I'm saying?" "I'm trying to get a feel for your argument," "I'm just tossing around some ideas." Which metaphor is emphasized has philosophic significance. Dewey preferred metaphors of understanding as manipulation over the more Platonic ones of vision. Herbert Schneider reports Dewey's comment at a dinner party: "I think this whole problem of understanding should be approached not from the point of view of the eyes, but from the point of view of the hands. It's what we grasp that matters."[40]

Far from being arbitrary, conventional metaphors like these are motivated and structured by the kinds of bodies we have and the environments in which we live out our lives. Some metaphors, such as visual metaphors for knowing, are shared across cultures due to the similarity of human bodies and brains. But due to different environing conditions, most metaphors are not universal. For example, in industrialized cultures, time is a valuable commodity. In American English, it can be wasted, saved, spent, invested, spared, budgeted, and squandered. We can live on borrowed time, and we can run out of time.[41] We can give valuable time to others by paying attention to them. This may be worth our while, and we are gratified when those we respect set aside or allot time to spend with us. The metaphor of time as a valuable commodity is constitutive of temporal experience among members of industrialized cultures in which time and monetary exchange are closely conjoined (a culture with hourly wages, etc.). Studies of cultures with different economic systems show that they do not understand and experience time in this way.[42]

Yet our bodies and environments do not utterly determine the metaphors we live by. Human interactive experience is far too fecund to predict in advance what metaphors will emerge in a culture. For example, in most languages the widely shared experience of motion-situations—as when I am on a path and literally see something "ahead of me"—motivates understanding the future as ahead of an observer and the past as behind. Time may be in motion relative to us ("Your birthday is fast approaching") or we may be in motion relative to it ("We're coming up on your birthday"). Yet in Aymara, a Chilean language of the Andes, the past is in front and the future is behind (thus *mayamara,* "eye year" or "front year," means "last year"). This appears to be motivated by the visible presence of an action's consequences and the invisibility of the future.[43]

Primary metaphors, which according to Lakoff and Johnson are blended to form complex metaphors, originate from literal sensorimotor concepts.[44] Here are some examples illustrated with a common linguistic expression:

Vision (Knowing is Seeing: "Do you see my point?")
Motion (Time is Motion: "Fall passed by quickly")
Reaching destinations (Purposes are Destinations: "Peace is a ways off, but they're getting there")
Object manipulation (Understanding is Grasping: "I'm trying to grasp your argument")
Exertion of force (Causes are Physical Forces: "I was pushed to do it")
Bounded regions (States are Locations: "She's in a depression")
Vertical orientation (More is Up/Less is Down: "Prices rose")
Bodily orientation (Happy is Up/Sad is Down: "I'm feeling down")

In contrast with much analytic philosophy, Lakoff and Johnson reveal that only a fraction of meaning is literal and propositional. In the absence of metaphor, literal concepts are fleshless. They write: "Imagine a concept of love without physical force—that is, without attraction, electricity, magnetism—and without union, madness, illness, magic, nurturance, journeys, closeness, heat, or giving of oneself. Take away all these metaphorical ways of conceptualizing love, and there's not a whole lot left. What's left is the mere literal skeleton."[45]

What these three findings of cognitive science add up to is an embodied realism that, in spite of shortcomings of Lakoff and Johnson's book,[46] meshes well with pragmatism's reconstruction of reason. As discussed in Part I, symbol-system realism and its compatriot, the correspondence theory, presuppose the mind-world, subject-object, conception-perception gap bequeathed to philosophy by Descartes and crystallized by Kant. Embodied realism, in contrast, "gives up on being able to know things-in-themselves, but, through embodiment, explains how we can have knowledge that, although it is not absolute, is nonetheless sufficient to allow us to function and flourish." The idea of a disembodied truth is arrogant and unrealistic because what makes knowledge possible, Lakoff and Johnson urge, "is our embodiment, not our transcendence of it, and our imagination, not our avoidance of it."[47]

Although it may initially seem wearisome to subsume a subject such as the metaphorization of experience under the steely guise of "cognitive science," this work is good theory. From the Greek *theamai,* to behold, a good theory enlarges and stimulates observations about how experience hangs together.

The upshot of metaphor for imagination is that our sense of who we are, how we understand situations, how we relate to others, and what we see as possible courses of action all depend significantly on culturally inherited metaphors and models. Most importantly, courses become options for us in part because the metaphor(s) used to make sense of a situation marks out these alternatives, so what is possible under one metaphor may not be possible under another.[48] George Eliot memorably underscored this in *Middlemarch,* as Casaubon's marriage to Dorothea drew near: "Poor Mr. Casaubon had imagined that his long studious bachelorhood had stored up for him a compound interest of enjoyment, and that large drafts on his affections would not fail to be honoured; for we all of us, grave or light, get our thoughts entangled in metaphors, and act fatally on the strength of them."[49] As Johnson argues in *Moral Imagination,* metaphor is "the locus of our imaginative exploration of possibilities for action."[50] Susan Sontag called attention to pitfalls of this in *Illness as Metaphor* and *AIDS and Its Metaphors:* "Of course, one cannot think without metaphors. But that does not mean there aren't some metaphors [such as illness as battle] we might well abstain from or try to retire."[51] Without denying the value of Sontag's consciously ironic pursuit of metaphor-free experience in the face of the inevitability of metaphoric interpretation, it is nonetheless a practical necessity to ask whether the metaphors that shape our moral imaginations are *trustworthy* when activated. Here are six straightforward examples:

In an argument, we may "gain" or "lose ground," "attack" or "defend a position," "win" or "lose." Not only do we use this agonistic language; we actually *experience* arguments as battles. Possible avenues for thought and action are opened up or closed off in accordance with understanding of one kind of thing (arguments) in terms of another (warfare). If this metaphor is operative in a predicament where there is a conflict of opinion or policy, truculent pathways are likely to seem inevitable, while possibilities for mutual growth through communication may be obscured. One's subconscious, unreflective, spontaneous tendency may, unchecked, be to belligerence. Taken by itself (in abstraction), this metaphor does not open up communicative possibilities as would, say, understanding differences of opinion in terms of jazz musicians catching each other's cadence.

With some metaphors the stakes are even higher. For example, a physician or medical researcher perceives one set of possibilities for medical diagnosis, treatment, and research if she conceives the body as a machine with highly specific, detachable parts that can break down and require localized adjustment, repair, or replacement. But she pictures different possibilities if she conceives the body as a homeostatic organism that adapts in a more general and coordinated way to disturbances so as to preserve functional equilibrium in its overall system. Widespread acceptance of the homeostatic metaphor significantly affected the course of twentieth-century medicine by opening up new avenues for inquiry. "The emergence of the new metaphorical structuring," Johnson asserts, "opened up new questions, made possible new discriminations, and suggested new connections."[52]

In a love relationship, one set of possible goals, expectations, and values will be highlighted when a relationship is conceived as a market exchange (e.g., "I *invested* a lot in that relationship, but I got nothing *in return*"), and quite another set will guide the deliberations of one who conceives it as, say, an organic unity.[53] If a relationship is an exploitable resource, investment, or commodity, the most sensible question is "What am I getting out of this?" Anthropologist Naomi Quinn observes of the couples she has interviewed: "They talk, for instance, of 'being short-changed in this relationship,' or of the possibility of divorce 'when the effort is more than the reward.' . . . [This] assumes that the parties to such a [voluntary] relationship will not continue in it unless benefits outweigh their costs, to render the relationship rewarding in net terms [for both spouses]."[54]

This presupposes atomistic individuals who meet each other's needs not out of sympathetic regard but because rules of fair exchange demand this. Creative possibilities for communication and empathy are ignored, shriveling the job of intelligence to incessant calculation of what is owed to each other. On the other hand, if a relationship is conceived in terms of the less libertarian metaphor of an organic unity, interrelatedness and interdependence are emphasized. A companion's desires and needs are treated with an inclusive eye to the way values elsewhere in the system are affected.

This recognition of the pitfalls of individualism has given rise to an ecological approach to the self-world relationship, of profound import for environmental policy. It is common knowledge in the biological sciences that organic beings live as integral parts of larger dynamic systems. A localized individual such as this flower or that bee is intelligible only in the context of relations with other parts of the dynamic biotic systems inhabited. For example, in one of many illustrations of ecological interdependence in *On the Origin of Species,* Darwin reported that there exists a species of flowering clover in England, the population of which depends in some measure on the population of cats in a region. From an ecological perspective this is not at all far-fetched. Many flowering plants require pollination if they are to produce seeds enabling them to reproduce. This particular clover is pollinated by bumblebees. Darwin inferred that an increase in a region's bumblebee population results in a proportional increase in the region's clover population, while a decrease in the number of bees results in a decrease in clover.

The plot thickens: "The number of humble-bees in any district," Darwin writes, "depends in a great measure upon the number of field-mice, which destroy their combs and nests." Other factors remaining the same, an increase in the ravenous field-mouse population decreases the bee population and therefore the clover population when it is underpollinated. Contrariwise, a decrease in the number of field mice leads to an increase in both the bee and clover populations. If a drought were drastically to reduce the clover population, many bees would starve and die for want of pollen. This decrease in the number of bees would deprive the field mice of a primary food source, drastically reducing their numbers. Cats of course eat the field mice, so that an increase in the number of cats results in fewer mice, more bees, and more clover. Darwin concludes: "Hence it is quite credible that the presence of a feline animal in large numbers in a district might determine, through the intervention first of mice and then of bees, the frequency of certain flowers in that district!"[55]

Similar studies in what is now called population ecology abound. For example, a 1990 article in *Nature* studied the ecosystem of Lake Mendota, Wisconsin, after "an unusually warm summer (1987) resulted in massive mortality of planktivorous fish." The authors write:

> Massive mortality of fish greatly reduced predation on zooplankton [animal organisms in the larger aggregate of floating organisms], resulting in an increase in the abundance of large *Daphnia* [fresh-water fleas], and a dramatic decrease in phytoplankton [plant organisms in the larger aggregate of floating organisms]. Our results demonstrate strong food web influences on phytoplankton, and support the idea that food web interactions can be managed to reduce phytoplankton abundance.[56]

In addition to setting the stage for "ecocentrism" in environmental ethics, a "moral" to these ecological stories is that such interdependence extends, at least as a metaphor, to sociocultural interactions. This is certainly not to propose a food-web model of morality. To invoke a turgid turn of phrase from Dewey, the ontological lesson is that experience is "transdermally transactional" (KK, LW 16:117). We live and think, Dewey says, across skins. We exist in and through others.[57] The metaphor of an ecological self serves as a powerful corrective to "ragged" individualism by making recognition of social and physical interdependence automatic.

Turning to politics, possibilities differ depending on what metaphor for government is uppermost. According to Lakoff, conservatives and progressives both conceive the nation as a family, but they tend to have opposing views about the role of the parent in this family. Is the government, on one hand, a strict father disciplining its progeny through distribution of rewards and punishments based on individual desert? If so, then oppose welfare programs because they reward rather than punish people for not working. Or is government, on the other hand, a nurturant parent establishing material and social conditions for the self-actualization of its offspring? If so, then support social programs that give people a leg up, lest they never reach sanctioned ends.[58]

A distinction between anthropocentric and non-anthropocentric perspectives toward nature pervades environmental ethics. On its own, the distinction is vague and skeletal, but metaphors underlie and give flesh to conflicting moral images of nature. Some prevalent anthropocentric metaphors include understanding nature as a resource (for immediate liquidation or for long-term sustainable human consumption), as property (a commodity to be owned and sold), as God's dominion (given to humans to subdue and rule over, or steward wisely), as a wild animal (to be tamed into submission for human use), as an adversary (to be conquered in self-defense), or as a taskmaster (that keeps us in slavery). Non-anthropocentrists tend instead to conceive nature as, for example, a mother (who provides for and nurtures her offspring), as Gaia (an all-enveloping superorganism to be revered and respected), as a victim of injury (who has been harmed and needs healing), as a living organism (with needs to be met if it is to survive), or as a whole (of which we are integral parts).[59]

To claim that dramatic rehearsals are guided in part by metaphorical projections such as these is not to say moral reasoning is ultimately arbitrary. These metaphors are social habits that emerge through embodied interactions as organized means of comprehension, adaptation, and adjustment. So they are tightly structured and checked by experience. Some are so ill-adapted to associated life or personal crises that, with Sontag, we long to escape their tyranny; others help us to communicate so we can coordinate a future together. We act on the basis of this understanding, the world answers back, and the metaphors in turn persist or change. Most of this takes place unconsciously, without the mediation of much intelligence.

In 1972, formal education became a legal right for British children with severe mental retardation. Mary Warnock was on a committee stumped in its attempt to morally buttress this as an entitlement. They were charged with addressing whether it really makes sense to speak of "educating" such children. She reports spontaneously seeing a "mental picture" or image: "I saw that education was a road down which every child had to walk, but there was only one road, with a common destination."[60] The metaphor of purposes as destinations tethered her moral imagination, highlighting possibilities.

An organization of avenues for acting would be largely unavailable if metaphorical understanding did not mark it out. Instead of a knee-jerk-reflex act, a coherent inquiry is organized along the lines highlighted by the metaphor (or, as is often the case, a tangled inquiry along the lines of conflicting metaphors). Possibilities not highlighted do not blink out of existence, but they are overshadowed by the brilliance of focal alternatives.

To ignore metaphor is to leave one of our primary moral resources drifting capriciously. The chief engineer of an interstate highway recently completed through the Appalachian Mountains remarked: "Those mountains have stood in the way of progress for far too long!" Conceiving nature as an obstacle on a journey toward "progress" is far more likely to maladapt us than conceiving it, for instance, as a home to be sustained. Offending habits will not politely evaporate upon request, a point illustrated in the story of Studs Lonigan. But with a greater knowledge of encultured metaphors—the variety of these organizational tools as well as their inner workings—we are supplied an inroad to disclosing formerly concealed cognitive processes so that they may be critically appraised. A degree of artful control over habit-formation, and thus over dramatic rehearsal, may then be exercised.

Much work remains to be done on the role of metaphoric thinking in conduct. In addition to further investigation of key metaphors that guide deliberations this way rather than that (metaphors used to frame situations), we need further exploration of metaphors that help to define such basic moral concepts as rights, justice, duty, and virtue.[61] Furthermore, alternatives to the predominant general metaphors for moral conduct need to be probed. Among many candidates, one of the most promising emphasizes the neglected imaginative dimension of moral life, morality as art.

According to Dewey's theory of the psychology of deliberation, imagination arises as the hunting phase of any situation involving perplexity. We probe optional futures and envision participating in them before acting overtly. A complete deliberation forecasts altered conditions that would ensue if this or that route were opted for, until an option is hit upon that can be trusted to integrate conflicting factors and restore equilibrium.

In contrast with an emotive outburst, imaginative rehearsal is guided by exigencies of a situation along with a vast array of internalized social habits. Conventional metaphors are crucial in this respect. It was shown in the discussion of James that it matters what order we throw realities into. Since there is no single correct way to take things, moral philosophers must ask about the effects of conceptual frames. Research on metaphor bears profoundly on pragmatist ethics since it advances Dewey's project of "intellectual disrobing," enabling us to critically inspect intellectual habits to see "what they are made of and what wearing them does to us" (EN, LW 1:40). Habits form characters, so ignorance of them leaves character to haphazard development. If we do not own metaphors imaginatively, they own us mechanically.

SIX

The Deweyan Ideal

The failures of philosophy have come from lack of
confidence in the directive powers that inhere in
experience, if men have but the wit and courage
to follow them.

—John Dewey, *Experience and Nature*

IMPROVISATIONAL MORAL INTELLIGENCE

Central to Dewey's approach is that ethics is understood as the art of helping people to live richer, more responsive, and more emotionally engaged lives.[1] This is closer to Aristotle than to Kant, who approaches ethics primarily as rational justification of an inherited moral system. Dewey's criticism is mitigated only slightly if the inherited system is correctly acknowledged—as it is for instance by Bernard Gert in contrast with Alan Donagan—to be embodied in imaginatively constituted and applied rules and ideals.

Pragmatist ethics acknowledges our inherited moral vocabulary, what Kant disparaged as "a disgusting mishmash of patchwork observations and half-reasoned principles."[2] But it is not so driven by what borders on an obsession to forge a less repelling system of this mishmash by, for example, attempting with Gert to describe in advance a conclusive test, procedure, or formula to define what can count as rational or irrational action.[3] This is not to say the creative endeavor of pragmatist ethics is free of obsessions. It is by temperament fixated on the world's qualitative ambiguity, on indeterminate, muddled situations and the imaginative virtues that fund our more admirable dealings with them.[4]

Martha Nussbaum's reintroduction of Aristotelian practical wisdom is significant in this context. In a poignant passage in *Love's Knowledge,* she observes that moral knowledge entails "seeing a complex, concrete reality in a highly lucid and richly responsive way; it is taking in what is there, with imagination and feeling."⁵ Moral decision making calls for refined sensitivity and immersion in events (in dialogue with a "rule-governed concern for general obligations," which on her view plays an essential though subordinate role).⁶ It is a matter of artistry. "A responsible action," she writes in a passage reminiscent of Havelock Ellis's 1923 *The Dance of Life,* "is a highly context-specific and nuanced and responsive thing whose rightness could not be captured in a description that fell short of the artistic."⁷

Considered in this light, jazz improvisation suggests an unconventional metaphor for the harmony and discord of daily interpersonal life. A jazz combo spotlights and illustrates the empathetic, impromptu, and inherently social dimensions of moral compositions. This is especially helpful in framing ideals for interpersonal relationships and group interactions, dimensions of most moral situations. The metaphor corrects Dewey's unfortunate slips into cephalocentric descriptions of dramatic rehearsal. Moreover, it compensates for a possible misreading of deliberation as rehearsal for a ready-made drama. To whatever extent improvisation is essential to mediating interpersonal circumstances, the jazz metaphor calls attention to habits we need to cultivate, and it enables construction of improvisational ideals for which to strive.

As metaphor, conceiving social interactions in terms of jazz is limited in scope. Improvisational intelligence may play only a minor role, for example, in adversarial relationships, conflict mediation, bioethics, or environmental policy; how central or peripheral this role is will not be taken up here. And cultural differences must be acknowledged. Nevertheless, the metaphor calls attention to subtleties of communal interaction that would otherwise go unnoticed.

Ferrying the logic of jazz over to interpersonal conduct may initially raise caution flags, and for good reason. There are two extremes to which conduct tends, one the opposite of improvisation and the other popularly identified with it. One relies on routine ends, fixed doctrines, or closed systems of ready-made principles. It engenders cultural rigidity, conformity, and dogmatism, or is compatible with dictatorial coerciveness. The other relies on no forethought or discipline and results in behavior that is slapdash, unorganized, cursory, and discontinuous. It is haphazardly *unrehearsed,* "improvised" in the dictionary sense of offhand. Both extremes can have a deadening effect on moral imagination, especially on the phase of dramatic rehearsal. Dewey similarly criticized "hasty improvisation" and "patchwork policies" in progressive education (LW 13:109; LW 17:53).⁸

The middle course is experimental intelligence. It is guided neither by fixed ends that anesthetize perception of emerging events nor by patchwork trial and error that excludes imaginative forethought. Key aspects of this middle course are embodied in jazz improvisation, including a rich, nuanced sort of imaginative rehearsal. The popular sense of improvisation as "spur of the moment" composition is of course there, particularly in some avant-garde jazz. But the extreme of offhanded recklessness and discontinuous drifting is alien to the jazz artist.

This becomes apparent when the stereotype of jazz artistry as anarchic is replaced by a realistic depiction of its tight structure and aesthetic richness. Unfortunately this was lost on Dewey, who implies that jazz and movies, like vulgar tabloids, are cheap arts sought out by the average person because fine art is held up as remote from ordinary experience (AE, LW 10:12).[9] This may be true of much art, but not jazz. Dewey also conceives improvisation as "jerky, discontinuous movement" (LW 3:263). Ironically, jazz may generally be even more organized and continuous than moral experience. This conceptual structure contributes to its richness and coherence as metaphor.

Such is the nature of a novelty that one can never be fully prepared for it. One must improvise. At our best, we skillfully respond to each other with the aim of harmonizing interests. But coordinated impromptu thinking is difficult. Jazz pianist Bill Evans discusses the challenge of group improvisation on new material, observing of his celebrated collaboration with Miles Davis on the album *Kind of Blue:* "Aside from the weighty technical problem of collective coherent thinking, there is the very human, even social need for sympathy from all members to bend for the common result."[10]

A jazz musician—also consider bluegrass, blues, drum circles, and the like, with notable parallels in dance and theater—takes up the attitude of others by catching a cadence from the group's signals while anticipating the group's response to her own signals.[11] Drawing on the resources of tradition, memory, and long exercise, she plays *into* the past tone to discover the possibilities for future tones in the way moral imagination enables us to see the old in terms of the possible. This is not simply casual drifting into the next note, but movement toward an emerging sonorous image that is felt to unify the composition.

No "right" way to do this can be spelled out, but it is far from arbitrary. Only a novice would imagine anything beautiful could come from, on one hand, reposing in rules of composition, or on the other hand, arbitrarily imposing rhythms or tones on the rest of the group. It would not romanticize jazz to observe that beauty in improvisation emerges as members revel in supporting others, not when they jockey for a solo.

Prima donnas in jazz, and there are many, never quite live up to their potentials as artists. The virtuoso in jazz is practiced in listening, and at her best—even if only for a few moments—puts vanity behind. This enables her in those moments to go beyond simple recognition of a cue to perceive and creatively respond to what it portends and signifies. Yet even the disciplined virtuoso may misread the tone of a composition. No matter how mutually sympathetic a community of musicians or moral-agents/patients may ideally be—and recall that the metaphor may be less applicable outside such a community—discordance is always possible. In fact, it is certain. This is both because the situation is existentially uncertain and because no amount of listening and learning can absolutely guarantee against misconstruing the "style" of another. Jazz musician and poet Michael Harper explains: "It's a matter of waiting for an opening rather than just rushing into what's happening. It's very much like a conversation. . . . The problem is that sometimes people don't always understand what the *tone* of the conversation is, but that happens to all of us in life, too."[12]

Moral-agents/patients must respond empathetically to each other instead of imposing insular designs, and they must rigorously imagine how others will respond to their actions. This is learned, with experience and practice. Only to the degree that we are immature, unexercised in thinking and uncultivated in perception, do we imagine anything enduringly good will come from immediate satisfaction of stray, self-interested desires. Mature deliberation faces problems as wholes and perceives the interdependence of parts. It shuns piecemeal and slapdash acts as much as ready-made solutions. In jazz as in conduct, a blueprint for action would impede the emergence of a unifying image charged with a felt direction of movement.

Simple recognition of cues that certain feelings or interests are at play—say, that someone is offended—is sufficient only for acting as customary propriety dictates. Within certain limits such rule-governed behavior may serve, as with everyday manners. But it falls far short of a "full perceptual realization" of particulars, in Dewey's helpful phrasing (AE, LW 10:182). Like most everyday perception, it is incomplete and oversimplified. It lacks deep perception—gained primarily through the give and take of communication—of individual causes and purposes: Why is she offended? How does this fit into the history of the life she is composing? Mere recognition of social cues also lacks the expanded perception of humane learning: In what way does her style differ from mine, perhaps due to race, gender, ethnicity, or nationality?[13] Without deep perception, you won't "get it." Moral imagination may collapse into a pseudo-empathy of the Golden Rule variety (in one common interpretation),[14] in which others' values and intentions are reduced to one's own. Yet even the most patient, communicative, and learned will honestly misread the tone of some situations, and no amount of cultivation of moral talent can guarantee against bad improvisations.

Moreover and perhaps most significantly, the tradition of the art form structures group improvisation and is remade through innovation, much as customs and principles may flexibly guide moral behavior. There is ample disagreement about the role of tradition in jazz as in morality, but no matter how avant-garde one aspires to be (say, the Free Jazz of Ornette Coleman versus the more measured Miles Davis), one does not experiment in a vacuum. Indeed, drawing from Mead's theory of the self, all people are in a sense born into a jazz combo and become differentiated as contributing members only as a result of participation in the group.[15]

The partnership between innovation and tradition is addressed by Nussbaum in a striking yet undeveloped contrast of images. On her (unsympathetic) view, for the symphony player

> all commitments and continuities are external; they come from the score and from the conductor. The player reads them off like anyone else. The jazz player, actively forging continuity, must choose in full awareness of and responsibility to the historical traditions of the form, and must actively honor at every moment his commitments to his fellow musicians, whom he had better know as well as possible as unique individuals. He should be more responsible than the score reader, and not less, to the unfolding continuities and structures of the work.[16]

Nussbaum neglects the role of imaginative perception in what Mary Reichling, in an essay on Dewey and musical imagination, calls the "sonorous image of the [composed] work that the performer wishes to achieve."[17] But Nussbaum rightly highlights that we can improvise, morally and artistically, only because we do not create in a vacuum. Styles, techniques, and visions are funded. Harper sums this up in a tribute to John Coltrane's influence: "You're *never* starting at ground zero. Somebody took you to the place where you now are."[18] The inescapability of cultural context in improvisational intelligence is distilled to delightful simplicity in a conversation between Charles Mingus and Timothy Leary, reported by Barry Kernfeld: "Mingus listens for a long time to Dr. Leary's anarchic approach to spontaneous art, Mingus's art, improvisation. 'You can't improvise on nothin' man,' Mingus says at last. 'You gotta improvise on somethin.'"[19]

THE DEWEYAN IDEAL

Inquiry, art, value, religion, and all other aspects of human existence are natural functions. They should be approached as such, despite the long-cherished faith in a nonnatural spring or a priori matrix for values and standards.

There is a great difference between something's being desired and its being judged worthy of approbation, between noncognitive prizing and critical appraising.[20] It is a fact that people want and admire many things, "food, a companion, money, fame and repute, health, distinction among their fellows, power, the love of friends, the admiration of rivals, etc." (1932 E, LW 7:181). But what is *satisfying* is not ipso facto *satisfactory.* "The fact that something is desired only raises the *question* of its desirability; it does not settle it. Only a child in the degree of his immaturity thinks to settle the question of desirability by reiterated proclamation: 'I want it, I want it, I want it'" (QC, LW 4:207–208).

In *Crime and Punishment,* Dostoyevsky's "superman" Raskolnikov emerges from prolonged brooding with a powerful desire that stimulates overt action. One suspects, however, that his repertoire of possibilities included an option preferable to an axe murder. In outline, then, what direction did Dewey provide for distinguishing (a) uncriticized desires from (b) critical judgments about what should be desired?

As Kekes observes in *The Morality of Pluralism,* imagination obviously reveals evil possibilities as well as good. So when is moral imagination, as a psychological capacity, moral, as an evaluative judgment? Kekes argues that "morality requires us to place limits on the exercise of moral imagination" and that these limits are found in the deep conventions of a moral tradition that only the most "extraordinary and abnormal" circumstances may override. While agreeing that imagination operates only within a biosociocultural matrix, as has been shown, Dewey breaks free of the hyper-dependency in ethics on protective limits and boundaries as trump cards. This especially includes limits preordained by convention, no matter how deep, as a fixed standard of behavior. At the same time, Dewey's alternative context acknowledges social limits as one irreducible factor of moral life (TIF, LW 5:285) that encompasses basic protections—"protection of life, physical security, and some freedom from undeserved violations"—rightly demanded by Kekes.[21]

Pragmatist ethics sanctions one disposition, action, or institution rather than another because one is judged (by reference to its interactions and connections) to serve or ameliorate experience. Something is estimated good, and thus to be perpetuated and made secure (QC, LW 4:208), only in proportion to its contribution to this amelioration. This is too open-ended as stated, but it nevertheless shows "Good" has more than a strictly emotive use. The feeling that something is good does not necessarily make it so, and the judgment that it is the good of *this* situation is a working hypothesis qualified by experimental confirmation or disconfirmation.

The words "ought" or "should" are variously used. "He should sing that an octave higher," "You should rotate your crops," and "She should be more considerate" are distinguishable in terms of their ends, but this does not entail there is any *peculiarly* moral meaning of "ought" that singles out all and only moral uses. To say "The act *ought* to be done" differs only verbally from saying "This act will meet the situation" (EW 3:108–109). Moral judgment, inasmuch as it is "the product of investigation of conditions and consequences," is not different in kind from judging that something "should" be done in farming, nutrition, or engineering (LW 13:219). The act is a fit means to a valued end. Judgments that claim a justification transcending pragmatic fittedness, which "descend out of the *a priori* blue" or "descend as an imperative from a moral Mount Sinai" (LW 13:219), are as inappropriate in ethics as in medicine.

Dewey generalizes an ideal end for moral deliberation. He does not seek a summum bonum to which all other goods in a hierarchy of ends are subservient. Moreover, he breaks with traditional theories of the good by denying that his own theory can establish a commensurable principle that unifies all that goes by the name of good, duty, and virtue. But neither does he shy away from discussing ideals to make moral reflection less specious, exclusive, "arbitrary, capricious, unreasoned" (EN, LW 1:320). So long as this is understood as a *direction* and not confused with a rationalistic principle or an attempt to delineate a latitude and longitude of moral rectitude, the Deweyan ideal can be summed up as inclusive, continuing growing.[22] With his ideal of growth, Dewey locates goodness in imaginative transitions, in "the continuous reconstruction of experience" (RP, MW 12:185). Virtues and obligations play a pivotal role as means. In this way he aspires to meet "the demands of impartial and far-sighted thought as well as satisfy the urgencies of desire" (1932 E, LW 7:191).[23]

Since moral life is prospective, moral judgment would be senseless without the possibility of growth or maturation, of education broadly construed. Dewey's most detailed articulation of the nature of growth is found in his theory of experience. Alexander explains: "There is, in short, a dynamic, rhythmic and growing nature to all interaction; experience exemplifies this in a heightened degree, and this aspect of experience itself becomes the basis for aesthetic experience and art."[24] This is too vague to operate as a model for intellectual and moral development. It is perhaps best fleshed out through the art of the novel, as with Farrell's *Studs Lonigan*. To offer a more substantive characterization of the Deweyan ideal within the limitations of philosophic prose, an artistic-aesthetic model of moral thinking is developed in the next chapter, personified by the archetypal figure of a moral artist. Before turning to this, the gist of Dewey's idea of growth in its social aspect can be clarified, as he intended, in light of his conception of the *democratic ideal*.

It is an ancient philosophic question whether acting for the social good has intrinsic worth. Is it a blessing unto itself, like health or happiness? Or is regard for the common welfare strictly a means to goods external to it? If it has no inherent worth, is social concern ultimately motivated by the stick of law's punishment and the carrot of rewards and reputation? Machiavelli, along with Hobbes, notoriously assumed this in his view of human nature: "all men are bad and ever ready to display their vicious nature, whenever they may find occasion for it."[25] Without sugar-coating, Plato took the other side. Pursuing justice (*dikaiosune*), Socrates urges against Thrasymachus in the *Republic,* is worthwhile regardless of the goods to which a reputation for it leads or its profitability to narrow self-interest. For Plato, as it is obviously better to *be* healthily constituted than merely to *seem* so, it is better to be just than simply to appear to others to be just.

Dewey sides with Plato, though he conceives right action as cooperative social interaction and inclusive growth, not in terms of a harmonious soul in which reason rules appetites. Contrary to Dewey's reception by critics like Brand Blanshard, he did not reject the idea of goods such as growth, joyfulness, learning, love, or the like being valued for themselves. He rejects the notion of intrinsic value *only* if it is taken to mean (1) that the valued end is beyond appraisal so that its attainment justifies any means, which is absurd (see TV, LW 13:227) or (2) that there are goods that *in no way* enrich future enjoyments, which is difficult to imagine. For example, a hungry child is normally motivated to eat because she recognizes food as a good of this concrete situation, not because she is conscious of nutritional ends served by eating (DE, MW 9:250). The violinist is inspired by goods internal to the act, not external to it, and the violin is literally "instrumental" to these goods.

Growing as a moral end—a good, duty, and right—is intimately connected for Dewey with cultivating the goods of social consciousness. Like Plato's idea of justice, growing has both intrinsic and extrinsic worth. There is a parallel in Mill's criticism of Bentham, who focused impersonally on quantifying anticipated pleasures and pains while ignoring factors of personal disposition "as *direct* sources and ingredients of happiness" (1932 E, LW 7:244). For Dewey, we can find direct satisfaction in conducting ourselves out of "regard for general welfare." He urges, "Infinite relationships of man with his fellows and with nature already exist. . . . Even in the midst of conflict, struggle and defeat a consciousness is possible of the enduring and comprehending whole" (HNC, MW 14:226). It is both possible and desirable to cultivate "a sympathetic imagination for human relations in action" (EW 4:57). This is reminiscent of Hume, who grounds moral sensibility not in our capacity for intellectual abstraction but in "an extensive sympathy with mankind."[26] Dewey, however, is more concerned than Hume to respond to others as wholes, as complex and often enigmatic bundles of experience.

"Look out for number one" is a principle of rootlessness and disloca-
tion. It does not grasp the value of active social concern. In contrast, Dewey
echoes the ancient Greeks in identifying the good of members with the
common welfare of society. His justification for this as a value—both immediately for itself and for ends beyond it—hinges on an insight discussed
in Part One: Humans rely on their sociocultural environment for physical
sustenance, for basic resources, and most importantly for meaning. Thus,
growing as a moral end is inseparable from the ties that bind us to others.

This can be stated as a social criterion for moral appraisal that helps us
judge what ought to be brought into or sustained in existence (LW 4:208–
209): "[T]he effects of acts upon the common welfare, the general well-
being, is the criterion for judging moral worth of personal acts and dispositions [as well as to social institutions and plans for social change]" (1932 E,
LW 7:344–345; cf. DE, MW 9:368). Dewey accommodates what is sound
in the utilitarian intuition that we should act so as to bring about the most
good for the most people. But he does not get mired in an ultimate moral
principle or supreme maxim that, when applied formulaically, can be
shown to violate basic rights, forgo colloquy, ignore cultural and personal
differences, and forsake the direct satisfactions of moral engagement.

Dewey is often characterized as proposing an ideal of "self-realization."
This is misleading. It is true that a distinction between habitual and ideal
selves is crucial (1908 E, MW 5:326), and Dewey is vehement in denounc-
ing Stalinist sacrifice of full and distinctive individuality to a "common
good" that is neither good nor shared (see 1932 E, LW 7:347). This is manifest in his critique of traditional education: "There is no opportunity for
each child to work out something specifically his own, while he, in turn,
participates in the productions of others" (MW 4:275). Nonetheless, there
are no separate selves to realize. "What sort of self is in the making" must
be identified with the question "what kind of world is in the making"
(HNC, MW 14:150). Jane Addams, whose Hull House community sharp-
ened and deepened Dewey's faith in democracy as a way of life, argues in
Democracy and Social Ethics that only those oblivious to actual circumstances fill themselves with pride in their personal morality in the face of
the pressing need for a social morality in which we join forces for practical
reform of socioeconomic and political institutions.[27] With Addams, personal ethics is transformed without remainder into social ethics.

On this view, the central goal of education is nurturance of a child's in-
satiable social curiosity into a communicative democratic faith. Democratic
moral education is committed not to consumerism and crass materialism,
but to liberation of students' energies so that they can realize their own potentials to be humane, compassionate, active, and informed members of a
world too often indifferent to their welfare.[28] Democratic education works

when such students, in turn, are committed to securing the material and social prerequisites for others to realize their potentials for intellectual vitality, humane feeling, environmental responsiveness, and aesthetic perceptiveness. This cannot establish a utopia, but it may at least avert disaster. And it will help us respond intelligently and humanely to disaster when it comes.

Contrary to Reinhold Neibuhr's influential indictment of Dewey as a group-centered thinker, Dewey and Addams were not collectivists, championing the French revolutionary demand for fraternity while ignoring liberty. Nor were they libertarians espousing the reverse, failing to grasp that freedom entails cooperative expression of individualities (FC, LW 13:79). Neither solidarity nor differentiation is decisive; both are constituents of human experience. The Deweyan ideal unites two historically antagonistic ideas, "liberation of individuals on one hand and promotion of a common good on the other" (1932 E, LW 7:349), in perpetual re-creation "of a freer and more humane experience in which all share and to which all contribute" (LW 14:230; Cf. 1932 E, LW 7:350). Individualism is not prima facie bad, and sociality is not beyond reproach. As irreducible constituents of experience each "serves to release and mature the other" (FC, LW 13:78).

Dewey's criterion in its political aspect is the democratic ideal. This ideal is refreshingly free of the emaciated usage of democracy to denote unfettered market capitalism, which is joined to a consumer individualism that makes it difficult to take responsibility for the rippling social and environmental consequences of daily choices.[29] "Cooperation," he explains, "is as much a part of the democratic ideal as is personal initiative" (FC, LW 13:78). The democratic ideal "simply projects to their logical and practical limit forces inherent in human nature and already embodied to some extent in human nature. It serves accordingly as basis for criticism of institutions as they exist and of plans of betterment" (1932 E, LW 7:349).

As stated, the democratic ideal is a Western cultural outgrowth, but if we have the humility to listen to what makes the practices of another culture intelligible to its members, the ideal can be an instrument (improvable like any other) with which any culture may inquire into the customs of another with an eye to ameliorating the ties that bind members of communities to each other. In this way, for example, Japanese criticisms of American individualism and American criticisms of Japanese collectivism have opened up possibilities for social inquiry and reconstruction. Any cultural milieu in some ways sustains and enriches, and in other ways hinders, the growth of relations.

James's influential essay "The Moral Philosopher and the Moral Life" helps to frame the democratic ideal. "It is a tragic situation, and no mere speculative conundrum," James notes, that all ideals and demands in a situation cannot be satisfied simultaneously (MPML, 203). Every imaginable good competes "for the possession of the same bit of space and time with some other imagined good. Every end of desire that presents itself appears exclusive of some other end of desire" (MPML, 202). There is a practical need for subordinating some of these demands to others. The work of moral philosophy lies in looking beyond mere partisan interests. Yet as traditionally practiced it has failed in its work by assuming an ideal universe in which all goods approved by Reason are compossibles. To be more responsive to the traits of existence, philosophical ethics must become situational and experimental: "For every real dilemma is in literal strictness a unique situation; and the exact combination of ideals realized and ideals disappointed which each decision creates is always a universe without a precedent, and for which no adequate previous rule exists" (MPML, 209).

We all profess to be experts at deciding which ideals should be realized (ours) and which disappointed (those that seem alien to us). The greatest moral failing is lack of empathy respecting points of view that differ from our own. They appear less significant, less real. James exclaims in "On a Certain Blindness in Human Beings": "Hence the stupidity and injustice of our opinions, so far as they deal with the significance of alien lives. Hence the falsity of our judgments, so far as they presume to decide in an absolute way on the value of other persons' conditions or ideals." He therefore cautions the moral philosopher: "Hands off: neither the whole of truth nor the whole of good is revealed to any single observer, although each observer gains a partial superiority of insight from the peculiar position in which he stands."[30]

To compensate for this tendency, what is needed, on James's view, is to actualize the largest set of compossibles. We should strive for what George Santayana called a harmony of desires. "Since all demands conjointly cannot be satisfied in this poor world" we must act so as "to satisfy at all times *as many demands as we can*" (MPML, 205), placing the highest value over that option which promises "the richer and the more inclusive arrangement" (MPML, 208). The best act is one that "makes for the *best whole*, in the sense of awakening the least sum of dissatisfactions" (MPML, 205). The philosopher Ralph Barton Perry, James's biographer, developed this as the "principle of inclusiveness."[31]

In its nascent form, this appears compatible with what Alexander Hamilton in *The Federalist Papers* called the "tyranny of the majority." In the context of James's other work, this is tempered by the fact that we must choose an action that fits and adapts us as individuals to the empirical situation. The gist of James's pluralistic criterion is stated in a more jaded tone by Isaiah Berlin: "[T]he best that one can do is to try to promote some kind of equilibrium, necessarily unstable, between the different aspirations of different groups of human beings—at the very least to prevent them from attempting to exterminate each other."[32]

Anticipating current criticisms of "preference utilitarianism," Dewey is more careful than James to avoid conflating the satisfying with the satisfactory, and he is more amenable than Berlin to subordinating some goods to others so long as none pretends to be absolute or definitive. The best act, what *should* be desired (1932 E, LW 7:192), is not merely the one that provokes the least dissatisfactions. "The true good is . . . an inclusive or expanding end. In substance, the only end which fulfills these conditions is the social good" (1908 E, MW 5:261). The aim of deliberation is "a working harmony among diverse desires" (HNC, MW 14:136) that ideally brings about "an inclusive and enduring satisfaction" (1932 E, LW 7:308).

As with the example of jockeying for a solo in jazz improvisation, to satisfy desires without an eye to their desirability in encompassing relationships—as commonly occurs when we take the attitude of others in order to decide what persona will best manipulate them[33]—can suppress and dull our development and theirs. It is undeniable that imagination is all too compatible with malicious intent and self-serving deception, but the predictable result is disintegrated selfhood (in which habits, such as seeking both friendship and dominance, do not internally support each other) and social fragmentation.

Procedural impartiality, as in Rawls's "original position," guards against such bias, but it can do so at the expense of social intelligence. From the standpoint of pragmatist social ethics, such as that of Jane Addams, the function of impartiality is best served through communicative, caring interaction in which no one's concerns are rejected out of hand. The blindfold of justice symbolizing the American legal ideal is a sign of what will serve when democratic trust and respect have broken down. As an ideal for equal treatment it is second best. Morality, as Dewey says of democracy, begins in conversation.

Asked in an interview what inescapable question faces the twenty-first century, the sociologist Robert Bellah said: "The most critical question is how can we give interdependence—which is so obvious in connection with everything we do—a moral meaning?"[34] As is, Bellah argues, our "habits of the heart"—received ways of thinking about ourselves and our relationships—are out of sync with demands of associated life.[35] As a prerequisite for enjoying the goods of community, we need to give coherent and positive meaning to interdependence and to enrich and diversify moral vocabularies so that expressing care and commitment to others does not unnerve us.

In a December news broadcast, a man in his thirties was interviewed at a Chicago post office as he sifted through some of the thousands of "Dear Santa" letters the post office receives. Each year, he explained, he takes gifts to a few impoverished children who write letters. Asked about his motives, this obviously caring person replied: "Because it makes me feel good inside. When I give gifts to these children it's really just a gift to myself."

Doubtless his actions were gratifying, but shall we take his remarks at face value? Was he motivated exclusively or even primarily by a selfish thirst for pleasure? Perhaps. But he may have been responding not just to his yearning for subjective delight but to an overall situation in which others' lives were interwoven with his own. Yet our individualistic language—what Bellah calls "the first language of American individualism"—did not provide him the means for telling the other-regarding half of the story.

Interactions in the so-called information age are astoundingly complex and social. Yet the concept of an individual remains so private and atomic that people are confused and maladapted, their aims frustrated. "I don't have kids," says the author of a typical letter to the editor, "so why should I have to pay to educate other people's offspring?"[36] This is more than meanness. In Addams's phrasing, it is an utter failure to comprehend the situation. Dewey lamented over eighty years ago that such ragged individualism leads to "aloofness and indifference. It often makes an individual so insensitive in his relations to others as to develop an illusion of being really able to stand and act alone—an unnamed form of insanity which is responsible for a large part of the remediable suffering of the world" (DE, MW 9:49).

We are far from what Edward Bellamy, the nineteenth-century utopian novelist Dewey deemed "a great American prophet," envisioned in *Looking Backward* and *Equality* for the year 2000, where "increasing the common stock" predominated "increasing the individual hoarde." During the Great Depression, Dewey wrote of Bellamy: "Many persons have indicted the present system. But what enabled Bellamy's books to circulate by the hundreds of thousands was that his indictment operated through imagination setting forth what was possible. The result is a sense of the terrible gulf between what is possible and what is actual" (LW 9:102). Shaking the invisible hand of free trade, vast resources in what Eric Schlosser has dubbed our "fast food nation" are channeled toward exclusionary interests of supposedly self-sufficing individuals or corporations instead of harnessing economic and technological power for "the liberation and enrichment of human life" (ION, LW 5:87; cf. 1932 E, LW 7:331–339).[37] There is, in John Steinbeck's words, "a failure here that topples all our success." It is a failure to develop on a wide scale and from multiple perspectives and idioms a social ethics of cooperative individualities.

It remains painfully true today that "the problem of constructing a new individuality consonant with the objective conditions under which we live is the deepest problem of our times" (ION, LW 5:56). It is crucial to guard individual creativity from being thwarted by the impingements of an over-organized social environment. Yet it is equally paramount to welcome the possibility of shared experience—across current boundaries of wealth and power, gender, race, ethnicity, nationality, sexual orientation, religion, and the like—as desirable and identify ourselves with its realization (see HNC, MW 14:209–215). In this way we move toward perceiving ourselves as a public (or as a plurality of publics) so that ideals and inquiries become, in Dewey's words, "the spontaneous function of a communal life" (ION, LW 5:81). Read in light of feminist social philosophy, such as Nel Noddings's controversial book *Caring,* it is evident why Seigfried asserts in *Pragmatism and Feminism* that pragmatist discourse "is more feminine than masculine, as is its valuing of inclusiveness and community over exaggerated claims of autonomy and detachment. The same can be said for its developmental rather than rule-governed ethics."[38]

These reflections on social ethics are embodied in the democratic ideal. Forms of social organization realize their fullest potentials to the extent that democracy becomes a way of life for their members.[39] "Regarded as an idea, democracy is not an alternative to other principles of associated life. It is the idea of community life itself. It is an ideal. . . . [D]emocracy in this sense is not a fact and never will be" (PP, LW 2:328). Far more than a form of government, Dewey writes in a frequently cited passage in *Democracy and Education,* democracy "is primarily a mode of associated living, of conjoint communicated experience" (MW 9:93). It is a way of life and a melioristic social hope that encourages intimacy in relationships while respecting individual liberties. When interests conflict, the democratic way of life elicits differences and gives them a hearing instead of sacrificing them on the altar of preconceived plans or biases. Democracy entails that we and the groups of which we are parts each, according to capacity, refer our "own action to that of others, and . . . consider the action of others to give point and direction" to our own (DE, MW 9:93). A democratic imagination opens up an expansive field of contact with which to flexibly interact so that goods of communal life are enjoyed rather than repressed, and difficulties can be treated comprehensively instead of in isolation.

This "greater diversity of stimuli" (DE, MW 9:93) opened by democratic imagination expands the sense of exigencies struggling for recognition. Democracy, in Reinhold Niebuhr's words, finds "proximate solutions for insoluble problems."[40] Despite Niebuhr's unsympathetic portrayal of Dewey as a universalizing "bourgeois liberal," they both agreed that perfect fulfillment is unattainable. Like community, democracy is a proximate ideal, hope, and standard, not a fact. "There is no short-cut to it, no single predestined road which can be found once for all and which, if human beings continue to walk in it without deviation, will surely conduct them to the goal" (1932 E, LW 7:350). Yet integrative values may emerge to reconstruct and harmonize, albeit tenuously, conflicting desires and appraisals so that different individuals and groups "reenforce one another and their values accord" (PP, LW 2:328). In sum, a *social* imagination—indeed an *ecological* imagination—integrates us as individuals even as we participate in the give-and-take of associated life.[41]

SEVEN

The Moral Artist

> Obtuseness is a moral failing; its opposite can be cultivated.
> —Martha Nussbaum, *Love's Knowledge*

MORAL CONDUCT AS ART

The student of imagination turns naturally to art and aesthetic experience for subject matter. The moral power of art is well known and as widely feared. Art challenges convention, educates emotions, rescues perception from numbness. Lionel Trilling perceived this in his 1947 remark that "for our time the most effective agent of the moral imagination has been the novel."[1]

Art can directly and literally contribute to moral imagination and character. The most famous account of this forms part of Plato's argument for censorship in the *Republic,* which begins with Socrates' claim that stories about gods "warring, fighting, or plotting against one another" are bad theology and set poor models for the young (378cd and 380c). Socrates goes on to argue that musical and poetic grace and harmony penetrate the soul to produce fine and beautiful moral character: "And gracelessness, bad rhythm, and disharmony are akin to . . . bad character, while their opposites are akin to . . . a moderate and good character" (401a). He concludes with the psychologically simplistic claim that "rhythm and harmony permeate the inner part of the soul more than anything else, affecting it most strongly and bringing it grace, so that if someone is properly educated in music and poetry, it makes him graceful, but if not, then the opposite" (401de).

It is a familiar thesis that art affects moral imagination. But as a *metaphor* or model for moral experience, artistic production and enjoyment have been overlooked. This is no small oversight, not because artists are more saintly than the rest of us, but because seeing imagination so blatantly manifested gives us new eyes with which to see what can be made of imagination in everyday life. In fact, as illustrated in the previous chapter with jazz improvisation, artistic creation offers a rich model for understanding the sort of social imagination that is essential to moral deliberation.

This suggests a more substantial way of expressing and advancing the Deweyan ideal than the somewhat vague idea of growth. It suggests what Hilary Putnam calls a "moral image of the world," a more apt and trustworthy metaphor—or better yet, myriad complementary metaphors—for organizing moral lives and giving meaning to ethical claims:

> A moral image, in the sense in which I am using the term, is not a declaration that this or that is a virtue, or that this or that is what one ought to do; it is rather a picture of how our virtues and ideals hang together with one another and of what they have to do with the position we are in. It may be as vague as the notions of 'sisterhood and brotherhood'; indeed, millions of human beings have found in those metaphors moral images that could organize their moral lives—and this notwithstanding the enormous problem of interpreting them and of deciding what it could possibly mean to make them *effective*.[2]

Putnam implies that ethics is better served by exploring such tethering centers than by constrictive argumentation that is insensitive to what James calls the world's "relational mosaic."

No moral image will prove ultimately satisfactory. Wallace Stevens exhorts: "It would be the merest improvisation to say of any image of the world, even though it was an image with which a vast accumulation of imaginations had been content, that it was the chief image. The imagination itself would not remain content with it nor allow us to do so. It is the irrepressible revolutionist."[3] Accordingly, the virtues and ideals of moral artistry are not final or definitive, but they embody the democratic ideal and contribute to a socially responsible, experimentally plausible, and ecologically sensitive moral image of the world. To the degree that these virtues and ideals are *justified*, it is not by the metaphor (which on its own can only highlight, not critically appraise) but by their actual contribution to interlocking lives. All moral theories, as with theories of farming, surgery, or navigation, need to be run through pragmatism's experimentalist winnowing fan in which "only chaff goes, though perhaps the chaff had once been treasured" (EN, LW 1:4; cf. LTI, LW 12:108).

The great challenge here is to respect the uniqueness of imagination, artistry, the aesthetic, and the moral as traits of lived experience, while also disclosing their relationships with one another. Central to Dewey's aesthetic theory—discussed more extensively in relation to morality in the final section of this chapter—is the claim that "art is the most direct and complete manifestation there is of experience *as* experience" (AE, LW 10:301).

Inquiry into artistic and aesthetic experience is revelatory of the nature of any complete experience because "esthetic experience is experience in its integrity" (AE, LW 10:278). The upshot is that moral experiences could be as richly developed as those consummated in the peaks of the arts.[4]

Art is conceived here along Dewey's lines as imaginative social communication through culturally refined skills. Inasmuch as art is popularly identified with physical products that stand apart from experience, the title of this chapter may be misleading, for the aim is to illuminate the *activity* of ethical engagement rather than its discrete outcomes. In lieu of the draconian step of expunging the word *art*, Dewey stipulates "the actual work of art is what the product does with and in experience" (AE, LW 10:9). Boisvert explains, "An art 'product' is potentially an art 'work.'"[5]

The working of art, Dewey declares with a little-recognized penchant for erotic metaphors, "is the impregnation of sensuous material with imaginative values" (AE, LW 10:297). It is *not* merely "the beauty parlor of civilization" (AE, LW 10:346) producing idyllic pleasantries, nor uproars of feeling. This must be borne in mind, since the latter would be a barren model.

The prevailing view of art as ethereal has contributed to its neglect by moral philosophers, since on this view artistic peaks are cut off from everyday life. But we ignore the moral analogue of artistic productions and appreciations to our detriment. To say that "art is more moral than moralities" (AE, LW 10:350) is to highlight our capacity to imaginatively outrun hardened habits of the status quo. This is exemplified by art not relegated to beauty parlor work. Moral reflection has always been ineliminatively imaginative, but this capacity has been restrained like an oak in a flowerpot by consigning morals and art to their own safe compartments. In art imagination finds its most complete expression as "the culminating event of nature" (EN, LW 1:8)—even more so than science, itself an art whose proper role is to serve aesthetic enjoyments (EN, LW 1:269). So we turn there to learn how best to spread the hitherto clipped wings of moral imagination.

Unfortunately, modeling ethical engagement on art brings us up against the dominant moral accounting metaphor, in which moral interactions are understood as business transactions. According to Johnson's analysis:

1. Moral deeds are objects in transactions ("In *return* for our kindness, she *gave* us nothing but trouble")
2. Well-being is wealth ("I've had a *rich* life")
3. The moral account is a record of transactions ("His despicable lying *counts against* him in my book")
4. Moral balance is a balance of transactions ("His noble deeds far *outweigh* his sins")

5. Doing moral deeds is accumulating credit ("I've got to *give you credit* for your sacrifices")

6. Benefiting from moral deeds is accumulating debt ("He is *indebted* to her for her help")

7. Doing immoral deeds is accumulating debt ("He *owes a debt* to society for his crimes")[6]

This suppresses qualitative aspects of moral thinking such as empathy and focuses exclusively on isolated actions of atomistic individuals seeking fixed ends. A wealth of alternative metaphors might be explored. For example, organic growth, evolutionary adaptation, scientific experimentation, technological innovation, and art are all key metaphors in Dewey's philosophy. Although no metaphor is alone sufficient, those of artistry provide a promising model. Yet, unlike the accounting metaphor, metaphors of morality (or more precisely, of moral conduct) as art are not in the mainstream. They could be, to the extent that customs are plastic. To appropriate the words of Lakoff and Johnson in *Metaphors We Live By*, they could "provide an organization of important [moral] experiences that our conventional conceptual system does not make available."[7]

Understanding ethical reflection as artistry is supported by the nature of our wisest everyday decisions. It highlights the role of an expansive imagination that enables sensitivity to social bearings and consequences, intervenes widely and deeply in experience, and brings diverse elements together in a unified experience (AE, LW 10:272). This is perhaps clearest when focusing on particular arts, as with jazz. The arts are not created equal in disclosing salient features of moral life. For example, interpersonal arts such as jazz single out colloquy and communication better than individual-centered arts such as sculpting. The jazz metaphor highlights an interpersonal ideal, yet it may be inadequate for comprehending situations in which parties are ill-intentioned.

Sculptors begin with a medium—stone, wood, clay, plaster, bronze. The beauty of the sculpture demands absolute respect for the medium; otherwise the art "product" will fail as an art "work." The medium suggests the formal possibilities for the artwork just as relatedness to others constrains possibilities for moral acts of grace and beauty. The sculpting metaphor aptly emphasizes the power of moral-agent/patients to form their environments; nonetheless, it downplays the tragic extent of human frailty in the face of impersonal environmental forces. (When it's you against the world, Kafka says, bet on the world.)[8] And thankfully, even the despot finds that people's purposes and nature's ways are less malleable than sculptors' clay, bronze, or wood. Others' aims, urges, and needs might be better conceived as threads to be collaboratively woven with other threads in a unified tapestry.

Or consider moral deliberation as dramatic writing. In a manner analogous to the creative imagination of a fiction writer or playwright (if understood in an Aristotelian vein), we run through a dramatic scene in imagination and thereby discover mediating courses that may temper initial inclinations. At our best, we do this with a cultivated awareness of human foibles and a deep respect for the consequences of events. The good dramatist rigorously imagines her characters thinking, feeling, and acting in ways continuous with their past behaviors, and she selects and rejects what happens next by shuttling in imagination back to what went before. To take a lowbrow example, Bill Watterson discusses his comic strip *Calvin and Hobbes:* "When I come up with a topic, I look at it through Calvin's eyes. Calvin's personality dictates a range of possible reactions to any subject, so I just tag along and see what he does."[9] Moral action, when it is not anesthetic, has this same growing meaning, and it likewise depends on continuity of character. Moreover, like good dramatists, good moral thinkers compose successive drafts before signing off on the product.[10] A refined moral imagination enables the moral dramatist to configure an action richly aware of connections and possibilities. Unfortunately, this metaphor of composing a life seems compatible with reducing others to the status of texts and downplaying colloquy.

We may be dramatists, but, as Shakespeare's fool expressed, we are also stage players: "All the world's a stage, and all the men and women merely players: They have their exits and their entrances; and one man in his time plays many parts."[11] MacIntyre uses the stage metaphor to underscore that a person is not an isolated entity, which underscores the role of community and the need for dialogue better than the dramatist metaphor:

> We are never more (and sometimes less) than the co-authors of our own narratives. Only in fantasy do we live what story we please. . . . We enter upon a stage which we did not design and we find ourselves part of an action that was not of our making. Each of us being a main character in his own drama plays subordinate parts in the dramas of others, and each drama constrains the others.[12]

Individual lives are dramatic narratives that interlock as major or minor characters in other dramas. MacIntyre states this more generally: "The narrative of any life is part of an interlocking set of narratives." We are not essentially private, rule-following animals, but social, story-telling animals. What we should do depends on the story or stories in which we find ourselves playing a part.[13] When gripped by the suspense of a story we ask, "What happens next?" not "What rule applies here?"

Yet the moral drama is not scripted in advance by a playwright; like a resourceful improvisational actor we must, Nussbaum exhorts, be "prepared to see and respond to any new feature that the scene brings forward" rather than viewing a situation "simply as the scene for the application of antecedent rules." Nussbaum forestalls criticism of improvisational morality as unprincipled or arbitrary: "The actress who improvises well is *not* free to do anything at all. She must at every moment—far more than one who goes by an external script—be responsively alive and committed to the other actors, to the evolving narrative, to the laws and constraints of the genre and its history." To discover how others' life-dramas can develop coordinately with one's own requires attention to the constraints imposed and possibilities made available by other dramas enacted on the same stage. Most importantly, one must be able to imaginatively take on the role of others if one is to excel at "taking what the other actor gives and going with it."[14] There is a crucial element of obligation or duty in this if the drama is to come off.

As we turn from particular arts to analysis of the generic metaphor of moral conduct as art, a healthy skepticism on the part of the reader will understandably attend any generalizations about art. But the generalizations that follow are intended to be operational, so the inevitable discovery of exceptions is "the antecedently conditioning means to further inquiries" (LTI, LW 12:197) rather than final grounds for abandonment.

Recall that, in contrast with the popular view, what Lakoff and Johnson call conceptual metaphors are far more than mere rhetorical flourishes, replaceable ornaments, or arresting comparisons. They are "cross-domain conceptual mappings" indispensable for human understanding and experience.[15] Thus an analysis does not simply compare pre-existing literal features of art and morality; it explores how the logic of artistry and aesthetic experience is ferried over to conduct so we conceive moral life in a new way.

In "Metaphor," John Searle followed the legacy of Max Black in criticizing the "comparison theory," the root of which is the idea that metaphors are elliptical similes. Searle deploys counterexamples such as the following: With "Sally is a block of ice," there are no literal similarities (relevant to the operation of the metaphor) between Sally and blocks of ice. Her "coldness," for instance, is a metaphorical rather than a literal feature. Likewise with "Richard is a gorilla." Richard may be ill-tempered and prone to violent outbursts, but this is part of our (exaggerated, as Dian Fossey showed) folk image of a gorilla rather than a constant literal feature.[16]

So, the following analysis does not simply compare pre-existing literal similarities of art and morality. In addition to being bad philosophy of language, the opposing view would make several suspect assumptions. First, it would assume that we can circumscribe in advance what behaviors will be morally significant and insignificant, or at least it would suppose that morality has a fixed form if not a finished content. The view that morality has a finished form or content hangs on the thread of suspect a priori assumptions. The view that the moral realm can be circumscribed in advance misses that any act, no matter how seemingly innocuous, could potentially have morally significant consequences.[17] Second, the comparison view here implies that analytically sophisticated specialists in ethics already know perfectly well what it means to be moral and can exhaustively analyze the nature and limits of moral conduct independent of any metaphorical understanding of it. This is far from apparent. Since the metaphor of morality as art, unlike the moral accounting metaphor, is not part of our cultural inheritance, neither is the concomitant way of thinking.

In fact, to the extent that there are *literal* similarities between moral conduct and art relevant to the operation of the metaphor, this stems from the fact that moral and artistic inquiries *are* structurally similar as forms of life-experience. They follow the "story" or "journey" structure already discussed. The same principle of development holds for "morals, politics, religion, science, philosophy itself, as well as the fine arts" (LW 16:397). Any literal description of the generic traits of experience is minimal and skeletal, which is why Dewey's corpus is so heavily dependent on artistic, technological, and biological metaphors, which lend differentiating hues to Dewey scholarship. The metaphor of moral conduct as art, with art understood as a form of social communication, is so revealing because artistic and aesthetic experiences illustrate the shared developmental traits of all experiences so well. It is probably "the simplest and most direct way to lay hold of what is fundamental in all the forms of experience" (LW 16:396).

Good artists are characterized, in part, by perceptiveness, creativity, expressiveness, and skill.[18] These parallels, although far from comprehensive, appear to be among the most salient. Of course, as Johnson admits, "there are many aspects of prototypical artistic activity that are not part of moral reasoning, and vice versa."[19] A brief analysis must seek to be evocative, not definitive.

Perceptiveness

Nussbaum's reintroduction of Aristotelian practical wisdom (*phronesis*) has contributed a great deal to refocusing moral philosophy on the concrete and particular. Although she may, in Alexander's words, lack Dewey's "robust theory of experimental moral conduct, conflict resolution, and the pluralistic, integrative ideals of the democratic life," she carries on the pragmatic spirit by retrieving moral theory from formalistic abstractions and returning it to worldly interactions.[20] She writes in *The Fragility of Goodness:*

Practical wisdom, then, uses rules only as summaries and guides; it must itself be flexible, ready for surprise, prepared to see, resourceful at improvisation. This being so, Aristotle stresses that the crucial prerequisite for practical wisdom is a long experience of life that yields an ability to understand and grasp the salient features, the practical meaning, of the concrete particulars. . . . Practical insight is . . . the ability to recognize, acknowledge, respond to, pick out certain salient features of a complex situation.[21]

Like Dewey's call to educate democratic imagination, Aristotle's ideal of citizen perceivers (his ideal for both public and private spheres) demands a great deal from public institutions. In *The Politics* he follows Thucydides in criticizing Spartan moral education for despotically drilling citizens to be subservient, and he praises the nobility of the Athenian system for cultivating personal intelligence and emotional engagement. On Aristotle's view, codified rules are a practical necessity for economizing effort, guarding against bias, and providing parameters for bad reasoners. But flexible practical wisdom, not unthinking subjugation to law, is the *ideal* for citizens, legislators, and judges.[22] Nussbaum explains:

Aristotelian education is aimed at producing citizens who are perceivers. It begins with the confident belief that each member of the heterogeneous citizenry is a potential person of practical wisdom, with the basic (that is, as yet undeveloped) ability to cultivate practical perception and to use it on behalf of the entire group. It aims at bringing these basic abilities to full actuality.[23]

Perception involves more than taking intellectual note of a situation's features; it is acknowledgment fused with appropriate feeling. Nussbaum clarifies Aristotle's theory of deliberation: "To have correct perception of the death of a loved one is not simply to take note of this fact with intellect or judgment. If someone noted the fact but was devoid of passional response, we would be inclined to say that he did not really *see, take in, recognize,* what had happened; that he did not acknowledge the situation for what it was."[24]

The great moral vice is not failure to universalize motives or calculate pleasurable consequences; it is obtuseness. Mill too hastily agreed with Enlightenment ethics when he asserted at the outset of *Utilitarianism,* "the morality of an individual action is not a question of direct perception, but of the application of a law to an individual case."[25] Better to heed Pericles who, in Nussbaum's words, "wants neither subservient followers nor calculating technocrats; he wants improvisers whose creativity is animated by passion."[26]

No decision tree or test can substitute for feeling one's way with a discerning imagination through a tangled web of relationships. Artists embody this receptiveness fused with orchestrating power. They disclose and create relations that otherwise go unnoticed, and it is especially for this that they are esteemed. The moral artist, like the prototypical artist, must have a dilated eye (to borrow Emerson's metaphor)[27]—an amplified receptivity to the potential of the present. People fail morally in part because, like Raskolnikov, their range of creative prospects becomes contracted. Resultant acts lack the Greek virtue of *kalokagathia:* They fail to blend the beautiful (*kalos*) and the good (*agathos*), so they are disproportionate, cacophonous, graceless. Contrariwise, Kierkegaard points out in *Either/Or* that imagination may also be overwhelmed by an *overabundance* of possibilities, to the same ill effect.[28]

Contraction of perception is attributable in part to a culture-wide inversion of the fact that moral engagement, like artistic activity, falls flat when product-orientation (a failure of Benthamite utilitarianism) supersedes process-orientation. It would not occur to anyone to think Louis Armstrong played his trumpet merely as a means to some future enjoyment, yet because people are so accustomed to mistaking moral and artistic experiences as disparate kinds, they ignore the immediacy of meaning in moral deliberation. This comes at a high price. Subordinating the present process—conceived not as a knife-edge, but as a complex, story-structured field event (HNC, MW 14:194–195)—to the future product indefinitely postpones goods. Consequently, as Moore criticized utilitarianism, the "here and now never has any value itself."[29] And such subordination limits one's capacity to forecast possible courses for attaining good in the future. Dewey implores: "[Is there] any intelligent way of modifying the future except to attend to the full possibilities of the present? Scamping the present in behalf of the future leads only to rendering the future less manageable. It increases the probability of molestation by future events" (HNC, MW 14:183–184).[30]

Buddhists have long understood that when mindfulness to the present is sacrificed, the quality of the product suffers, at least so long as we are not hypnotized by the swirling confusion around us. Products emerge as present conditions are transformed in light of latent possibilities. A Japanese Zen garden takes on its form through the alternating appreciations and productions of gardening. Lest the garden be poor and artless, exactly what form the product will take is patiently discovered through raking the sand and placing the stones. In kind, thinking of moral ends as "out there," and of deliberation as recognizing a familiar case to be lumped under a predetermined class of ends, anesthetizes imagination. This leads to artless behavior. Much moral reflection is not immediately experienced as significant, so it has no instrumental worth in the pregnant sense that playing a musical instrument has worth. In this case, things are not appreciated in their particularities and relations. In aesthetic terms, because we do not have a "cultivated taste" (EN, LW 1:299), we merely recognize without perceiving (AE, LW 10:30).[31]

The artist does not subordinate the present to a remote outcome. Dewey defines art with respect to "the relation of means and consequence, process and product, the instrumental and consummatory. Any activity that is simultaneously both, rather than in alternation and displacement, is art" (EN, LW 1:271). As the instrumental and consummatory are fused in the art of the Zen gardener, they are fused in the art of conduct. Rich imaginations achieve the "nuance and fine detail of tone" of perceptive moral communication.[32] Sequestering art and the aesthetic from everyday reflection, far from celebrating imagination, is a recipe for moral sterility, fragmentation, and alienation. Imagination cannot be democratic when it is "flat and toneless and lifeless," so it has historically turned either to radically individual pursuits or to promotion of authoritarian control.

Creativity

Artists make things that transform cultural perceptions. The best artists break out of old ruts or explore new directions in order to experiment with novel ways in which to see, hear, feel, and think.[33] "The architect, the musician, and the dancer," Boisvert notes, "explore untapped possibilities in the uses of space, sound, and movement."[34] They do not merely duplicate conventions or gift-wrap sanctioned ideals.

Conceived in this way, moral action is an ongoing experiment with novel possibilities. We venture beyond moral canons, often in playful ways common to art yet inconceivable on the accounting metaphor. In spite of the sad fact that educational, religious, and political institutions have tended to be deaf to the need for flexible mores and have conditioned against improvisational thinking, the "flexible logic" of human imagination occasionally comes up with "imaginative new forms of personal and institutional relationships."[35] Yet moral creativity all too easily succumbs to the inertia of habit. Dewey cautions:

> Conversion into doctrinal teachings of the imaginative relations of life with which great moral artists have dowered humanity has been the great cause of their ossification into harsh dogmas; illuminating insight into the relations and goods of life has been lost, and an arbitrary code of precepts and rules substituted. (EN, LW 1:322)

Contrary to a popular view of artistic creativity, formal possibilities of art are not radically free impositions by an artist on chaos. Artistic forms are achieved in a cultural and historical context, and they are constrained by a medium that has definite properties. To the extent that creative expressions are spontaneous, they are at least preceded by a period of subconscious maturation (AE, LW 10:79). This sociocultural, historical, and personal context of artistic production is a fit source for conceiving the complex horizon of moral judgments.

The recalcitrance of the artist's medium gives rise to another parallel. Social experience resists throwing it into just any order, so one must be perceptive of the encompassing whole. The whole, Thomas McCollough observes in *The Moral Imagination and Public Life,* "is not only the complex interrelated functional aspects of society, economic, political, social institutions. It is also the traditions, beliefs, values, ideals, and hopes of its members, who constitute a community with a stake in the good life and a hopeful future."[36] This whole is situated within the larger whole of the natural environment. The moral artist responds—as a normative ideal, though not in fact—to the entire system of exigencies in a troubled scene, deals with conflicts of long-range ends and short-range ends-in-view, attends to pressing interests of self and others, negotiates contingencies, and cares for her ecological household. Freed of the myopic demand for an authoritative first principle, she relies on the authority of circumstantial pressures. "Social pressure is but a name for the interactions which are always going on and in which we participate, living so far as we partake and dying so far as we do not" (HNC, MW 14:223–224). Moral imagination is the means for perceiving these pressures and investigating effectual prospects in a broadened and deepened context.

Expressiveness

Disturbances to habits often incite knee-jerk reactions or a spewing of feelings, "as meaningless as a gust of wind on a mudpuddle" (HNC, MW 14:65). But if enthusiasms are controlled, something more than sound and fury may result. Disturbances may kindle us to exert ourselves, as James says, toward "newly taken and freshly understood" ends (PP, I, 255). The former is a case of venting, the latter, if married to makings, an act of expression. "A gush of tears may bring relief, a spasm of destruction may give outlet to inward rage. But when there is no administration of objective conditions, no shaping of materials in the interest of embodying the excitement, there is no expression" (AE, LW 10:68).

Both artists and moral thinkers must have courage to discover, through what Keats speaks of as "innumerable compositions and decompositions," forms that will effect a controlled transformation from old ways of thinking and feeling to new ways. This probing yields expressive forms—as opposed to blind, wasteful spasms—that redefine the world. Morality, as Johnson insists, is "one of our primary forms of self-expression and self-definition. It is the main arena in which we project ourselves and pursue our sense of what we hope to become."[37] Artistic investigation is an expressive activity through which the artist struggles to configure emotions, desires, images, and the like. The art product opens up possibilities that awaken and enliven. Analogously, the best conduct coherently expresses overall character rather than blindly giving way to either custom or fleeting impulse. These acts may be appreciated for revealing possibilities that refresh life and restore courage. Seen as an expression of character, such acts become role models.

Skill

Delicately refined skills—habits, for Dewey—are the tools of artistic and moral imagination. On a pragmatic view, it is not the quantity of possibilities available to imagination, but their fittedness to the situation that counts for wise deliberation. To skilled perception, possibilities come in neither droughts nor floods. Rules are indispensable here. In the way rules of composition in painting (say, that there should be a focal point, positional and color balance, flow) economize discrimination of workable possibilities, social rules are helps to moral reflection. Skilled use of rules as instruments is the mean proportional between obeisance and flouting. Moral skillfulness also funds intuition, a habituated felt sense of the rightness of a projected action that parallels an artist's trained sense of the rightness of an artistic act. Effective moral habits may then be understood in terms of masterful artistic technical skills. Habits are intelligent rather than routine in art, and in this sense morality *is* art.

Response of the Other

An artist's anticipation of an audience (along with the actual response of that audience) enables a dialectical interaction that gives point and focus to art. Communication is called forth, whether or not it is intended.[38] In fact, an artist responds to herself as an audience as she selects and rejects. The artist, and analogously one engaged in ethical deliberation, "embodies in himself the attitude of the perceiver while he works" (AE, LW 10:55). Moreover, a moral agent's forecast of others' responses to a proposed act informs her deliberations, while their actual responses inform future deliberations. And the art world's criticism of the artwork is analogous to communal appraisal of a moral act. The social world furnishes materials for the act of expression and also reacts.

Highlighting and Hiding

All metaphors highlight and hide. Touching on several possible limitations of the art metaphor suggests a course for further criticisms. To begin with, contemporary artists often revel in values that seem exactly opposite of virtues and ideals important to moral life. They may value expressive acts of discord and imbalance rather than harmony and equilibrium; creative deconstructions instead of prototypically beautiful productions; perceptive subversion, not preservation and stability; skillful presentations of discontinuity rather than continuity. But the generic traits of artistry are more stable. The product may be fractured or subversive, but if there is cause for taking it more seriously than a temper tantrum, it is a skillful presentation of disharmony, or a perceptive shattering of the status quo. Art that attempts to problematize customary meanings, "to unexpress the expressible"[39]—is not the end-result of an uncontrolled evincing of raw feeling. As an act of expression its production involves skill, creativity, and perceptiveness. These are traits that also characterize admirable ethical reflection.

Another concern is that artists typically have finished products, but the moral artist's work is always in process. In response to this, consider that an artist's life is not a series of finished projects, but is instead an ongoing exploration with consummations of projects along the way. Just so, moral conduct is an ongoing process characterized by consummated experiences, each having their beginnings, middles, and closures.

Artistic actions might be blotted out or painted over. It is possible that an artistic decision will irreversibly change the character of the work or world, but an overt mistake is not generally as irrevocable in art as it might be in conduct. This is a minor detail, overshadowed by the fact that, as Kekes points out, the main corrective available for imaginative rehearsal, moral or artistic, is assessment of past counterproductive mistakes.

A more substantial criticism of the metaphor is that in conduct there is often a demand to produce in the tempestuous present without studio-like reflection. Dewey observes in a 1917 letter: "There are situations in which action is required to clear the air; in which continued deliberation and discussion simply weave a spell."[40] Additional criticisms can be piled on, but they are mitigated by clarifying the thesis: it is the generic logic of artistry, not the manifold details, that is revelatory of the potencies of moral inquiry. That an artist interacts perceptively with a medium is crucial; that this may take place in a studio, even through the hands of a wild-eyed misanthrope, is of marginal interest. What is crucial, as will be clarified in the next section on aesthetics and ethics, is to observe the way the arts, and aesthetic experiences deliberately cultivated in the arts, exemplify the aesthetic phase found as a primary dimension of *all* human experience.

THE AESTHETIC AND THE MORAL

In a contemporaneous review of Dewey's 1932 *Ethics,* Dewitt H. Parker spoke of "one great defect": "an insufficient sense for the tragic in moral conflicts, with the related absence of any appreciation of the bearing of . . . art (except historically) on ethical problems."[41] These are sound demands. It is by now evident that the latter criticism is unfounded, but what of the former?

Art is popularly associated with the idyllic and pleasant, the stuff of Grandma Moses's nostalgic paintings of rural Vermont and New York life. Does bringing it to bear on morals imply that moral reflection is invariably a pretty or pleasant affair? An adequate moral theory must respond to the inherent ambiguities of moral judgment, to the genuineness of tragic moral conflict, and to the pitfalls often encountered in even the best of decisions. Can a theory of moral artistry pass muster?

To associate art and aesthetic experiences strictly with pleasure is of course unwarranted. In the domain of art narrowly construed, Wordsworth's "The Daffodils" is delightful:

> I wander'd lonely as a cloud,
> That floats on high o'er vales and hills,
> When all at once I saw a crowd,
> A host of golden daffodils,
> Beside a lake, beneath the trees,
> Fluttering and dancing in the breeze.

Tolstoy's *The Death of Ivan Ilyich* is not:

> For three straight days, during which time ceased to exist for him, he struggled desperately in that black sack into which an unseen, invincible force was thrusting him. He struggled as a man condemned to death struggles in the hands of an executioner, knowing there is no escape.[42]

Ivan Ilyich's horrific encounter with his mortality was intensely aesthetic in what Dewey would call its "consummatory phase," but it was hardly pleasant. Encounter with this novel is painful yet transformative. The reader experiences moral growth permeated with dread. Dewey speaks to this:

> For "taking in" in any vital experience is something more than placing something on top of consciousness over what was previously known. It involves reconstruction which may be painful. Whether the necessary undergoing phase is by itself pleasurable or painful is a matter of particular conditions.

It is indifferent to the total esthetic quality, save that there are few intense esthetic experiences that are wholly gleeful. (AE, LW 10:48)

Moral artistry is not an idyllic ideal. Deliberation may be consummated in a moral outcome of unconventional beauty. When an addict is given methadone to help curb an addiction to crack, this may be artistry. Its beauty may be wrenching, but there is no immunization that would make the moral life a series of rosy events. Deliberations are sometimes consummated in the face of insurmountable contingencies when the better route is not one marked by smooth terrain. The best course discernable—if one is discernable at all—may lead to dissatisfying employment, ruptured friendships, harassment, political imprisonment. A moral theory can contribute to better lives, but it cannot "do away with moral struggle and defeat. It would not make the moral life as simple a matter as wending one's way along a well-lighted boulevard" (HNC, MW 14:10).

To more directly address Parker's criticism: Moral artistry deals as responsibly with the tragic dimension of experience—that is, situations with incompatible yet genuine goods—as with the comic. Universalist moral philosophies, even when confronting complex issues of distributive justice, have taught that human reason is capable of sifting through a merely apparent competition of values to discover the "Right" channel that will satisfy all rational agents (i.e., those using the right critical principle). This assumes an ideal universe in which all "legitimate" desires (those in accord with duty) can blossom into action simultaneously. A truly moral education forges tools needed to face conflicts and dilemmas rather than taking refuge in a phantom universe that explains away tragic conflicts when they arise. And it does not pretend situations come prepackaged with one and only one right solution.

Theoretical strategies such as the utilitarian or Kantian are designed to purify moral reasoning of attention to practical conflicts and moral dilemmas. But these theories gain the virtues of clarity and simplicity at the expense of much genuine amelioration. They wish, as a norm for moral reasoning, to rise above and pinpoint "the ethical issue" and formulate the right response. As an unintended result, they ignore virtues of vigilant perception and dismiss as morally irrelevant whatever exigencies do not fit into their hardened schemes.[43]

In *Moral Dilemmas,* Walter Sinnott-Armstrong distinguishes "moral requirement conflicts" from "moral dilemmas." Requirements in moral *conflicts* may be realistically ranked, whereas in genuine moral *dilemmas* "neither moral requirement overrides the other." He argues compellingly that we can be more responsible and tolerant if we "admit the inexactness of moral requirements and the possibility of moral dilemmas."[44] In a thoroughgoing naturalistic empiricism, discovering an integrative value is an ideal for which to strive, though success is uncertain. The mediation of intelligence will not always discover a channel for contending values, no matter how critically reflective and socially responsible these values may be. Real incompatibles emerge, and this is the source of tragic situations. We may be torn between moral requirements: do not kill yet be loyal to country and bring "evildoers" to justice, be kind to other species yet support medical science, be ecologically responsible yet travel afar to be with family. These are incompatible values in which no duty clearly overrides another (cf. 1932 E, LW 7:164–165). Choices like these are not the exclusive domain of high Greek drama: Should Antigone betray the State by burying her brother? Should Agamemnon sacrifice his daughter Iphigenia to keep his promises and responsibilities? Incompatible values are the norm, and the demand for moral artistry increases proportionally. Art, approached along the lines of the Greek *techne,* is after all "the sole alternative to luck" (EN, LW 1:279).

There are also occasions, equally tragic, when legitimate aspirations compete and cannot be simultaneously fulfilled. Sometimes no action under the sun will allay the slings and arrows of fortune from falling more heavily on some roofs than on others. The theme of unrequited love in poetry and literature serves as a reminder of this. In his own poetry Dewey lamented "the woes of fresh made hells" that arose when he had to be satisfied not with romantic fulfillment, but with bittersweet memories. A mutually traversable path must be discovered, but it may not be a happy one, and no two moral artists would necessarily choose alike.

We need to respond to tragedy in a way that neither embitters us nor leaves us with an impotent, mono-focused moral schema. What is needed is twofold: (1) to wrest the complete meaning from situations so that we are better prepared for future events, and (2) to transform crippling conditions that may yield to reconstruction so that the future might not merely repeat the past.[45] In imagination, we see beyond confused and dizzying conditions so that we may eventually construct more desirable circumstances.

Approaching moral conduct from the standpoint of art and aesthetic experience may still strike some as, at best, incoherent. Worse, it may appear to be an opening for "anything goes" relativism. This prejudice is conditioned by our Enlightenment heritage, which teaches that artistic-aesthetic and moral experiences are discontinuous. The contrast with the ancient Greek moral-aesthetic ideal of *kalokagathia*—grace and harmony in comportment, entwined with virtues such as wisdom, courage, and self-mastery—is palpable. Kant can be held up as a model of Enlightenment thinking: Understanding (*Verstand*), according to Kant, is constrained by our universal conceptual structure and has nothing to do with feeling. In understanding, fixed concepts functioning in a purely formal realm enable classification of a presented image in the material realm. An aesthetic judgment, by contrast, has no such determinateness. It is a matter of subjective feeling (albeit "common" or universal feeling, for Kant). With the aesthetic, Kant writes in the *Critique of Judgment*, "the basis determining [the judgment] is the subject's feeling and not the concept of an object."[46] Meanwhile, he argues in *Grounding for the Metaphysics of Morals*, in a moral judgment "moral concepts have their seat and origin completely *a priori* in reason [*Vernunft*]."[47] Thus Kant subjectivizes the aesthetic and severs it from a transcendental rationality that legislates moral laws that are "unconditioned and indeed objective and hence universally valid."[48]

The assumptions surrounding Kant's conception of a morality based on transcendental rationality were, as has been discussed, powerfully criticized by the classical pragmatists. Despite growing disrepute and incompatibility with empirical findings, assumptions about reason dominant in seventeenth- and eighteenth-century Europe still set the context for moral inquiries, for both the person on the street and the moral philosopher. Consequently, any attempt to decompartmentalize the supposedly autonomous spheres of the moral and aesthetic, treating them as "dominantly different" (AE, LW 10:44) features of a unified field of value, raises a suspicious eyebrow because it is mistakenly taken to radically subjectivize moral reflection.[49]

Compartmentalization leads us to suppose there is something contrived about seeing moral conduct as an art. Art, *because* it is imaginative, is widely thought to be a radically spontaneous overflow of feeling untarnished by everyday habits. But Dewey treats aesthetic experience as paradigmatic of *all* experience. This is why Dewey exclaims: "There is no test that so surely reveals the one-sidedness of a philosophy as its treatment of art and esthetic experience. . . . All the elements of our being that are displayed in special emphases and partial realizations in other experiences are merged in esthetic experience" (AE, LW 10:278).

Moral and artistic-aesthetic experiences follow the same story-structured pattern from beginning to middle to consummatory end, but they are guided by different ends, emphasize different materials, and are furthered by different activities and considerations of relevance. Moral experience is suffused with emotion but has a distinctively practical bearing, while artistic thinking and aesthetic appreciation are more distinctively emotional (distinguished from raw feeling, in Dewey's terminology), yet still at least indirectly practical (AE, LW 10:44).[50] Reflection has moral import—as potentially all conduct does—to the degree in which alternatives arise that may impact the lifeworld and so must be appraised as better or worse, thereby giving cause for evaluating character. Reflection on this impact is dyed with emotion, but its dominant quality is not aesthetic.

An experience *as lived* is "neither emotional, practical, nor intellectual." But reflection may find that "one property rather than another was sufficiently dominant so that it characterizes the experience as a whole" (AE, LW 10:44). This property gives the experience its qualitative distinctiveness. Enrico Fermi's experiment on fission was intellectual, and he may have experienced the qualitative spread of the event with less immediacy than would an artist, but in its "actual occurrence" it was "emotional as well" (AE, LW 10:44; LW 10:80). Distinguishing the moral from the aesthetic in this reconstructed way helps to reframe what was of value in the traditional split: the mere fact that an experience has a primary aesthetic phase is inadequate as a test for whether conclusions will be seaworthy when set in motion.

Far from being a lofty, elite, or contrived ideal, what is cultivated in moral artistry already goes on incessantly: "the dynamic interpenetration of aesthetic discernment and artistic execution."[51] Dewey distinguishes the "artistic," which "refers primarily to the act of production," from the "esthetic," which refers to acts of "perception and enjoyment" (AE, LW 10:53). Moral experience includes both simultaneously. This operational distinction helps to illuminate limiting factors in conduct. With acts that destroy, divide, or dull there is usually production (the *potentially* artistic) with a minimum of perception (the aesthetic phase), or vice versa. When there is no mean proportional between activity and receptivity, experiences are distorted by lust for action or fanciful sentimentality (AE, LW 10:51). Experiences are cut short in their development so that inclusive and enduring ends escape notice. "Unbalance on either side blurs the perception of relations and leaves the experience partial and distorted, with scant or false meaning" (AE, LW 10:51).

Moreover, the stilted perception of anesthetic experience is a sure route to miserable behavior because as imagination shrinks, foresight and critical appraisal are abandoned to the inertia of mechanical habit. The aesthetic quality may also be funded so narrowly that receptiveness to the encompassing whole is eclipsed by obsessive focus (see HNC, MW 14:138). We rightly call such experiences (im)moral rather than (an)aesthetic in order to emphasize their practical rather than immediately felt effects, but these effects are palpable.

The aesthetic is not merely subjective. Both as a natural phase of everyday experiences and as developed in the arts, it involves (a) a felt opening of awareness of a situation's objective potentialities in which (b) something of the world is revealed. Its unitary quality "is attained only when, by some means, terms are made with the environment" (AE, LW 10:23). And it emerges from ordinary life rather than being the exclusive domain of formalized art. In one commentator's helpful phrasing, "aesthetic experience is a critical, adaptive felt response, revealing value in the world."[52]

In *Art as Experience* Dewey shows how an ordinary job interview is aesthetically guided and fundamentally imaginative:

> The employer sees by means of his own emotional reactions the character of the one applying. He projects him imaginatively into the work to be done and judges his fitness by the way in which the elements of the scene assemble and either clash or fit together. The presence and behavior of the applicant either harmonize with his own attitudes and desires or they conflict and jar. Such factors as these, inherently esthetic in quality, are the forces that carry the varied elements of the interview to a decisive issue. They enter into the settlement of every situation, whatever its dominant nature, in which there are uncertainty and suspense. (AE, LW 10:50)

Although the employer's decision making is not properly labeled an aesthetic experience, it has an inescapable and indispensable aesthetic character. To understand the unifying quality of an interview experience we turn not to a treatise on management psychology but to drama or fiction (AE, LW 10:49). The same holds for moral experiences: their nature is best expressed not by an account ledger or by the "Nash equilibrium," but by art. Dewey summarizes his position: "I have tried to show . . . that the esthetic is no intruder in experience from without, . . . but that it is the clarified and intensified development of traits that belong to every normally complete experience" (AE, LW 10:52–53). It is as much a feature of a decision of reproductive choice as of writing a poem.

This emphasis on artistic-aesthetic experience helps to make moral theory more relevant to bewildering circumstances. Far from collapsing into extreme subjectivism, decompartmentalization revitalizes moral theory and opens the door to a more responsible ethic.

This can be further illuminated in light of Dewey's theory of experience. For deliberation of any sort to be brought to a resolution, it must develop so as to have a form that expresses coherently the conflicts that originally set the problem for inquiry. When experience becomes sufficiently demarcated to be called *an* experience (as when we say "Now that was an experience!"), a coherent story may be told, from commencement to culmination, about a problematic situation.

In focusing on this pattern of artful development Dewey is simply clarifying the colloquial way of talking about an experience in the singular. Each experience has a story to tell: "For life is no uniform uninterrupted march or flow. It is a thing of histories, each with its own plot, its own inception and movement toward its close, each having its own particular rhythmic movement; each with its own unrepeated quality pervading it throughout" (AE, LW 10:42–43; cf. MW 10:321–324). There is a drive to complete these stories, though interruptions and lethargy often bring us up short. This is why we generally remember things that are unfinished or that do not have closure, as when an unfinished job nags at us.[53] Dewey clarifies:

> We have *an* experience when the material experienced runs its course to ful-fillment. Then and then only is it integrated within and demarcated in the general stream of experience from other experiences. A piece of work is fin-ished in a way that is satisfactory; a problem receives its solution; a game is played through; a situation, whether that of eating a meal, playing a game of chess, carrying on a conversation, writing a book, or taking part in a politi-cal campaign, is so rounded out that its close is a consummation and not a cessation. Such an experience is a whole and carries with it its own individu-alizing quality and self-sufficiency. It is *an* experience. (AE, LW 10:42)

Consummatory experiences are exemplified by the deliberate produc-tions and perceptions of art, useful or fine (a distinction Dewey disdained [EN, LW 1:271–272]). Art celebrates the consummatory (AE, LW 10:18). The failure of experience to be artfully developed is for Dewey "the human tragedy, for it signifies that most experience is unconsummated in its mean-ing."[54] Whether we focus ecstatically on a future end or plod along in a lethargic daze, imagination may become so contracted that we do not at-tend to the world's potentialities. Dewey observes that in such experiences "one thing replaces another, but does not absorb it and carry it on. There is experience, but so slack and discursive that it is not *an* experience" (AE, LW 10:47).

On Dewey's (questionable)[55] view, all experiences share the same gener-ic pattern, whether they involve "genuine initiations and concludings" or anesthetic beginnings and cessations (AE, LW 10:46–47). The concern at hand is to consider moral experience in this light. If "rival claimants for lik-ing" (EN, LW 1:320) are ignored, the moral experience will be incomplete and underdeveloped. Moral deliberation can be artfully developed only through a socially responsive imagination that skillfully perceives paths of mutual growth. Essentially, Joseph Kupfer explains, "we judge whether our imaginative projection of alternative futures proceeds in an *aesthetically complete way*."[56]

Any decision that resolves a state of doubt, whether for good or for ill, has some aesthetic quality. This is the reason we are often taken in by our own poor, unartful judgments. Dostoyevsky's Raskolnikov asks why a worthless pawnbroker should go on living when her murder would elimi-nate her future pettiness. Raskolnikov rehearses what to do, and his choice to commit murder is surely accompanied by the aesthetic stamp. But his ex-perience is incomplete and underdeveloped. It lacks depth and breadth, fails to grasp inherent connections and relationships, is "partial and distort-ed, with scant or false meaning" (AE, LW 10:51). It is not *art*. "An artist, in comparison with his fellows, is one who is not only especially gifted in powers of execution but in unusual sensitivity to the qualities of things. This sensitivity also directs his doings and makings. . . . What is done and what is undergone are thus reciprocally, cumulatively, and continuously instrumental to each other" (AE, LW 10:56–57).

Not all consummations are "devoutly to be wished." Buddhism points out that much of the drive toward consummation is spent assuaging childlike cravings of desperate, confused lives, outwardly purposeful yet destitute of growth. Dewey contends: "There is interest in completing an experience. The experience may be one that is harmful to the world and its consummation undesirable. But it has esthetic quality" (AE, LW 10:46). The dramatic rehearsals of Napoleon or Caesar, Dewey observes, had aesthetic quality while stifling the interests of all but the state. They failed in artistry.

In his *Commentaries* on the Gallic Wars, Julius Caesar records the slaughter of hundreds of thousands of Gauls. Caesar dealt effectually with the situation by eradicating those who experienced the world differently. As a result, two hundred years of relative peace were forced upon Gaul, and the Roman borders were secured. To be sure, Caesar was aware of the threat to his inflexible ends of Roman border extension, acquisition of fertile land, and personal glory if he did not deal with the warlike and nomadic Gauls. But he wove his tapestry of exclusively Roman and Caesarian strands. Even if one argues that this reinforcement of Roman militarism was an improvement, its effectiveness was one-sided. It was "pragmatic" only in the vulgar sense. The experience had aesthetic quality, but it fell short of art. Modern Caesars should reevaluate their ideals accordingly.

The best moral decisions deal sensitively yet critically with others' valuings. Their consummations are not individualistic and fleeting. Inclusive consummation is not a mere drug-like mental state, but a transformed situation in which the individual contrives an organic equilibrium with her social and natural surroundings. Gouinlock notes, "It is hence *situations* that become an organic whole; our powers as human beings are effectively engaged with the environment and fulfilled therein."[57] In aesthetically complete ethical reflection, existential factors are woven into a tapestry most likely to persist and grow.[58]

Conceiving the aesthetic as a phase of everyday experiences aids the development of moral ideals consonant with the central role of imagination. Intelligent dramatic rehearsals are directed toward the ultimate art of bringing about democratic consummations in experience. This is not a mechanical measure or a necessary and sufficient condition of moral value of the "X is good, Y is bad" variety. It is an ideal to strive for to consummate and revivify meaning and value.

It has been urged that, in addition to investigating metaphors that guide deliberations and structure shared moral concepts, we must explore alternative metaphors for morality. Morality as art emphasizes the aesthetic dimension of morally significant behavior ignored by the moral accounting metaphor. It is not possible to magically will away habits of cold-blooded accounting and cost-benefit calculating. But drawing from artistic production, experience, and evaluation does reveal imaginative dimensions of ethical reflection hitherto left to chance development. Conceiving moral conduct as art highlights, for instance, that we imagine most effectively when we live in an aesthetically funded present.

It is widely recognized that many today think of value commitments as simply my opinion against yours. Responding to this, most moral philosophers share a sense of urgency about the need to fortify moral intelligence. But their carefully argued diagnoses and prescriptions typically ignore imagination. This is a sure route to obtuseness. A revitalized ethics requires a central focus on imaginative inquiry.

In imagination not only do we forecast consequences for ourselves, but also, as Mead points out, we dramatically take the attitude of others whose lives interlace with our own.[59] Especially through colloquy, we place ourselves in the emerging dramas of others' lives to discover actions that may meaningfully continue their life-stories alongside our own.[60] Lacking this, we may weave an aesthetically incomplete tapestry, or, equally likely, leave initially tangled circumstances in unmanageable knots. Such moral failure is largely remediable and is due to maldeveloped imagination and botched artistry. To be sensitive and perceptive, aided by critically examined principles and rules, is a realizable ideal in a social milieu that cultivates and sustains moral imagination.

The moral of the arts is that everyday moral decisions can be as richly consummated as artistic productions. The distance is narrowed between this ideal and actual deliberations to the degree that a culture focuses beyond sedimented moral criteria to education of aesthetic virtues of sensitivity, perceptiveness, discernment, creativity, expressiveness, courage, foresight, communicativeness, and experimental intelligence. "One great defect in what passes as morality," Dewey observes, "is its anesthetic quality. Instead of exemplifying wholehearted action, it takes the form of grudging piecemeal concessions to the demands of duty" (AE, LW 10:46).

In much mainstream ethical theory, particulars must be scrutinized only when anomalies make subordination to a governing principle troublesome. Faced with irregularities, the normative theorist adjusts lists of precepts and proposes new ways to apply them. But it is increasingly recognized that, on its own, this leaves imagination coarse and monochromatic.

In *John Dewey's Pragmatic Technology,* Larry Hickman cites Edwin A. Burt's suggestion that "if he had to pick a single word to typify Dewey's philosophical work, it would be 'responsibility.'"[61] Calculation and disengaged judgment are not responsible enough. What Dewey dubbed "the bleakness and harshness often associated with morals" is gradually dissipating as moral philosophers become resensitized to aesthetic values of "grace, rhythm, and harmony as dominant traits of good conduct" (1932 E, LW 7:271).

NOTES

INTRODUCTION

1. James Gouinlock critiques absolutism and relativism as "Janus faces of the same assumption," in *Rediscovering the Moral Life* (Buffalo, N.Y.: Prometheus, 1993), 24.

2. As examples of this shift in focus outside the increasingly vital philosophical tradition that includes classical pragmatism, I have in mind such works as Charles Taylor's "The Diversity of Goods," in *Utilitarianism and Beyond*, ed. Bernard Williams and Amartya Sen (Cambridge, U.K.: Cambridge University Press, 1982), 129–144; Bernard Williams's *Moral Luck* (Cambridge, U.K.: Cambridge University Press, 1981) and *Ethics and the Limits of Philosophy* (Cambridge, Mass.: Harvard University Press, 1985); Nel Noddings, *Caring: A Feminine Approach to Ethics and Moral Education* (Berkeley: University of California Press, 1984); Alasdair MacIntyre's *After Virtue*, 2nd ed. (Notre Dame: University of Notre Dame Press, 1984) and *Whose Justice? Which Rationality?* (Notre Dame: University of Notre Dame Press, 1988); Martha Nussbaum's *The Fragility of Goodness: Luck and Ethics in Greek Tragedy and Philosophy* (Cambridge, U.K.: Cambridge University Press, 1986) and *Love's Knowledge* (Oxford: Oxford University Press, 1990); Owen Flanagan's *Varieties of Moral Personality: Ethics and Psychological Realism* (Cambridge, Mass.: Harvard University Press, 1991); and Mark Johnson's *Moral Imagination* (Chicago: University of Chicago Press, 1993).

3. The most notable exception is Thomas Alexander's "John Dewey and the Moral Imagination: Beyond Putnam and Rorty toward a Postmodern Ethics," *Transactions of the Charles S. Peirce Society* 29, no. 3 (1993): 369–400. The most comprehensive recent study of Dewey's theory of intelligence is Michael Eldridge's *Transforming Experience* (Nashville: Vanderbilt University Press, 1998).

4. Gregory Pappas's comprehensive treatment of Dewey's moral theory, *John Dewey's Ethics: Morality As Experience* (in preparation), will help to address this need. For detailed engagement with Anglo-American metaethics, see Todd Lekan, *Making Morality: Pragmatist Reconstruction in Ethical Theory* (Nashville: Vanderbilt University Press, 2002).

1. HABIT AND CHARACTER

1. John J. McDermott, *Streams of Experience: Reflections on the History and Philosophy of American Culture* (Amherst: University of Massachusetts Press, 1986), 128.

2. John Calvin, *Institutes of the Christian Religion,* trans. Henry Beveridge (Edinburgh: Calvin Translation Society, 1845), 806.

3. In *Freedom and Culture,* Dewey helpfully identifies at least six chief factors of culture (FC, LW 13:79): (1) law and politics, (2) industry and commerce, (3) science and technology, (4) the arts of expression and communication, (5) "morals, or the values men prize and the ways in which they evaluate them, (6) social philosophy, "the system of general ideas used by men to justify and to criticize the fundamental conditions under which they live." In *The Evolution of Culture in Animals* (Princeton, N.J.: Princeton University Press,

1980), John Bonner offers a more inclusive definition suitable for ethological study: "Certain kinds of information can only be transmitted by behavioral means. . . . If the transmission of this difficult kind of information is adaptive, then there would be strong selection pressure for culture" (183). For a sustained criticism of the claim that survival strategies in nonhumans are genetically hard-wired rather than cultural, see Frans de Waal, *The Ape and the Sushi Master* (New York: Basic Books, 2001). For a troubling and decisive critique of biodeterminism, see Stephen Jay Gould, *The Mismeasure of Man*, 2nd ed. (New York: W. W. Norton, 1996).

4. Maurice Merleau-Ponty, *The Phenomenology of Perception,* trans. Colin Smith (Atlantic Highlands, N.J.: Humanities Press, 1962), 87.

5. Mary Pipher, *Reviving Ophelia: Saving the Selves of Adolescent Girls* (New York: Ballantine Books, 1994), 23. Cf. Pipher, *Hunger Pains: The American Woman's Tragic Quest for Thinness* (New York: Ballantine Books, 1995).

6. For a psychological account of the emergence of the self in infancy compatible with Dewey's work, see Daniel Stern's *The Interpersonal World of the Infant* (New York: Basic Books, 1985). Humans are not the only animals to have evolved cultures. See Bonner, *Evolution of Culture in Animals;* de Waal, *The Ape and the Sushi Master.*

7. George Herbert Mead, "The Social Self," in *Selected Writings,* ed. Andrew Reck (Chicago: University of Chicago Press, 1964), 146.

8. This does not entail that, so long as a culture sanctions it, anything goes. See Chapter 6.

9. Thomas Alexander, *John Dewey's Theory of Art, Experience, and Nature: The Horizons of Feeling* (Albany: SUNY Press, 1987), 235.

10. Cf. MW 9:34–35.

11. Alfred North Whitehead, *Science and the Modern World* (1925; New York: Macmillan, 1953), vii.

12. From "Memories of John Dewey by James Farrell" (November 5, 1965). Morris Library, Southern Illinois University at Carbondale. Used by permission. This quotation is a conglomeration of relevant passages in pages 3–7. Priscilla Hill addresses some aspects of Dewey's work in relation to Farrell in "Aesthetics and the Novel: A Study of the Relation of John Dewey's Philosophy and the Novels of James T. Farrell" (Ph.D. diss., Southern Illinois University at Carbondale, 1986).

13. James T. Farrell, *Studs Lonigan* (Champaign: University of Illinois Press, 1993). Originally published as a trilogy: *Young Lonigan* (1932), *The Young Manhood of Studs Lonigan* (1934), and *Judgment Day* (1935).

14. Edgar M. Branch, *James T. Farrell* (New York: Twayne Publishers, 1971), 44.

15. Isaiah Berlin, "The Pursuit of the Ideal," in *The Crooked Timber of Humanity,* ed. Henry Hardy (New York: Knopf, 1991), 13.

16. Branch, *James T. Farrell,* 47.

17. Branch, *James T. Farrell,* 39, 43.

18. In *Knowing and the Known* (LW 16), Dewey and Arthur Bentley distinguish "interaction" from "transaction." The former term, which had served Dewey for over three decades, is observed to retain a residue of the very subject/object dichotomy it was meant to transcend. "Transaction" is proposed as a replacement. Although "transaction" may be etymologically superior to "interaction," the two terms are here used somewhat loosely and interchangeably.

19. John B. Watson, *Psychology from the Standpoint of a Behaviorist,* 2nd ed. (Philadelphia: J. B. Lippincott, 1924), 10.

20. B. F. Skinner, *Walden Two* (New York: Macmillan, 1976), 274.

21. B. F. Skinner, *The Behavior of Organisms,* (New York: D. Appleton-Century, 1938), 10. In his experimental writings Skinner follows Dewey in criticizing the reflex arc model, which he identifies with the extreme "environmentalism" of Watson.

22. Example drawn from an unpublished lecture by John E. Smith.

23. Farrell, *Studs Lonigan,* 404–405.

24. Farrell, *Studs Lonigan,* 409.

25. Vincent Colapietro, presentation at the Summer Institute for American Philosophy, Burlington, Vermont, July 1998.

26. Robert Coles, *The Call of Stories: Teaching and the Moral Imagination* (Boston: Houghton Mifflin, 1989), 108.

27. David Hume, *A Treatise of Human Nature,* ed. L. A. Selby-Bigge (Oxford: Clarendon Press, 1978).

28. Farrell, *Studs Lonigan,* 439–440. I have condensed this passage, along with most others included here.

29. Plato, *Statesman,* trans. J. B. Skemp (Indianapolis: Hackett, 1992), 66.

30. From James, *Memories and Studies,* quoted in McDermott, *Streams of Experience,* 44. James acknowledges the "social self" as one aspect of the self, but, unlike Dewey and Mead, he does not advance far beyond the fact that humans are "gregarious animals" (see PP, I, 281–283; 293–296 and PP, II, 1047; 430 and PP, I, 300–302; 314–317). In "The Will to Believe" he writes that our "pre-existing tendencies" to believe this or that grow in an "intellectual climate" in which "[o]ur social system backs us up" (WB, 18; 9). He takes this up again in the *Varieties* via Jonathan Edwards's encultured schemas of religious conversion (VRE, 165; 165). But he immediately returns to "first hand and original" experiences of individuals. Cf. PM, 71; 67 and PM, 139; 130. See John McDermott's "The Promethean Self and Community in the Philosophy of William James" in *Streams of Experience,* 44–58.

31. Cf. James Campbell's discussion in *Understanding John Dewey* (Chicago: Open Court, 1995), 124.

32. Walpola Rahula, *What the Buddha Taught* (New York: Grove Weidenfeld, 1974), 54.

33. Farrell, *Studs Lonigan,* 440.

34. Farrell, *Studs Lonigan,* 317–320.

35. Farrell, *Studs Lonigan,* 326–327.

36. Farrell, *Studs Lonigan,* 359–360.

37. Farrell, *Studs Lonigan,* 450.

38. See McDermott, *Streams of Experience,* 128–131.

39. Farrell, *Studs Lonigan,* 486.

40. F. Matthias Alexander was the innovator of the "Alexander Technique," which Dewey took to be a scientifically established method for enhancing human well-being. He explains Alexander's view: "The assumption is that if a man is told to stand up straight, all that is further needed is wish and effort on his part, and the deed is done. He pointed out that this belief is on a par with primitive magic in its neglect of attention to the means which are involved in reaching an end. And he went on to say that the prevalence of this belief, starting with false notions about the control of the body and extending to control of mind and character, is the greatest bar to intelligent social progress" (HNC, MW 14:23). See Dewey's glowing introduction to one of Alexander's books: F. Matthias Alexander, *The Resurrection of the Body: The Writings of F. Matthias Alexander,* ed. Edward Maisel (New York: Dell Publishing, 1969). Richard Shusterman discusses Alexander in *Pragmatist Aesthetics: Living Beauty, Rethinking Art,* 2nd ed. (Oxford: Blackwell, 2000). Jo Ann Boydston offers personal reflections on the Alexander Technique at http://www.alexandercenter.com/jd/deweyalexanderboydston.html.

41. George Herbert Mead, "The Philosophical Basis of Ethics," in *Selected Writings,* 92. Cf. Heather Keith, "Feminism and Pragmatism: George Herbert Mead's Ethics of Care," *Transactions of the Charles S. Peirce Society* 35, no. 2 (1999).

42. Geoffrey Canada, *Fist Stick Knife Gun: A Personal History of Violence in America* (Boston: Beacon Press, 1995), 127.

43. Friedrich Nietzsche, *On The Genealogy of Morals,* trans. W. Kaufmann (1887; New York: Vintage, 1989), 85. It had become common for European thinkers to conclude that the civilization they had erected must have been the result of taming the wildness thought to be manifest in "savages" they were encountering overseas. In this context, the theory of the social contract and of enlightened self-interest came to full flower.

44. See LW 5:288; 1908 E, MW 5:328ff.; LW 13:286–293.

45. This is the will to create a higher self by partly destroying the old self, not a will-to-overpower, as Dewey crudely misconstrues it. For Dewey's misconceptions of Nietzsche, see 1908 E, MW 5:332–337 and HNC, MW 14:97–99. He later recants (FC, LW 13:75).

46. Gouinlock, *Rediscovering the Moral Life,* 205, 233, 211, 119, 218. Such claims are decisively criticized by Stephen Jay Gould in *The Mismeasure of Man.*

47. Gouinlock, *Rediscovering the Moral Life,* 214, 206, 170, 207, 169, 208.

48. See the influential study by Eleanor Maccoby and J. A. Martin on punitive enforcement of rules. "Socialization in the Context of the Family: Parent-Child Interaction," in *Handbook of Child Psychology,* Vol. 4: *Socialization, Personality, and Social Development,* 4th ed., ed. P. H. Mussen and E. M. Hetherington, (New York: Wiley, 1983), 1–101. Gouinlock writes as though it is universally self-evident what functions as a reward and what functions as punishment. But according to behavioral psychology, whatever functions to strengthen a behavior is ipso facto reinforcement, and this is relative to idiosyncrasies of individuals and situations. We cannot specify in advance exactly what will be rewarding or punishing for a class of people.

49. Undesired consequences stemming from punishment (as opposed to simple removal from the ordinary stream of reinforcement) include increased aggression, escape from or aversion to the punishment situation, a strong tendency toward abuse, and modeling of aggressive behavior begetting aggressiveness.

50. Gouinlock, *Rediscovering the Moral Life,* 179, 183, 193.

51. Gouinlock concedes in passing that our nature is not strictly a given, but he insists that Dewey let "his enthusiasms run ahead of his evidence." *Rediscovering the Moral Life,* 199, 209, 229, 28.

52. The claim that Dewey's social philosophy has utopian tendencies is investigated by Raymond Boisvert, "The Nemesis of Necessity: Tragedy's Challenge to Deweyan Pragmatism," in *Dewey Reconfigured: Essays on Deweyan Pragmatism,* ed. Casey Haskins and David I. Seiple (Albany: SUNY Press, 1999), 151–168. Cf. Donald Morse, "Pragmatism and The Tragic Sense of Life," *Transactions of the Charles S. Peirce Society* 37, no. 4 (2001): 555–572, and Boisvert's response, "Updating Dewey: A Reply to Morse," in the same volume, 573–583.

2. THE PRAGMATIC TURN

1. John Rawls, *A Theory of Justice* (Cambridge, Mass.: Harvard University Press, 1971). Cf. Rawls, *Justice as Fairness: A Restatement,* ed. Erin Kelly (Cambridge, Mass.: Belknap Press, 2001).

2. See Richard Rorty, *Philosophy and the Mirror of Nature* (Princeton, N.J.: Princeton University Press, 1979).

3. See Daniel Kahneman, Paul Slovic, and Amos Tversky, *Judgment under Uncertainty: Heuristics and Biases* (New York: Cambridge University Press, 1982).

4. In George Lakoff and Mark Johnson, *Philosophy in the Flesh* (New York: Basic Books, 1999), 521. This analysis is based on Lakoff and Johnson's critique, 515–538.

5. Compare to Sigmund Freud, *Beyond the Pleasure Principle* (New York: W. W. Norton, 1961), 1: "The course of [mental] events is invariably set in motion by an unpleasur-

able tension, and . . . it takes a direction such that its final outcome coincides with a lowering of that tension" (1). This is Freud's "pleasure principle," which he counters with the "reality principle."

6. The other installment of Bain's two-volume magnum opus was *The Senses and the Intellect*, published in 1855. In the mid-nineteenth century, John Stuart Mill and Bain (1818–1903) were the two standard English psychologies, both associationist. Herbert Spencer and Bain shared this influence in the latter nineteenth century. See Max Fisch's essay "Alexander Bain and the Genealogy of Pragmatism," in *Peirce, Semeiotic, and Pragmatism*, ed. Kenneth Ketner and Christian Kloesel (Bloomington: Indiana University Press, 1986), 79–109.

7. Bain, *The Emotions and the Will* (New York: D. Appleton, 1899), 505, 507.

8. James's marginal query in his copy of Bain's *Emotions,* in Fisch, "Alexander Bain and the Genealogy of Pragmatism," 92. James is referring to Bain, *Emotions and the Will,* 509.

9. Although he did not compellingly work out the details of his anti-subjectivism, Bain repeatedly stresses that "nothing can be set forth as belief that does not implicate in some way or other the order, arrangements, or sequences of the universe." Bain, *Emotions and the Will,* 506.

10. Fisch, *Peirce, Semeiotic, and Pragmatism,* 84. See Bain, *Emotions and the Will,* 312.

11. Cf. Bain, *Emotions and the Will,* 512–513, Peirce, "What Pragmatism Is," in *The Essential Peirce: Selected Philosophical Writings,* vol. 2, ed. Nathan Houser and Christian Kloesel (Bloomington: Indiana University Press, 1998), 336, and George Santayana, *Scepticism and Animal Faith* (New York: Dover, 1955), chs. 15–16.

12. In Fisch, *Peirce, Semeiotic, and Pragmatism,* 93.

13. According to Fisch, Bain's psychology was well received by Metaphysical Club members prior to the club's outset. Fisch, "Alexander Bain and the Genealogy of Pragmatism," 93. Cf. Max Fisch, "Was There a Metaphysical Club in Cambridge?" in *Studies in the Philosophy Charles Sanders Peirce: Second Series,* ed. Edward Moore and Richard Robin (Amherst: University of Massachusetts Press, 1964), 3–32, and Fisch's "Was There a Metaphysical Club in Cambridge? A Postscript," *Transactions of the Charles S. Peirce Society* 17, no. 2 (1981): 128–130. Joseph Brent's *Charles S. Peirce: A Life* (Bloomington: Indiana University Press, 1993) contains an account of controversies about the Metaphysical Club period.

14. Louis Menand, *The Metaphysical Club: A Story of Ideas in America* (New York: Farrar, Straus and Giroux, 2001), 225. Menand helpfully points to the influence of James Fitzjames Stephen's *A General View of Criminal Law in England.*

15. *Essential Peirce,* vol. 1, 29. Peirce later writes: "The mere putting of a proposition into the interrogative form does not stimulate the mind to any struggle after belief. There must be a real and living doubt, and without this all discussion is idle." *Essential Peirce,* vol. 1, 115. Dewey agrees that problems "grow out of an actual situation." "Problems that are self-set are mere excuses for seeming to do something intellectual" (LTI, LW 12:112).

16. In 1868, Peirce identified thought with abstract cognition (*Essential Peirce,* vol. 1, 39). In 1877, while preserving his semiotic view of mind, he identified thought more broadly with *inquiry,* motivated by "the irritation of doubt." *Essential Peirce,* vol. 1, 127, 114. On Karl-Otto Apel's view, this transition marked the birth of pragmatism. See Karl-Otto Apel's *Charles S. Peirce: From Pragmatism to Pragmaticism* (Amherst: University of Massachusetts Press, 1981), 129.

17. *Essential Peirce,* vol. 1, 114.

18. *Essential Peirce,* vol. 1, 15; 114, 128.

19. *Essential Peirce,* vol. 1, 129, 114, 115. Cf. EEL, MW 10:327.

20. *Essential Peirce,* vol. 1, 116, 122.

21. *Essential Peirce,* vol. 1, 118.

22. Immanuel Kant, "What Is Enlightenment?" in *Sources of Western Tradition*, 4th ed., ed. Marvin Perry, Joseph Peden, Theodore Von Laue (Boston: Houghton Mifflin, 1999), 54–55.

23. *Essential Peirce*, vol. 1, 119, 29, 48, 119.

24. *Essential Peirce*, vol. 1, 53. In Peirce's system, the cyclical belief-doubt-inquiry-belief continuum is revealed by categories of *firstness, secondness,* and *thirdness:* Doubt, as a capacity for refiguring beliefs through disruption, is understood through secondness. A habit is a stable pattern of matter or mind that enables organization to emerge, traits of thirdness. Because a belief settles, resolves, and interprets, it is categorized with habit. Belief is a mostly unconscious "habit of mind," not "a momentary mode of consciousness" (*Essential Peirce,* vol. 2, 337). But a belief also has a qualitative, affective character, a trait of firstness. Belief is succeeded without end by doubt, inquiry, and new belief. In his 1905 essays "What Is Pragmatism?" and "Issues of Pragmaticism," Peirce downplays the psychological fact that doubt is an "irritant," and he is almost single-mindedly concerned with the instrumental value of doubt for the laboratory-minded. The ideal scientific thinker (the critical common-sensist) "is not content to ask himself whether he does doubt, but he invents a plan for attaining to doubt, elaborates it in detail, and then puts it into practice." Moreover, the critical common-sensist is a *fallibilist* who acknowledges that "his indubitable beliefs may be proved false" (vol. 2, 353).

25. See James Campbell's summary of Dewey's scientific spirit in *Understanding John Dewey,* 99–110.

26. In contrast, Bain regarded the stream of thought as a discontinuous sequence of distinct ideas.

27. Charles M. Bakewell, review of *Pragmatism, Philosophical Review* 16 (1907): 625.

28. See "What Makes a Life Significant?" on "the element that gives to the wicked outer world all its moral style, expressiveness and picturesqueness,—the element of precipitousness, so to call it, of strength and strenuousness, intensity and danger." John J. McDermott, ed., *The Writings of William James* (Chicago: University of Chicago Press, 1977), 647–648. Cf. PM, 106; 100 and Dewey, AE, LW 10:65.

29. Charlotte Perkins Gilman, *Herland* (1915; New York: Dover, 1998), 84, 87.

30. Fisch accuses Dewey of "having forgotten his Bain" (100). Yet Dewey quotes from Bain's *The Emotions and the Will* at several points in *Ethics* (MW 5). Dewey's appropriation of this theme came primarily from James's *Principles of Psychology,* his hands-on experience at the Laboratory School in Chicago, and his interactions with Jane Addams at Hull House. Charlene Haddock Seigfried argues compellingly that the history of pragmatism owes as much to its grandmothers as to its grandfathers. See *Pragmatism and Feminism* (Chicago: University of Chicago Press, 1996). In her introduction to the reissued edition of Addams's *Democracy and Social Ethics* (Champaign: University of Illinois Press, 2002), ix–xxxviii, Seigfried persuasively suggests that Addams's concept of "perplexity" directly influenced Dewey.

31. See Thomas Alexander, *John Dewey's Theory of Art, Experience, and Nature,* 127.

32. On inquiry as art, see Jim Garrison, *Dewey and Eros: Wisdom and Desire in the Art of Thinking* (New York: Teachers College Press, 1997).

33. Hickman, "Nature as Culture: John Dewey's Pragmatic Naturalism," in *Environmental Pragmatism,* ed. Andrew Light and Eric Katz (London: Routledge, 1996), 50. Other relevant works by Hickman include *Philosophical Tools for Technological Culture: Putting Pragmatism to Work* (Bloomington: Indiana University Press, 2001), "Dewey's Theory of Inquiry," in *Reading Dewey: Interpretations for a Postmodern Generation,* ed. Larry Hickman (Bloomington: Indiana University Press, 1998), and his earlier defense of a pragmatic view of technology in *John Dewey's Pragmatic Technology* (Bloomington: Indiana University Press, 1990), 13ff. One of the best general elaborations of Dewey's pragmatism is Ralph Sleeper's *The Necessity of Pragmatism* (New Haven, Conn.: Yale University Press, 1986).

3. PRAGMATISM'S RECONSTRUCTION OF REASON

1. Charlene Seigfried, presentation at the Summer Institute in American Philosophy, Burlington, Vermont, July 1998. See Seigfried, *William James's Radical Reconstruction of Philosophy* (Albany: SUNY Press, 1990) for a discussion of James's hesitancy. Seigfried argues, for instance, that James thought he could give pure, unprejudiced, objective descriptions of the way phenomena present themselves to consciousness.

2. E. M. Adams, *The Metaphysics of Self and World* (Philadelphia: Temple University Press, 1991), 30.

3. Dewey had little patience with James's religious apologetics. See John B. Westbrook, *John Dewey and American Democracy* (Ithaca: Cornell University Press, 1991), 131-132, for a helpful contrast of James and Dewey. For insight into harmonies and tensions among James, Peirce, and Dewey with respect to the "will to believe" hypothesis, see William Gavin, *William James and the Reinstatement of the Vague* (Philadelphia: Temple University Press, 1992), chs. 5–6. Gavin argues that similarities between Peirce and James on the role of affective experience have been undervalued.

4. On controversies surrounding Dewey's theory of knowledge, see John Shook, *Dewey's Empirical Theory of Knowledge and Reality* (Nashville: Vanderbilt University Press, 2000); Gerard Deledalle, *John Dewey* (Paris: Presses Universitaires de France, 1995); Thomas Burke, *Dewey's New Logic: A Reply to Russell* (Chicago: University of Chicago Press, 1994); and Christopher Kulp, *The End of Epistemology: Dewey and His Current Allies on the Spectator Theory of Knowledge* (Westport, Conn.: Greenwood Press, 1992).

5. On the sculpting metaphor, see PM, 119; 112 and PP, I, 277; 288–89. Cf. PU, 9–10 and WB, 103. James uses numerous other metaphors to emphasize distinctive features of consciousness, a fact discussed by Seigfried in *William James's Radical Reconstruction of Philosophy,* 209–235.

6. Adams, *Metaphysics of Self and World,* 30.

7. For a contemporary misreading of James and Dewey along these lines, see Roderick Chisolm, *The Foundations of Knowing* (Minneapolis: University of Minnesota Press, 1982), 190.

8. D. M. Armstrong, *Belief, Truth and Knowledge,* (Cambridge, U.K.: Cambridge University Press, 1973).

9. Charles Taylor similarly observes: "We can draw a neat line between my *picture* of an object and that object, but not between my *dealing* with that object and that object." Charles Taylor, "Overcoming Epistemology," in *Philosophical Arguments* (Cambridge, Mass.: Harvard University Press, 1995), 12.

10. Edward Tivnan, *The Moral Imagination: Confronting the Ethical Issues of Our Day* (New York: Simon & Schuster, 1995), 237.

11. See Dewey's scathing "William James's Morals and Julien Benda's: It Is Not Pragmatism That Is Opportunist" (LW 15:19–26).

12. Eric Schlosser, *Fast Food Nation* (New York: Houghton Mifflin, 2001), 41.

13. This prejudice is helpfully addressed by Gregory Pappas in "The Latino Character of American Pragmatism," *Transactions of the Charles S. Peirce Society* 34, no. 1 (1998): 93–112.

14. Paul Carus, *Truth on Trial* (Chicago: Open Court, 1911), 7.

15. In Gerald E. Myers, *William James: His Life and Thought* (New Haven, Conn.: Yale University Press, 1986), 414. Horace M. Kallen, a former student of James's who helped to popularize his thought, writes in "Mussolini, William James, and the Rationalists": "The opportunity . . . came in the fall of 1926 when I had a chance to ask Mussolini directly what he had read of William James's. His only answer was a show of irritation; it was apparent that whatever Mussolini meant by 'pragmatism' was not based on anything he had gotten from James." Kallen continues: "I could not reconcile the great pragmatist's individualism,

pluralism, radical empiricism with fascist totalitarianism . . . and dogmatic rationalism. . . . I could not see how James's tolerance, his scrupulous concern that alternatives should have an equal freedom to make good their claims, could spawn the authoritarian intolerance, the coercion and destruction of alternatives integral to fascism." In Myers, *William James: His Life and Thought*, 414–415.

16. On James's threefold distinction, see, e.g., PM, 102; 96, 119; 111–112, and MT, 129.

17. E.g., PM, 101; 95 and PM, 119; 111. It is difficult to see how an "eternal" conceptual world could be consistent with James's contention that "relations of ideas" are not "without the human touch." James does not carry his thought to its logical fruition and finds himself involved in contradictions.

18. Hilary Putnam, *The Many Faces of Realism* (Chicago: Open Court, 1987), 16–21. Cf. Putnam's *Realism with a Human Face*, (Cambridge, Mass.: Harvard University Press, 1992).

19. On the "horizon," see Harvard edition PP, I, 246–247, 249–250, 270–271, 446–447, PP, II, 695; Dover edition PP, I, 255–256, 258–259, 281–282, 472–473, PP, II, 49. The notion of a "horizon" has been more fully articulated since James. Dewey elaborates it as a pervasive, "underlying qualitative character that constitutes a situation" (LW 5:248). It is the field of experience upon which all meaning is dependent. In his introduction to *Essays in Experimental Logic*, Dewey criticizes James's use of the "penumbra" and "fringe" metaphors because they suggest something peripheral to rather than suffusing experience. Hans-Georg Gadamer writes of his and Husserl's use of the term: "According to *Husserliana* VI, p. 267, the concepts of 'horizon' and of 'horizon consciousness' were in part suggested by William James' idea of 'fringes.'" *Truth and Method* (New York: Seabury Press, 1975), 521, 138n.

20. See E. Thompson, *Colour Vision: A Study in Cognitive Science and the Philosophy of Perception* (London: Routledge, 1995). Cf. Lakoff and Johnson, *Philosophy in the Flesh*, 23–26.

21. James's *The Meaning of Truth* is a sustained defense of pragmatic realism. He refutes "the slanderous charge [by Bertrand Russell] that we deny real existence. . . . [T]he existence of the object, whenever the idea asserts it 'truly,' is the only reason, in innumerable cases, why the idea does work successfully, if it work at all" (MT, 8).

22. James even speaks of schematic structures of imagination that emerge from our embodiment. For example: "In reasoning I find that I am apt to have a kind of vaguely localized diagram in my mind, with the various fractional objects of the thought disposed at particular points thereof; and the oscillations of my attention from one of them to another are most distinctly felt as alternations of direction in movements occurring inside the head" (PP, 287–288; I, 300–301). Cf. PP, 288; I, 301–302. His account is in some respects less developed than that of Merleau-Ponty, and cognitive science has far surpassed his once cutting-edge knowledge of neurophysiology. For a look at recent work in cognitive science on the embodied basis of cognition, see Varela, Thompson, and Rosch's *The Embodied Mind* (Cambridge, Mass.: MIT Press, 1991).

23. On Rosch's theory of basic-level categories, see George Lakoff, *Women, Fire and Dangerous Things* (Chicago: University of Chicago Press, 1987), 39–55.

24. According to Peirce, the greatest mistakes of metaphysics stem from failure to recognize this. We must not, says Peirce, look at the future "as something that will have been past." Peirce, "Letters to Lady Welby," in *Charles S. Peirce: Selected Writings*, ed. Philip Weiner (New York: Dover, 1958), 386. We must not, James echoes with a less scientific bent, "pretend that the eternal is unrolling, that the one previous . . . truth [is] simply fulgurating and not being made" (PM, 116; 110).

25. John McDermott's phrasing, unpublished presentation. See PP, 246; I, 255 and PP, 238; I, 245–246.

26. See "Does 'Consciousness' Exist?" and "La Notion de Conscience," in *Essays in Radical Empiricism*. In the second part of "La Notion de Conscience," James suggests that we try to understand consciousness not by presupposing the heterogeneity of the mental and physical, but by starting with *the stuff of experience* as such. If we take undifferentiated experience as our starting point we find that subject-object dualism is in fact a purely contextual phenomenon. The same root experience (which James calls a "pure experience") *becomes* either a mental or a physical phenomenon because of the practical context. Thus the notion of consciousness is functional, not ontological. Consciousness does not substantially "exist." On controversies surrounding the first appearance of James's theory of pure experience, see Eugene Taylor and Robert H. Wozniak, *Pure Experience: The Response to William James* (Bristol: Thoemmes Press, 1996).

27. See James's *Psychology: Briefer Course* (New York: Henry Holt, 1892), 164. For the most comprehensive treatment, see Gavin, *William James and the Reinstatement of the Vague*.

28. Eugene Fontinell, *Self, God, and Immortality: A Jamesian Investigation* (Philadelphia: Temple University Press, 1986), 64. In Gavin, *William James and the Reinstatement of the Vague*, 3.

29. Quine famously argues in *Word and Object* (Cambridge, Mass.: MIT Press, 1960) that formulations do not exhaust the existent. There is no one-to-one correspondence between language and fact. Our concern must be with the importance of a given statement within our larger web of beliefs. Contrary to "sense-data" theorists, one *can* go astray in simply describing the appearance of things, so such descriptions must be seen in the larger context of our belief systems. Because the denial of certain claims demands an overhaul of our belief system, we must discover in what ways a belief will either jostle or harmonize with this system.

30. Nietzsche, *On the Genealogy of Morals*, sec. 3, pp. 12, 119.

31. Antonio R. Damasio, *Descartes' Error: Emotion, Reason, and the Human Brain* (New York: Avon Books, 1994), and *The Feeling of What Happens: Body and Emotion in the Making of Consciousness* (Fort Worth: Harcourt Brace, 1999).

32. Martha C. Nussbaum, *Upheavals of Thought: The Intelligence of Emotions* (Cambridge, U.K.: Cambridge University Press, 2001).

33. This article, as printed in *The Will to Believe* (1897), is a composite of two articles. The original was printed in *Mind*, 1879, 4, 317–346. McDermott writes in the bibliography of *The Writings of William James*: "About one-fifth of this [original] essay was combined with [a second article from] 1888 . . . and reprinted in 1897." (819)

34. See Rorty's *Consequences of Pragmatism* (Minneapolis: University of Minnesota Press, 1982) and *Philosophy and the Mirror of Nature*.

35. For engaging criticisms of pseudoscientific claims, see Carl Sagan, *The Demon-Haunted World* (New York: Random House, 1995), and Michael Shermer, *Why People Believe Weird Things* (New York: W. H. Freeman, 1997).

36. Stephen Pepper, *World Hypotheses* (Berkeley: University of California Press, 1942), 239.

37. See MacIntyre, *After Virtue*, and Paul Ricoeur, *Time and Narrative*, trans. K. McLaughlin and D. Pellauer (Chicago: University of Chicago Press, 1984), especially vol. 1, ch. 3, "Time and Narrative: Threefold *Mimesis*." Also see Johnson's *Moral Imagination*, 150–184. Johnson writes: "Narrative in my sense is not merely linguistic and textual. Rather, I shall argue that *narrative characterizes the synthetic character of our very experience,* and it is prefigured in our daily activities and projects" (163).

38. For a scholarly critique of James's sexism and ethnic prejudices, see Seigfried, *Pragmatism and Feminism*.

39. In *A Treatise of Human Nature*, Hume concludes by a process of elimination that reason is "incapable of . . . disputing the preference with any passion or emotion." This conclusion is necessary because only a contrary impulse can "oppose or retard the impulse of

passion." Reason cannot provide this combative impulse because it has no "original influence" on the will. Reason would have to be able "to cause, as well as hinder any act of volition," and Hume assumes we know reason does not have this power. Therefore reason is the slave of the passions. Since we know as a matter of fact that morals do incite action, and it has been inferred that morals "cannot be deriv'd from reason," Hume deduces that moral actions are stimulated by passionate sentiment and not by reason. Reason is an "inactive" principle, and "an active principle can never be founded on an inactive." As a result, moral education must turn to the education of strong sentiments, especially the sentiment of sympathy, that incline us toward kindness. Hume, *A Treatise of Human Nature*, 415, 457.

40. Supplemental citations for *A Pluralistic Universe* are to the London: Longmans, Green, 1909 edition.

41. For a more thorough discussion of the aesthetic dimension of rationality, in its aspects of *unity or simplicity* (the drive behind theoretic attempts to construct logically coherent, free floating systems) and *clarity* (a drive for exactness and particularity), see Seigfried's *William James's Radical Reconstruction of Philosophy*, 30ff. In James, see especially the first (1879) version of "The Sentiment of Rationality," which makes distinctions concerning the aesthetic that are not found in James's revised essay. It is reprinted in the Harvard edition, *Essays in Philosophy*.

4. IMAGINATION IN PRAGMATIST ETHICS

1. This is R. M. Hare's claim for his Kantian utilitarian ethical theory. R. M. Hare, "Why I Am Only a Demi-Vegetarian," in *Singer and His Critics*, ed. Dale Jamieson (Oxford: Blackwell, 1999), 247–268.

2. See MacIntyre's restatement of his position, partly critical of his earlier *After Virtue*. Alasdair MacIntyre, *Dependent Rational Animals: Why Human Beings Need the Virtues* (Chicago: Open Court Books, 2000).

3. A noteworthy treatment of this is Gary Varner's "Can Animal Rights Activists Be Environmentalists?" in Gary E. Varner, *In Nature's Interests?* (Oxford: Oxford University Press, 1998), 111–120.

4. Alan Donagan, *The Theory of Morality* (Chicago: University of Chicago Press, 1977), 7.

5. For a survey of areas of ongoing empirical research relevant to developing psychologically realistic moral theories, see Mark Johnson, "Ethics," in *A Companion to Cognitive Science*, ed. William Bechtel and George Graham (Oxford: Blackwell, 1998), 691–701.

6. "Quick Study: Philosophy" (Boca Raton, Fla.: BarCharts, 1994).

7. T. O. Beidelman, *Moral Imagination in Kaguru Modes of Thought* (Bloomington: Indiana University Press, 1986), 4–5.

8. Gert, *Morality: Its Nature and Justification* (Oxford: Oxford University Press, 1998).

9. See Jürgen Habermas, *Moral Consciousness and Communicative Action* (Cambridge, Mass.: MIT Press, 1990).

10. Boisvert, *John Dewey: Rethinking Our Time* (Albany: SUNY Press, 1998), 34.

11. For a guide to European theories of imagination predating the current flurry of writing on the subject, see Mary Warnock, *Imagination* (Berkeley: University of California Press, 1976), 10. She identifies the "essence" of imagination as the creation of mental images. Cf. Warnock's *Imagination and Time* (Oxford: Blackwell, 1994), which contains her 1992 Gifford Lectures.

12. See Rudolf Makkreel, *Imagination and Interpretation in Kant* (Chicago: University of Chicago Press, 1990).

13. Kant, *Lectures on Ethics*, trans. Louis Infield (Indianapolis: Hackett, 1979), 140. On faculty psychology, see Lakoff and Johnson, *Philosophy in the Flesh*, 427. They analyze this picture as embodying the metaphor of a "Society of Mind."

14. Nussbaum, *Love's Knowledge,* 76.

15. According to Hume, through "a great effort of imagination" we enter deeply into the sentiments of others and, as a direct and natural response, we do not merely believe something about them, but feel their sentiments as our own concerns. See Hume's *Enquiries Concerning Human Understanding and Concerning the Principles of Morals,* 3rd ed. (Oxford: Clarendon Press, 1975), 184, 227, 229n, 272, and *Treatise of Human Nature,* 381–386. Cf. Annette C. Baier, *A Progress of Sentiments: Reflections on Hume's Treatise* (Cambridge, Mass.: Harvard University Press, 1991). See also Adam Smith's 1759 *The Theory of Moral Sentiments.*

16. Jonathan Levin, *The Poetics of Transition: Emerson, Pragmatism, and American Literary Modernism* (Durham, N.C.: Duke University Press, 1999), 87.

17. John Searle, *Intentionality* (Cambridge, U.K.: Cambridge University Press, 1983). See ch. 5, "The Background." For a critique of Searle's account of imagination, see Mark Johnson, *The Body in the Mind* (Chicago: University of Chicago Press, 1987), 178–191.

18. Warnock, *Imagination,* 9.

19. Yi-Fu Tuan, *Morality and Imagination: Paradoxes of Progress* (Madison: University of Wisconsin Press, 1989), 4.

20. Charles Larmore, "Moral Judgment," *Review of Metaphysics* 35 (1981): 275–296. Quoted in Patricia Werhane, *Moral Imagination and Management Decision-Making* (Oxford: Oxford University Press, 1999), 92. Cf. Larmore's *The Morals of Modernity* (Cambridge, U.K.: Cambridge University Press, 1996).

21. On Hare, see Thomas Alexander, "John Dewey and the Moral Imagination," 375–376.

22. Oliver Williams, S.J., ed., *The Moral Imagination: How Literature and Films Can Stimulate Ethical Reflection in the Business World* (Notre Dame: University of Notre Dame Press, 1997), 6.

23. Werhane, *Moral Imagination and Management Decision-Making,* 93, 90, 111.

24. Tivnan, *Moral Imagination,* 250–51. Tivnan offers a nice example of empathy:

Following a tour of burned-out neighborhoods in South Central Los Angeles after the riots in the spring of 1992, President George Bush admitted, "I can hardly imagine—I try, but I can hardly imagine the fear and the anger that people must feel to terrorize one another and burn each others' property." It is not surprising that a sixty-eight-year-old Connecticut-born son of a U.S. Senator and an alumnus of Andover, Yale, the U.S. Congress, and the Central Intelligence Agency cannot put himself into the sneakers of a looter in South Central L.A. (248)

Tivnan rightly implies that he had better try. Cf. J. E. Tiles, *Dewey* (London: Routledge, 1988), 175, and HNC, MW 14:140ff.

25. Thomas McCollough, *The Moral Imagination and Public Life: Raising the Ethical Question* (Chatham, N.J.: Chatham House Publishers, 1991), 16–17.

26. John Kekes, *The Morality of Pluralism* (Princeton, N.J.: Princeton University Press, 1993, 99–117.

27. Lionel Trilling, *The Liberal Imagination* (New York: Charles Scribner's, 1950), vii–viii. Quoted in John Kekes, *The Morality of Pluralism* (Princeton, N.J.: Princeton University Press, 1993), 100.

28. Kekes, *Morality of Pluralism,* 99–117.

29. CP 6.286. Quoted in Vincent Colapietro, *Peirce's Approach to the Self* (Albany: SUNY Press, 1989), 114.

30. Stuart Hampshire, *Innocence and Experience* (Cambridge, Mass.: Harvard University Press, 1989), 126.

31. Dewey also frequently speaks of "imagination" simply to *locate* activity as going forth in inner vision—"in imagination"—versus activity proceeding overtly and irretrievably.

32. On this creative function of imagination, see Boisvert, *John Dewey: Rethinking Our Time*, 127–129, 139. On art and imagination, Dewey writes: "Possibilities are embodied in works of art that are not elsewhere actualized; this *embodiment* is the best evidence that can be found of the true nature of imagination" (AE, LW 10:272).

33. I am grateful to Ray Boisvert for this observation. See HWT, LW 8:208–209, on the past and future in imaginative "suggestions." Cf. J. J. Chambliss, "John Dewey's Idea of Imagination in Philosophy and Education," *Journal of Aesthetic Education* 25, no. 4 (1991): 43–49.

34. Thomas Alexander, "John Dewey and the Moral Imagination," 387.

35. Dewey writes: "It is sympathy which saves consideration of consequences from degenerating into mere calculation, by rendering vivid the interests of others and urging us to give them the same weight as those which touch our own honor, purse, and power" (1932 E, LW 7:270–271). In *Dewey*, J. E. Tiles discusses difficulties of taking up the viewpoint of others so long as we conceive the mind "as independent of and logically antecedent to the body" (75–76). Tiles implies in his analysis that empathy can be construed as a sort of rehearsal, whereby we approximate in our "dispositions and attitudes the unity of organic action to be found" in another person.

36. Immanuel Kant, *Grounding for the Metaphysics of Morals*, trans. James W. Ellington, 3rd ed. (Indianapolis: Hackett, 1993), 11–12. Cf. Keith, "Feminism and Pragmatism."

37. Thomas Alexander, "John Dewey and the Moral Imagination," 384–386.

38. Peter Singer, *Ethics into Action* (Lanham, Md.: Rowman & Littlefield, 1998), 184.

5. DRAMATIC REHEARSAL

1. To reconstruct Dewey's theory of deliberation one must look beyond his few uses of the term "dramatic rehearsal." Still, such passages in Dewey are fertile: 1908 *Ethics*, MW 5:293; *Human Nature and Conduct*, MW 14:132–133; 1932 *Ethics*, LW 7:275; *How We Think*, LW 8:200. Also see his correspondence, letter 03525; 1915/5/7,8,9; to Scudder Klyce. For earlier discussions of "imaginative rehearsal," see *The Study of Ethics: A Syllabus* (EW 4:251–252), and Donald F. Koch, ed., *John Dewey's Lectures on Ethics: 1900–1901* (Carbondale: Southern Illinois University Press, 1991), 141–143, 226–229. The main discussions of dramatic rehearsal in the literature on Dewey are James Gouinlock, *John Dewey's Philosophy of Value* (Atlantic Highlands, N.J.: Humanities Press, 1972), 302–304; Gouinlock, "Dewey's Theory of Moral Deliberation," *Ethics* 88, no. 3 (1978): 218–228; Joseph Kupfer, *Experience as Art* (Albany: SUNY Press, 1983), 141–170; Victor Kestenbaum's Preface to *Theory of the Moral Life* (New York: Irvington Publishers, 1980), xvii–xviii; Thomas Alexander, *John Dewey's Theory of Art, Experience, and Nature*, 148–150, 260–262; Tiles, *Dewey*, 185–187; William R. Caspary, "Ethical Deliberation as Dramatic Rehearsal: John Dewey's Theory," *Educational Theory* 41, no. 2 (1991): 175–188; Thomas Alexander, "John Dewey and the Moral Imagination"; Jennifer Welchman, *Dewey's Ethical Thought* (Ithaca, N.Y.: Cornell University Press, 1995), 168–177; Steven Fesmire, "Dramatic Rehearsal and the Moral Artist: a Deweyan Theory of Moral Understanding," *Transactions of the Charles S. Peirce Society* 31, no. 3 (1995): 568–597.

2. Welchman, *Dewey's Ethical Thought*, 168–177.

3. This issue is taken up in Chapter 6.

4. Dewey's contribution to the 1932 *Ethics*, co-authored with Tufts, was reissued as *Theory of the Moral Life*.

5. On high-functioning autism, see Oliver Sacks's engaging discussion of livestock specialist Temple Grandin in *An Anthropologist on Mars* (New York: Alfred A. Knopf, 1995), 244–296. On mental retardation and deliberation, I have been aided by Heather Keith and Kenneth Keith, *Consequences of Reason: Philosophical Roots of Dehumanization* (manuscript in process).

6. Clyde Edgerton, *Walking Across Egypt* (New York: Ballantine Books, 1987), 217–218.

7. Dewey's writings from 1882 through 1893, though relevant to the development of his theory of deliberation, are beyond this chapter's scope. James's *Principles* marked a transition in Dewey's thought from idealism toward pragmatism in the 1890s. For a discussion of Dewey's early work in ethics, see Welchman, *Dewey's Ethical Thought.*

8. Cf. James, PP, II, 562–565 on being in "some fiery passion's grasp." This is quoted by Dewey in 1908 E, MW 5:188 and HNC, MW 14:136. Likewise, James asserts: "Now into every one's deliberations the representation of one alternative will often enter with such sudden force as to carry the imagination with itself exclusively, and to produce an apparently settled decision in its own favor. These premature and spurious decisions are of course known to everyone" (PP, II, 530).

9. Kekes, *Morality of Pluralism,* 109.

10. In Koch, ed., *John Dewey's Lectures On Ethics: 1900–1901,* 245. Cf. Donald F. Koch, ed., *John Dewey's Lectures on Psychological and Political Ethics: 1898* (New York: Hafner Press, 1976). Some other important early sources are *The Study of Ethics: A Syllabus* (in EW 2) and *Outlines of a Critical Theory of Ethics* (in EW 3).

11. In Koch, *John Dewey's Lectures on Ethics: 1900–1901,* 226, 141.

12. In Koch, *John Dewey's Lectures on Ethics: 1900–1901,* 229, 142. Compare to Bain, *Emotions and the Will:* "In anticipating a want, we forecast at the same time the natural sequence that is to be the medium of supplying it, and, in that predicament wherein we are said to have confidence or trust in such a medium, we enjoy a positive satisfaction in the total absence of painful forebodings" (508).

13. Charles L. Stevenson, *Ethics and Language* (New Haven, Conn.: Yale University Press, 1944), 259. Dewey responded to Stevenson's *Ethics and Language* in a 1945 article, "Ethical Subject-Matter and Language" (LW 15:127–140).

14. Having accepted Stevenson's account of dramatic rehearsal, Welchman tries to save Dewey from Hobbesian implications by arguing that, for Dewey, "[d]ramatic rehearsal is *not* the only method of reasoning that has a place in ethics" (173).

15. Kestenbaum, "Preface," in *Theory of the Moral Life.*

16. In *Charles Sanders Peirce: A Life,* Brent discusses Peirce's view of habits and thought experiments. He maintains: "Beginning with a suggestion from Berkeley's work on vision, Peirce conceived the possibility of forming habits from imaginary practice. . . . He claimed that by exercising the imagination, we can visualize the occurrence of a stimulus and mentally rehearse the results of different responses. That which appears most satisfactory will influence actual behavior as effectively as a habit produced by reiteration in the outside world" (45).

17. Throughout his corpus Dewey echoes the prejudice of his contemporaries that all nonhuman animals act out of blind habit. See MW 14:146, LW 1:215, LW 1:276–278, LW 1:146, LW 10:83, LW 10:276, LW 13:250, LW 17:257–258. For one engrossing look at the cognitive abilities of chimpanzees, including language, tool use, and social intelligence, see Roger Fouts and Stephen Tukel Mills, *Next of Kin: My Conversations with Chimpanzees* (New York: Avon Books, 1997). Cf. Paola Cavalieri and Peter Singer, *The Great Ape Project* (New York: St. Martin's Press, 1993). Dewey's view that "scientific men are under definite obligation to experiment upon animals" was typical for the 1920s. See "The Ethics of Animal Experimentation" (LW 2:98–103; cf. LW 13:333). See my "Pragmatism and Animal Ethics," in Erin McKenna and Andrew Light, eds., *Animal Pragmatism* (Bloomington: Indiana University Press, forthcoming).

18. This is discussed under the heading "Deliberation as Dramatic Rehearsal" in the 1908 *Ethics* (MW 5:292).

19. G. E. Moore, *Principia Ethica* (1903; Cambridge, U.K.: Cambridge University Press, 1929), 40, 6.

20. In 1932 E, LW 7:273, Dewey contrasts "intuition" (which rests on attained habits) and "conscientiousness" (which is on a quest for something better than habits already attained).

21. Thomas Alexander, "John Dewey and the Moral Imagination," 371.

22. Micah Hester, unpublished manuscript. See Micah Hester, *Community as Healing: Pragmatist Ethics in Medical Encounters* (Lanham, Md.: Rowman & Littlefield, 2001). Cf. Mark Kuczewski, "Bioethics' Consensus on Method: Who Could Ask for Anything More?" in *Stories and Their Limits*, ed. H. L. Nelson (New York: Routledge, 1997), 134–149.

23. MacIntyre, *After Virtue*, 216.

24. Immanuel Kant, *Lectures on Ethics* (New York: Harper & Row, 1963), 66. Quoted in Gouinlock, *Rediscovering the Moral Life*, 244.

25. Ricoeur, *Time and Narrative*, vol. 1, 66. Quoted in Johnson, *Moral Imagination*, 166 (Johnson's emphases).

26. Thomas Alexander, *John Dewey's Theory of Art, Experience, and Nature*, 128.

27. This was brought to my attention by the late Lyle Eddy, Emeritus Professor of Education at the University of Nebraska and a former student of Dewey's. Letters in the files at the Center for Dewey Studies at Southern Illinois University at Carbondale (such as those between Dewey and Eddy) support that this was a prevailing view during the 1940s. Dewey corroborated that his language had tended toward mentalism and that Bentley and others had recognized and corrected this tendency.

28. Stevenson, *Ethics and Language*, 264.

29. Mead, "The Social Self," in *Selected Writings*, 146.

30. Thomas Alexander, *John Dewey's Theory of Art, Experience, and Nature*, 149.

31. Gouinlock, *Rediscovering the Moral Life*, 130.

32. Kant, *Grounding for the Metaphysics of Morals*, 15, Ak. 403. Emphasis is Gouinlock's, *Rediscovering the Moral Life*, 134.

33. Cognitive semantics is founded on the methodological assumption that any theory of meaning, concepts, reasoning, or language must be congruous with our most reliable empirical inquiries into the nature of human cognition. This coincides with a "generalization" commitment whereby any satisfactory theory of these aspects of cognition must offer empirically criticizable generalizations about human conceptualization, inference, and language. George Lakoff, "The Invariance Hypothesis," *Cognitive Linguistics* 1, no. 1 (1990): 40. See the first issue of the *Cognitive Linguistics* journal (1, no. 1 [1990]).

34. For example, see George Lakoff and Mark Johnson's *Metaphors We Live By* (Chicago: University of Chicago Press, 1980), Lakoff's *Women, Fire and Dangerous Things*, Johnson's *Body in the Mind*, and Lakoff and Johnson's comprehensive *Philosophy in the Flesh*.

35. Lakoff and Johnson, *Philosophy in the Flesh*, 515, 12, 414.

36. Lakoff and Johnson, *Philosophy in the Flesh*, 538, 136.

37. Lakoff and Johnson, *Philosophy in the Flesh*, 20, 77, 81–86, 43–44.

38. Lakoff and Johnson, *Philosophy in the Flesh*, 59. On metaphors as "ferrying" meaning, see William Eddy, *The Other Side of the World: Essays and Stories on Mind and Nature* (Lynchburg, Vt.: Stinehour Press, 2001).

39. Lakoff and Johnson, *Metaphors We Live By*, 48.

40. In Corliss Lamont, ed., *Dialogue on John Dewey* (New York: Horizon Press, 1959), 95.

41. Lakoff and Johnson, *Metaphors We Live By*, 8.

42. George Lakoff's *Women, Fire, and Dangerous Things* contains crosscultural studies of metaphors and categorization principles.

43. Lakoff and Johnson, *Philosophy in the Flesh*, 141.

44. Lakoff and Johnson, *Philosophy in the Flesh*, 141, 49–57.

45. Lakoff and Johnson, *Philosophy in the Flesh*, 71–72.

46. Critical reviews of *Philosophy in the Flesh,* as in the *New York Times Book Review* (Feb. 21, 1999) and *Civilization* (Feb./March 1999), harken back to perpetually reinvented, sophistical misunderstandings of classical American pragmatism. Lakoff and Johnson dismiss external reality, truth, morality, and philosophy, clamor objectivists. They throw our compass overboard by "echoing the multicultural clamor of contemporary America" in their rejection of absolute objectivity. Or conversely, they remain squarely within the totalizing confines of scientism, say some postmodernists. Such dismissive criticisms stall inquiry. But there are numerous problems meriting further investigation, including the distracting tendency of Lakoff and Johnson to lapse into a non-pluralistic voice, their odd implication that philosophy prior to cognitive science was only 5 percent relevant to understanding who we are (*Philosophy in the Flesh,* 12–13ff.), the fact that their enthusiasm for analyzable conceptual structure at times outstrips their evidence, their Kantian language and the neo-Kantian tone of their theory of primary metaphor (they at times seem to be identifying a universal core of human categories transcending cultures), their relegation of Dewey as merely good "for his time" (xi), and their unexamined tension between coherentist and pragmatic views of truth.

47. Lakoff and Johnson, *Philosophy in the Flesh,* 95, 93.

48. Phrase paraphrased from Johnson, *Body in the Mind,* 136.

49. George Eliot, *Middlemarch* (Boston: Houghton Mifflin, 1956), 63.

50. Johnson, *Moral Imagination,* 35. On the relation of cognitive semantics to Dewey, see Johnson's "Knowing Through the Body," *Philosophical Psychology* 4, no. 1 (1991).

51. Susan Sontag, *Illness as Metaphor* and *AIDS and Its Metaphors* (New York: Doubleday, 1990), 93.

52. Johnson, *Body in the Mind,* 132–136. This is drawn from Johnson's analysis of the work of Hans Selye on stress reactions in the context of Walter B. Cannon's homeopathic theory.

53. Johnson analyzes Love as a Market Transaction versus Love as an Organic Unity in *Moral Imagination,* 53–61.

54. Naomi Quinn, "Convergent Evidence for a Cultural Model of American Marriage," in Dorothy Holland and Naomi Quinn, eds., *Cultural Models In Language and Thought* (Cambridge, U.K.: Cambridge University Press, 1987), 173–192.

55. Charles Darwin, *The Origin of Species,* vol. 11, Harvard Classics (New York: P. F. Collier & Son, 1909), 87–88. Originally published in 1859.

56. Michael J. Vanni, Chris Luecke, James F. Kitchell, Yvonne Allen, Jo Temte, and John J. Magnuson, "Effects on Lower Trophic Levels of Massive Fish Mortality," *Nature* 344, no. 22 (1990).

57. Shannon Sullivan, *Living Across and Through Skins: Transactional Bodies, Pragmatism, and Feminism* (Bloomington: Indiana University Press, 2001). Cf. Johnson, "Ethics," 698.

58. For a comprehensive look at conservative vs. liberal metaphors in American politics, see George Lakoff's *Moral Politics* (Chicago: University of Chicago Press, 1996).

59. See Lakoff's illuminating analyses of these metaphors in *Moral Politics,* 212–221.

60. Mary Warnock, *An Intelligent Person's Guide to Ethics* (London: Gerald Duckworth, 1998), 15.

61. Lakoff and Johnson's *Philosophy in the Flesh* contains the most comprehensive account of work in this area.

6. THE DEWEYAN IDEAL

1. For a helpful overview of Dewey's ethics that takes stock of recent scholarship, see Gregory F. Pappas, "Dewey's Ethics: Morality as Experience," in *Reading Dewey: Interpreta-*

tions for a Postmodern Generation, ed. Larry Hickman (Bloomington: Indiana University Press, 1998), 100–123. See also Pappas's article on the ethical upshot of Dewey's method of naturalistic empiricism, "Dewey's Moral Theory: Experience as Method," *Transactions of the Charles S. Peirce Society* 33, no. 3 (1997): 520–556.

2. Kant, *Grounding for the Metaphysics of Morals,* 21.

3. Bernard Gert's work is a Kant-steeped attempt to render our moral inheritance rationally defensible. His goal is not to provide definite answers to dilemmas, for which he criticizes Alan Donagan, but to define the limits our inherited moral system places on conduct. Gert's conceptual analyses are often compelling, but my thesis is that this does not necessarily help us to act more intelligently, responsibly, and sensitively in everyday moral situations. See Gert, *Morality: Its Nature and Justification.*

4. Following are some examples of pragmatist ethicists tackling issues in practical ethics: Eugenie Gatens-Robinson, "The Private and Its Problem: A Pragmatic View of Reproductive Choice," in *Dewey Reconfigured,* 169–192; Light and Katz, eds., *Environmental Pragmatism;* Glenn McGee, ed., *Pragmatist Bioethics* (Nashville: Vanderbilt University Press, 1999); Rogene A. Buchholz and Sandra B. Rosenthal, *Business Ethics: The Pragmatic Path beyond Principles to Process* (Upper Saddle River, N.J.: Prentice Hall, 1997); Larry Hickman, "Making the Family 'Functional': The Case for Legalized Same-Sex Domestic Partnerships," *Philosophy of the Social Sciences,* 29, no. 2 (1999): 231–247.

5. Nussbaum, *Love's Knowledge,* 152. Cf. Johnson, *Moral Imagination,* 210–211.

6. Nussbaum, *Love's Knowledge,* 154. Nussbaum explores Henry James's *The Golden Bowl* to show "the relationships between the fine-tuned perception of particulars and a rule-governed concern for general obligations: how each, taken by itself, is insufficient for moral accuracy; how (and why) the particular, if insufficient, is nonetheless prior; and how a dialogue between the two, prepared by love, can find a common 'basis' for moral judgment" (157).

7. Nussbaum, *Love's Knowledge,* 154.

8. For Dewey's critique of "drift and casual improvisation" in progressive education, see LW 5:323, LW 11:37, LW 11:173–179, LW 11:196, LW 13:13, LW 13:52.

9. Cf. LW 13:367. James Tufts, who authored most of the first and third parts of Dewey and Tufts's *Ethics,* goes beyond innuendo: "The moving pictures, the jazz music, the comic strips, and various other forms of popular entertainment, are not an object of pride to those who have learned to know good art, good music, and good literature. A civilization, in which the average man spends his day in a factory and his evening at a movie, has still a long way to go" (1932 E, LW 7:434).

10. Bill Evans, liner notes from original 1959 release of Miles Davis's *Kind of Blue* (Columbia Records). Evans compares jazz improvisation to the Japanese art of calligraphy and implies that it is a form of communication in which deliberation can "interfere." The gist of this point is compatible with Dewey's broad conception of deliberation and habit.

11. George Herbert Mead's theory of the self provides a useful framework for these insights. See Mead, *Mind, Self, and Society,* ed. Charles Morris (Chicago: University of Chicago Press, 1934), chs. 18–20. Cf. ch. 5 of Dewey's *Experience and Nature* (EN, LW 1:132–161).

12. In Bill Moyers, *The Language of Life* (New York: Doubleday, 1995), 173.

13. See Thomas Kochman, *Black and White Styles in Conflict* (Chicago: University of Chicago Press, 1981), 25–29.

14. The Christian concept of *agape* is more compellingly stated by R. M. Hare: "What it requires is that we should treat the ends of others as of equal weight with our own ends." In Hare, "Why I Am Only a Demi-Vegetarian," 235.

15. Pointed out by Heather Keith, in a commentary on my paper at a meeting of the American Philosophical Association.

16. Nussbaum, *Love's Knowledge,* 155.

17. On imagination and compositional music, see Reichling's critical reading of Dewey's aesthetic theory through the metaphor of three counterpoints of a fugue: composer, performer, and listener. Mary Reichling, "Dewey, Imagination, and Music: A Fugue on Three Subjects," *Journal of Aesthetic Education* 25, no. 3 (1991): 61–78. The classic work in this area is Aaron Copland, *Music and Imagination* (Cambridge, Mass.: Harvard University Press, 1952).

18. In Moyers, *The Language of Life*, 175.

19. Barry Kernfeld, *What to Listen for in Jazz* (New Haven, Conn.: Yale University Press, 1995), 119.

20. See LW 4:207–208; LW 7:264, 181–182, 192; LW 12:174–175; LW 13:195. For a helpful analysis of this distinction, see Campbell, *Understanding John Dewey*, 128ff.

21. Kekes, *Morality of Pluralism*, 120.

22. In *Experience and Education,* Dewey elaborates (though not entirely satisfactorily) on growth as a criterion for discrimination among experiences: "The objection made is that growth might take many different directions: a man, for example, who starts out on a career of burglary may grow in that direction, and by practice may grow into a highly expert burglar. Hence it is argued that 'growth' is not enough; we must also specify the direction in which growth takes place, the end towards which it tends. . . . That a man may grow in efficiency as a burglar, as a gangster, or as a corrupt politician, cannot be doubted. But . . . the question is whether growth in this direction promotes or retards growth in general. Does this form of growth create conditions for further growth, or does it set up conditions that shut off the person who has grown in this particular direction from the occasions, stimuli, and opportunities for continuing growth in new directions? What is the effect of growth in a special direction upon the attitudes and habits which alone open up avenues for development along other lines?" (EE, LW 13:19–20).

23. For a refreshing discussion of imaginative transitions in American philosophy and poetry, see Levin, *Poetics of Transition*.

24. Thomas Alexander, *John Dewey's Theory of Art, Experience, and Nature,* 127.

25. Machiavelli, from *Discourse upon the First Decade of Livy,* in *Social and Political Philosophy,* ed. John Somerville and Ronald Santoni (Garden City, N.Y.: Anchor Books, 1963), 137.

26. Hume, *Treatise of Human Nature,* 619.

27. Jane Addams, *Democracy and Social Ethics* (Champaign: University of Illinois Press, 2002), 6. Cf. 1932 E, LW 7:315. On Addams giving a "sharper and a deeper meaning" to Dewey's democratic faith, see Jane M. Dewey, "Biography of John Dewey," in *The Philosophy of John Dewey,* ed. Paul Arthur Schilpp and Lewis Edwin Hahn (Chicago: Open Court, 1989; 1939), 29–30. Cited in Seigfried, "Introduction," *Democracy and Social Ethics*.

28. Adapted in part from Thomas Alexander, private correspondence.

29. For an inspired muckraking of America's contemporary failures to live up to a democratic ideal, see Schlosser, *Fast Food Nation*.

30. In McDermott, ed., *Writings of William James*, 630, 645.

31. Ralph Barton Perry, *General Theory of Value* (New York: Longman's, Green, 1926).

32. Berlin, *Crooked Timber of Humanity*, 47. Quoted in Tivnan, *Moral Imagination*, 236.

33. See Beidelman, *Moral Imagination in Kaguru Modes of Thought*, 7ff.

34. In Bill Moyers, *A World of Ideas* (New York: Doubleday, 1989), 279.

35. Robert N. Bellah et al., *Habits of the Heart: Individualism and Commitment in American Life*, 2nd ed. (Berkeley: University of California Press, 1996).

36. Quoted in Barbara Kingsolver, *High Tide in Tucson* (New York: Harper-Collins, 1995), 105.

37. The Bellamy reference is to *Looking Backward* (New York: Signet Classics, 1960), 166. For Dewey's critique of economic individualism, see also *The Public and Its Problems*

(LW 2) and *Liberalism and Social Action* (LW 11). The communist Bellamy exerted a significant, though little explored, influence on Dewey, who wrote of Bellamy's *Looking Backward* (1888) and *Equality* (1897): "What *Uncle Tom's Cabin* was to the anti-slavery movement Bellamy's book [*Equality*] may well be to the shaping of popular opinion for a new social order" (LW 9:106). Dewey wrote that Bellamy "was imbued with a religious faith in the democratic ideal" (LW 9:103).

38. Seigfried, *Pragmatism and Feminism*, 32. Quoted in Heather Keith, "Feminism and Pragmatism: George Herbert Mead's Ethics of Care," 328.

39. Vincent Colapietro elaborates that democracy is "the form in which the nature, assumptions and implications of community are most fully realized and thus most easily discernible." Colapietro, "Art and Philosophy: A Fateful Entanglement," *Reason, Subjectivity, and Agency: Postmodern Themes and Pragmatic Challenges* (Albany: SUNY Press, forthcoming), ch. 3. Quoted from working draft.

40. Reinhold Niebuhr, *The Children of Light and the Children of Darkness* (New York: Charles Scribner's Sons, 1944), 118. Cf. Cornel West, *Race Matters* (New York: Vintage Books, 1994), 158. Dewey's realistic hope for human community is captured in Erin McKenna's *The Task of Utopia: A Pragmatist and Feminist Perspective* (Lanham, Md.: Rowman & Litttlefield, 2001).

41. The most comprehensive study of Dewey's democratic credo is Robert B. Westbrook's acclaimed biography, *John Dewey and American Democracy*. Also see Michael Eldridge, "Dewey's Faith in Democracy as Shared Experience," *Transactions of the Charles S. Peirce Society* 32, no. 1 (1996): 11–30, with a response by Westbrook, "Democratic Faith: A Response to Michael Eldridge." For an upbeat study of the potential for Deweyan democracy in a multicultural setting, see Judith M. Green, *Deep Democracy: Community, Diversity, and Transformation* (Lanham, Md.: Rowman & Littlefield, 1999).

7. THE MORAL ARTIST

1. Trilling, *Liberal Imagination*, 222. Quoted in Tivnan, *Moral Imagination*, 9.

2. Putnam, *Many Faces of Realism*, 51.

3. Wallace Stevens, *Collected Poetry and Prose*, ed. Frank Kermode and Joan Richardson (New York: Library of America, 1997), 736. Quoted in Levin, *Poetics of Transition*, 88.

4. As used here, the art metaphor complements, not supersedes, other metaphors explored in Dewey scholarship, such as Hickman's emphasis on technology metaphors in *John Dewey's Pragmatic Technology* and Boisvert's preference for organic metaphors of "life, living systems, cells, adaptation" (161) in *John Dewey: Rethinking Our Time*. The most comprehensive interpretation of Dewey's corpus from the standpoint of his theory of art is Thomas Alexander's *John Dewey's Theory of Art, Experience, and Nature*.

5. Boisvert, *John Dewey: Rethinking Our Time*, 131.

6. Johnson, *Moral Imagination*, 45–46.

7. Lakoff and Johnson, *Metaphors We Live By*, 141.

8. In Kingsolver, *High Tide in Tucson*, 32.

9. Bill Watterson, *The Calvin and Hobbes Tenth Anniversary Book* (Kansas City, Mo.: Andrews & McMeel, 1995), 20.

10. On the creative imagination of the fiction writer, see John Gardner, "Moral Fiction," in John Garnder, *On Moral Fiction* (New York: Basic Books, 1978), 105–126.

11. Shakespeare, *As You Like It* 2.7.141–144.

12. MacIntyre, *After Virtue*, 213.

13. MacIntyre, *After Virtue*, 218, 216. On story telling and imagination, see Coles, *Call of Stories*. Coles quotes a mentor from the beginning of his psychiatric career: "The people who come to see us bring us their stories. They hope they tell them well enough so that we

understand the truth of their lives. They hope we know how to interpret their stories correctly. We have to remember that what we hear is *their story*" (7).

14. Nussbaum, *Love's Knowledge,* 157, 155, 157.

15. On the history of theories of metaphor, see the introduction to *Philosophical Perspectives on Metaphor,* Mark Johnson, ed. (Minneapolis: University of Minnesota Press, 1981). Also see George Lakoff, "The Contemporary Theory of Metaphor," in *Metaphor and Thought,* 2nd ed., ed. Andrew Ortony (Cambridge, U.K.: Cambridge University Press, 1994).

16. John Searle, *Expression and Meaning* (Cambridge, U.K.: Cambridge University Press, 1979), 76–116. A defense of the comparison theory in opposition to Searle and to Lakoff and Johnson can be found in Robert J. Fogelin, *Figuratively Speaking* (New Haven, Conn.: Yale University Press, 1988).

17. See HNC, MW 14:194, and 1932 *Ethics,* LW 7:169.

18. These categories are similar to those in Johnson's discussion of the morality-as-art metaphor in *Moral Imagination,* 210–215.

19. Johnson, *Moral Imagination,* 210.

20. Alexander, "John Dewey and the Moral Imagination," 395.

21. Nussbaum, *Fragility of Goodness,* 305.

22. Nussbaum, *Love's Knowledge,* 99.

23. Nussbaum, *Love's Knowledge,* 103. Cf. Nussbaum, *Upheavals of Thought.*

24. Nussbaum, *Fragility of Goodness,* 309.

25. John Stuart Mill, *Utilitarianism* (Indianapolis: Hackett, 1979; 1861), 2.

26. Nussbaum, *Love's Knowledge,* 98–99.

27. See, e.g., "Nature," 193, 204, in *Selected Writings of Ralph Waldo Emerson* (New York: Signet Classic, 1965). A dilated mind's eye has an enlarged receptivity to ideas and sentiments latent in a situation just as a dilated pupil has an enlarged receptivity to light.

28. Søren Kierkegaard, *Either/Or,* ed. and trans. Howard Hong and Edna Hong (Princeton, N.J.: Princeton University Press, 1988).

29. Moore, *Principia Ethica,* 106.

30. This is implicitly a critique of calculation theories of deliberation, but it is also a damning cultural critique. Workers, blue or white collar, are divorced from a direct interest in the ends of production, so daily activities are anesthetic. Dewey insists on conditions in which acts of production are aesthetically enhanced for all individuals so that the "realization of their capacities may be the law of their life" (LSA, LW 11:41). A stirring passage from *Experience and Nature* clarifies this: "The existence of activities that have no immediate enjoyed intrinsic meaning is undeniable. They include much of our labors in home, factory, laboratory, and study. By no stretch of language can they be termed either artistic or esthetic. . . . So we optimistically call them 'useful' and let it go at that. . . . If we were to ask useful for what? we should be obliged to examine their actual consequences, and when we once honestly and fully faced these consequences we should probably find ground for calling such activities detrimental rather than useful" (EN, LW 1:271–272). The tragic flaw of much current educational practice is that it systematically inculcates this habit of sacrificing the aesthetic. "As traditionally conducted, [education] strikingly exhibits a subordination of the living present to a remote and precarious future. To prepare, to get ready, is its keynote. The actual outcome is lack of adequate preparation, of intelligent adaptation" (HNC, MW 14:185).

31. See Philip W. Jackson's discussion of perception in *John Dewey and the Lessons of Art* (New Haven, Conn.: Yale University Press, 1998), 57–67.

32. Nussbaum, *Love's Knowledge,* 154.

33. See Johnson, *Moral Imagination,* 212.

34. Boisvert, *John Dewey,* 129.

35. Johnson, *Moral Imagination,* 213.

36. McCollough, *Moral Imagination and Public Life*, 16.

37. Johnson, *Moral Imagination*, 211.

38. Because of our cultural inheritance, "Expression of experience is public and communicating because the experiences expressed are what they are because of experiences of the living and the dead that have shaped them. It is not necessary that communication should be part of the deliberate intent of an artist. . . . But its function and consequence are to effect communication, and this not by external accident but from the nature he shares with others" (AE, LW 10:275). "Expression strikes below the barriers that separate human beings from one another" (AE, LW 10:277).

39. Attributed to Jonathan Culler, in Beidelman, *Moral Imagination in Kaguru Modes of Thought*, 7.

40. Letter 02991; 1917/10/10; to Edwin R. A. Seligman. The Center for Dewey Studies, Carbondale, Illinois.

41. Dewitt H. Parker, review of *Ethics, Philosophical Review* 43 (1934): 525. Reinhold Niebuhr likewise accuses Dewey of ignoring the tragic.

42. Leo Tolstoy, *The Death of Ivan Ilyich* (1886; New York: Bantam Classics, 1981), 131.

43. For an opposing view, see R. M. Hare's discussion of Archangels and Proles in *Moral Thinking* (Oxford: Oxford University Press, 1981). Nussbaum criticizes Hare in *Love's Knowledge*, 66.

44. Walter Sinnott-Armstrong, *Moral Dilemmas* (Oxford: Oxford University Press, 1989), 219, 222. Cf. Williams, *Moral Luck*.

45. "[O]nly by extracting at each present time the full meaning of each present experience are we prepared for doing the same thing in the future. This is the only preparation which in the long run amounts to anything" (EE, LW 13:29–30). Cf. John McDermott, ed., *The Philosophy of John Dewey* (Chicago: University of Chicago Press, 1981), xix.

46. Immanuel Kant, *Critique of Judgment*, trans. W. Pluhar (1790; Indianapolis: Hackett, 1987), S. 17, Ak. 231.

47. Kant, *Grounding for the Metaphysics of Morals*, 22, Ak. 411. In the *Critique of Judgment* Kant nonetheless probes theoretical links (even analogical mappings) between aesthetic and moral judgments. See Casey Haskins, "Kant and the Autonomy of Art," *Journal of Aesthetics and Art Criticism* 47, no 1. (1989): 43–54.

48. Kant, *Grounding for the Metaphysics of Morals*, 26, Ak. 416.

49. On this "aestheticist turn" in value inquiry, see Casey Haskins, "Dewey's Art As Experience: The Tension between Aesthetics and Aestheticism," *Transactions of the Charles S. Peirce Society* 28, no. 2 (1992): 217–259.

50. Dewey writes: "Construction that is artistic is as much a case of genuine thought as that expressed in scientific and philosophical matters, and so is all genuine esthetic appreciation of art, since the latter must in some way, to be vital, retrace the course of the creative process" (QT, LW 5:262).

51. Colapietro, "Art and Philosophy: A Fateful Entanglement."

52. See Jeffrey Petts's insightful article on this theme, "Aesthetic Experience and the Revelation of Value," *Journal of Aesthetics and Art Criticism* 58, no. 1 (2000): 61–71.

53. Psychologists label this the "Zeigarnik effect," named for Bluma Zeigarnik.

54. Thomas Alexander, *John Dewey's Theory of Art, Experience, and Nature*, 198.

55. Dewey's aesthetic theory primarily values those experiences that are developed toward consummation. He distinguishes this from momentary "seizures." Yet seizures—for example, being captivated by the colors of leaves in autumn—do not beg for further development. Indeed, as Santayana appreciates better than Dewey, such an attempt would destroy their aesthetic quality.

56. Kupfer, *Experience as Art*, 142.

57. Gouinlock, *Rediscovering the Moral Life*, 54. Cf. Gouinlock, *John Dewey's Philosophy of Value*.

58. For a critique of some aspects of my view, see Gregory Fahy, "Being Properly Affected: Emotion in John Dewey's Virtue Ethics," Society for the Advancement of American Philosophy, http://www.american-philosophy.org/archives/2002_Conference/2002_papers/tp-6.htm.

59. See Mead, *Mind, Self, and Society*, chs. 18–20.

60. This aspect of imagination is explored by Gadamer in *Truth and Method*. Genuine "understanding," which is the consummating phase of the "logic of question and doubt," is essentially a "fusion of horizons." In this way, past "prejudices" are transformed into new ones. See, e.g., 273–274.

61. Hickman, *John Dewey's Pragmatic Technology*, 196. Cf. Boisvert, *John Dewey*, 26.

.

BIBLIOGRAPHY

Adams, E. M. *The Metaphysics of Self and World.* Philadelphia: Temple University Press, 1991.

Addams, Jane. *Democracy and Social Ethics.* Champaign: University of Illinois Press, 2002.

Alexander, F. Matthias. *The Resurrection of the Body: The Writings of F. Matthias Alexander.* Ed. Edward Maisel. New York: Dell Publishing, 1969.

Alexander, Thomas. *John Dewey's Theory of Art, Experience, and Nature: The Horizons of Feeling.* Albany: SUNY Press, 1987.

———. "Pragmatic Imagination." *Transactions of the C. S. Peirce Society* 26, no. 3 (1990): 325–348.

———. "John Dewey and the Moral Imagination: Beyond Putnam and Rorty toward a Postmodern Ethics." *Transactions of the Charles S. Peirce Society* 29, no. 3 (1993): 369–400.

Apel, Karl-Otto. *Charles S. Peirce: From Pragmatism to Pragmaticism.* Amherst: University of Massachusetts Press, 1981.

Aristotle. *Nicomachean Ethics.* Trans. Martin Ostwald. Englewood Cliffs, N.J.: Prentice-Hall, 1962.

Armstrong, D. M. *Belief, Truth and Knowledge.* Cambridge, U.K.: Cambridge University Press, 1973.

Baier, Annette C. *A Progress of Sentiments: Reflections on Hume's Treatise.* Cambridge, Mass.: Harvard University Press, 1991.

Bain, Alexander. *The Emotions and the Will,* 4th ed. New York: D. Appleton, 1899.

Bakewell, Charles M. Review of *Pragmatism. Philosophical Review* 16, no. 3 (1907): 625.

Beidelman, T. O. *Moral Imagination in Kaguru Modes of Thought.* Bloomington: Indiana University Press, 1986.

Bellah, Robert N., et al. *Habits of the Heart: Individualism and Commitment in American Life.* 2nd ed. Berkeley: University of California Press, 1996.

Bellamy, Edward. *Looking Backward.* New York: Signet Classics, 1960.

Berlin, Isaiah. *The Crooked Timber of Humanity.* Ed. Henry Hardy. New York: Knopf, 1991.

Boisvert, Raymond. *John Dewey: Rethinking Our Time.* Albany: SUNY Press, 1998.

———. "The Nemesis of Necessity: Tragedy's Challenge to Deweyan Pragmatism." In *Dewey Reconfigured: Essays on Deweyan Pragmatism,* ed. Casey Haskins and David I. Seiple, 151–168. Albany: SUNY Press, 1999.

———. "Updating Dewey: A Reply to Morse." *Transactions of the Charles S. Peirce Society,* 37, no. 4 (2001): 573–583.

Bonner, John T. *The Evolution of Culture in Animals.* Princeton, N.J.: Princeton University Press, 1980.

Boydston, Jo Ann. "John Dewey and the Alexander Technique." Available: http://www.alexandercenter.com/jd/deweyalexanderboydston.html [December 5, 2002].

Branch, Edgar M. *James T. Farrell.* New York: Twayne Publishers, 1971.

Brent, Joseph. *Charles Sanders Peirce: A Life.* Bloomington: Indiana University Press, 1993.

Buchholz, Rogene A., and Sandra B. Rosenthal. *Business Ethics: The Pragmatic Path Beyond Principles to Process.* Upper Saddle River, N.J.: Prentice Hall, 1997.

Burke, Thomas. *Dewey's New Logic: A Reply to Russell.* Chicago: University of Chicago Press, 1994.

Calvin, John. *Institutes of the Christian Religion.* Trans. Henry Beveridge. Edinburgh: Calvin Translation Society, 1845.

Campbell, James. *Understanding John Dewey.* Chicago: Open Court, 1995.

Canada, Geoffrey. *Fist Stick Knife Gun: A Personal History of Violence in America.* Boston: Beacon Press, 1995.

Carus, Paul. *Truth on Trial.* Chicago: Open Court, 1911.

Caspary, William R. "Ethical Deliberation as Dramatic Rehearsal: John Dewey's Theory." *Educational Theory* 41, no. 2 (1991): 175–188.

Cavalieri, Paola, and Peter Singer. *The Great Ape Project.* New York: St. Martin's Press, 1993.

Chambliss, J. J. "John Dewey's Idea of Imagination in Philosophy and Education." *Journal of Aesthetic Education* 25, no. 4 (1991): 43–49.

Chisolm, Roderick. *The Foundations of Knowing.* Minneapolis: University of Minnesota Press, 1982.

Colapietro, Vincent. *Peirce's Approach to the Self.* Albany: SUNY Press, 1989.

———. *Reason, Subjectivity, and Agency: Postmodern Themes and Pragmatic Challenges.* Albany: SUNY Press, forthcoming.

Coles, Robert. *The Call of Stories: Teaching and the Moral Imagination.* Boston: Houghton Mifflin, 1989.

Copland, Aaron. *Music and Imagination.* Cambridge, Mass.: Harvard University Press, 1952.

Damasio, Antonio R. *Descartes' Error: Emotion, Reason, and the Human Brain.* New York: Avon Books, 1994.

———. *The Feeling of What Happens: Body and Emotion in the Making of Consciousness.* Fort Worth: Harcourt Brace, 1999.

Darwin, Charles. *The Origin of Species.* Vol. 11 of Harvard Classics. New York: P. F. Collier, 1909.

De Waal, Frans. *The Ape and the Sushi Master.* New York: Basic Books, 2001.

Deledalle, Gerard. *John Dewey.* Paris: Presses Universitaires de France, 1995.

Dewey, Jane M. "Biography of John Dewey." In *The Philosophy of John Dewey,* ed. Paul Arthur Schilpp and Lewis Edwin Hahn, 3–45. Chicago: Open Court, 1989.

Dewey, John. *The Collected Works of John Dewey.* Ed. Jo Ann Boydston. 37 vols. Carbondale: Southern Illinois University Press, 1969–1991. (See List of Abbreviations.)

Donagan, Alan. *The Theory of Morality.* Chicago: University of Chicago Press, 1977.

Eddy, William. *The Other Side of the World: Essays and Stories on Mind and Nature.* Lynchburg, Vt.: Stinehour Press, 2001.

Edgerton, Clyde. *Walking Across Egypt.* New York: Ballantine Books, 1987.

Eldridge, Michael. *Transforming Experience.* Nashville: Vanderbilt University Press, 1998.

———. "Dewey's Faith in Democracy as Shared Experience." *Transactions of the Charles S. Peirce Society* 32, no. 1 (1996): 11–30.

Eliot, George. *Middlemarch.* Boston: Houghton Mifflin, 1956.

Ellis, Havelock. *The Dance of Life.* Boston: Houghton Mifflin, 1923.

Emerson, Ralph Waldo. *Selected Writings of Ralph Waldo Emerson.* New York: Signet Classic, 1965.

Evans, Bill. Liner notes, Miles Davis: *Kind of Blue.* Columbia Records, 1959.

Fahy, Gregory. "Being Properly Affected: Emotion in John Dewey's Virtue Ethics." Available: http://www.american-philosophy.org/archives/2002_Conference/2002_papers/tp-6.htm [December 5, 2002].

Farrell, James T. *Studs Lonigan.* Champaign: University of Illinois Press, 1993.

————. "Memories of John Dewey by James Farrell." Interview. November 5, 1965. Morris Library, Southern Illinois University at Carbondale.

Fesmire, Steven. "Dramatic Rehearsal and the Moral Artist: A Deweyan Theory of Moral Understanding." *Transactions of the Charles S. Peirce Society* 31, no. 3 (1995): 568–597.

Fisch, Max. "Was There a Metaphysical Club in Cambridge?" In *Studies in the Philosophy of Charles Sanders Peirce: Second Series,* ed. Edward Moore and Richard Robin, 3–32. Amherst: University of Massachusetts Press, 1964.

————. "Was There a Metaphysical Club in Cambridge? A Postscript." *Transactions of the Charles S. Peirce Society* 17, no. 2 (1981): 128–130.

————. "Alexander Bain and the Genealogy of Pragmatism." In *Peirce, Semeiotic, and Pragmatism,* ed. Kenneth Ketner and Christian Kloesel, 79–109. Bloomington: Indiana University Press, 1986.

Flanagan, Owen. *Varieties of Moral Personality: Ethics and Psychological Realism.* Cambridge, Mass.: Harvard University Press, 1991.

Fogelin, Robert J. *Figuratively Speaking.* New Haven, Conn.: Yale University Press, 1988.

Fontinell, Eugene. *Self, God, and Immortality: A Jamesian Investigation.* Philadelphia: Temple University Press, 1986.

Fouts, Roger, and Stephen Tukel Mills. *Next of Kin: My Conversations with Chimpanzees.* New York: Avon Books, 1997.

Freud, Sigmund. *Beyond the Pleasure Principle.* New York: W. W. Norton, 1961.

Gadamer, Hans-Georg. *Truth and Method.* New York: Seabury Press, 1975.

Gardner, John. "Moral Fiction." In John Gardner, *On Moral Fiction,* 105–126. New York: Basic Books, 1978.

Garrison, Jim. *Dewey and Eros: Wisdom and Desire in the Art of Thinking.* New York: Teachers College Press, 1997.

Gatens-Robinson, Eugenie. "The Private and Its Problem: A Pragmatic View of Reproductive Choice." In *Dewey Reconfigured,* ed. Casey Haskins and David I. Seiple, 169–192. Albany: SUNY Press, 1999.

Gavin, William J. *William James and the Reinstatement of the Vague.* Philadelphia: Temple University Press, 1992.

Gert, Bernard. *Morality: Its Nature and Justification.* Oxford: Oxford University Press, 1998.

Gilman, Charlotte Perkins. *Herland.* New York: Dover, 1998.

Gouinlock, James. *John Dewey's Philosophy of Value.* Atlantic Highlands, N.J.: Humanities Press, 1972.

————. "Dewey's Theory of Moral Deliberation." *Ethics* 88, no. 3 (1978): 218–28.

————. *Rediscovering the Moral Life.* Buffalo, N.Y.: Prometheus, 1993.

Gould, Stephen Jay. *The Mismeasure of Man.* 2nd ed. New York: W. W. Norton, 1996.

Green, Judith. *Deep Democracy: Community, Diversity, and Transformation.* Lanham, Md.: Rowman & Littlefield, 1999.

Habermas, Jürgen. *Moral Consciousness and Communicative Action.* Cambridge, Mass.: MIT Press, 1990.

Hampshire, Stuart. *Innocence and Experience.* Cambridge, Mass.: Harvard University Press, 1989.

Hare, R. M. *Moral Thinking.* Oxford: Oxford University Press, 1981.

————. "Why I Am Only a Demi-Vegetarian." In *Singer and His Critics,* ed. Dale Jamieson, 247–268. Oxford: Blackwell, 1999.

Haskins, Casey. "Kant and the Autonomy of Art." *Journal of Aesthetics and Art Criticism* 47, no. 1 (1989): 43–54.

————. "Dewey's Art As Experience: The Tension between Aesthetics and Aestheticism." *Transactions of the Charles S. Peirce Society* 28, no. 2 (1992): 217–259.

Hester, Micah. *Community as Healing: Pragmatist Ethics in Medical Encounters.* Lanham, Md.: Rowman & Littlefield, 2001.

Hickman, Larry. *John Dewey's Pragmatic Technology.* Bloomington: Indiana University Press, 1990.

———. "Nature as Culture: John Dewey's Pragmatic Naturalism." In *Environmental Pragmatism,* ed. Andrew Light and Eric Katz, 50–72. London: Routledge, 1996.

———. "Dewey's Theory of Inquiry." In *Reading Dewey: Interpretations for a Postmodern Generation,* ed. Larry Hickman, 166–186. Bloomington: Indiana University Press, 1998.

———. "Making the Family 'Functional': The Case for Legalized Same-Sex Domestic Partnerships." *Philosophy of the Social Sciences* 29, no. 2 (1999): 231–247.

———. *Philosophical Tools for Technological Culture: Putting Pragmatism to Work.* Bloomington: Indiana University Press, 2001.

Hill, Priscilla. "Aesthetics and the Novel: A Study of the Relation of John Dewey's Philosophy and the Novels of James T. Farrell." Ph.D. diss., Southern Illinois University at Carbondale, 1986.

Hume, David. *Enquiries Concerning Human Understanding and Concerning the Principles of Morals.* 3rd ed. Oxford: Clarendon Press, 1975.

———. *A Treatise of Human Nature.* Ed. L. A. Selby-Bigge. Oxford: Clarendon Press, 1978.

Jackson. Philip W. *John Dewey and the Lessons of Art.* New Haven, Conn.: Yale University Press, 1998.

James, William. *Psychology: Briefer Course.* New York: Henry Holt, 1892.

———. *The Principles of Psychology.* 2 vols. New York: Dover, 1950.

———. *The Works of William James.* Ed. Frederick H. Burkhardt, Fredson Bowers, and Ignas K. Skrupskelis. Cambridge, Mass.: Harvard University Press, 1975–. (See List of Abbreviations.)

———. *Pragmatism.* Indianapolis: Hackett, 1981.

Johnson, Mark. "Introduction." In *Philosophical Perspectives on Metaphor,* ed. Mark Johnson, 3–47. Minneapolis: University of Minnesota Press, 1981.

———. *The Body in the Mind.* Chicago: University of Chicago Press, 1987.

———. "Knowing through the Body." *Philosophical Psychology* 4, no. 1 (1991): 3–18.

———. *Moral Imagination.* Chicago: University of Chicago Press, 1993.

———. "Ethics." In *A Companion to Cognitive Science,* ed. William Bechtel and George Graham, 691–701. Oxford: Blackwell, 1998.

Kahneman, Daniel, Paul Slovic, and Amos Tversky. *Judgment under Uncertainty: Heuristics and Biases.* New York: Cambridge University Press, 1982.

Kant, Immanuel. *Lectures on Ethics.* Trans. Louis Infield. Indianapolis: Hackett, 1979.

———. *Critique of Judgment.* Trans. W. Pluhar. Indianapolis: Hackett, 1987.

———. *Grounding for the Metaphysics of Morals.* Trans. James W. Ellington. 3rd ed. Indianapolis: Hackett, 1993.

———. "What Is Enlightenment?" In *Sources of Western Tradition,* ed. Marvin Perry, Joseph Peden, Theodore Von Laue, 54–55. 4th ed. Boston: Houghton Mifflin, 1999.

Keith, Heather. "Feminism and Pragmatism: George Herbert Mead's Ethics of Care." *Transactions of the Charles S. Peirce Society* 35, no. 2 (1999): 328–344.

Kekes, John. *The Morality of Pluralism.* Princeton, N.J.: Princeton University Press, 1993.

Kernfeld, Barry. *What to Listen For in Jazz.* New Haven, Conn.: Yale University Press, 1995.

Kestenbaum, Victor. "Preface." In *Theory of the Moral Life,* pp. xvii–xviii. New York: Irvington Publishers, 1980.

Kierkegaard, Søren. *Either/Or,* ed. and trans. Howard Hong and Edna Hong. Princeton, N.J.: Princeton University Press, 1988.

Kingsolver, Barbara. *High Tide in Tucson.* New York: Harper-Collins, 1995.

Koch, Donald F., ed. *John Dewey's Lectures on Psychological and Political Ethics: 1898.* New York: Hafner Press, 1976.

————. *John Dewey's Lectures on Ethics: 1900–1901.* Carbondale: Southern Illinois University Press, 1991.

Kochman, Thomas. *Black and White Styles in Conflict.* Chicago: University of Chicago Press, 1981.

Kulp, Christopher. *The End of Epistemology: Dewey and His Current Allies on the Spectator Theory of Knowledge.* Westport, Conn.: Greenwood Press, 1992.

Kupfer, Joseph. *Experience as Art.* Albany: SUNY Press, 1983.

Lakoff, George. *Women, Fire and Dangerous Things.* Chicago: University of Chicago Press, 1987.

————. "The Invariance Hypothesis." *Cognitive Linguistics* 1, no. 1 (1990): 40.

————. "The Contemporary Theory of Metaphor." In *Metaphor and Thought,* ed. Andrew Ortony, 2nd ed., 202–251. Cambridge, U.K.: Cambridge University Press, 1994.

————. *Moral Politics.* Chicago: University of Chicago Press, 1996.

Lakoff, George, and Mark Johnson. *Metaphors We Live By.* Chicago: University of Chicago Press, 1980.

————. *Philosophy in the Flesh: How the Embodied Mind Challenges Western Conceptions of Reason.* New York: Basic Books, 1999.

Lamont, Corliss, ed. *Dialogue on John Dewey.* New York: Horizon Press, 1959.

Larmore, Charles. "Moral Judgment." *Review of Metaphysics* 35, no. 2 (1981): 275–296.

————. *The Morals of Modernity.* Cambridge, U.K.: Cambridge University Press, 1996.

Lekan, Todd. *Making Morality: Pragmatist Reconstruction in Ethical Theory.* Nashville: Vanderbilt University Press, 2002.

Levin, Jonathan. *The Poetics of Transition: Emerson, Pragmatism, and American Literary Modernism.* Durham, N.C.: Duke University Press, 1999.

Light, Andrew, and Eric Katz, eds. *Environmental Pragmatism.* London: Routledge, 1996.

Maccoby, Eleanor, and J. A. Martin. "Socialization in the Context of the Family: Parent-Child Interaction." In *Handbook of Child Psychology,* Vol. 4: *Socialization, Personality, and Social Development,* 4th ed., ed. P. H. Mussen and E. M. Hetherington, 1–101. New York: Wiley, 1983.

McCollough, Thomas. *The Moral Imagination and Public Life: Raising the Ethical Question.* Chatham, N.J.: Chatham House Publishers, 1991.

McDermott, John J. *Streams of Experience: Reflections on the History and Philosophy of American Culture.* Amherst: University of Massachusetts Press, 1986.

————, ed. *The Writings of William James.* Chicago: University of Chicago Press, 1977.

————. *The Philosophy of John Dewey.* Chicago: University of Chicago Press, 1981.

McGee, Glenn, ed. *Pragmatist Bioethics.* Nashville: Vanderbilt University Press, 1999.

MacIntyre, Alasdair. *After Virtue.* 2nd ed. Notre Dame: University of Notre Dame Press, 1984.

————. *Whose Justice? Which Rationality?* Notre Dame: University of Notre Dame Press, 1988.

————. *Dependent Rational Animals: Why Human Beings Need the Virtues.* Chicago: Open Court Books, 2000.

McKenna, Erin. *The Task of Utopia: A Pragmatist and Feminist Perspective.* Lanham, Md.: Rowman & Littlefield, 2001.

McKenna, Erin, and Andrew Light, eds. *Animal Pragmatism.* Bloomington: Indiana University Press, forthcoming.

Makkreel, Rudolf. *Imagination and Interpretation in Kant.* Chicago: University of Chicago Press, 1990.

Martin, Mike. *Everyday Morality.* Stamford, Conn.: Wadsworth, 2001.

Mead, George Herbert. *Mind, Self, and Society.* Ed. Charles Morris. Chicago: University of Chicago Press, 1934.

————. *Selected Writings.* Ed. Andrew Reck. Chicago: University of Chicago Press, 1964.

Menand, Louis. *The Metaphysical Club: A Story of Ideas in America.* New York: Farrar, Straus and Giroux, 2001.

Merleau-Ponty, Maurice. *The Phenomenology of Perception.* Trans. Colin Smith. Atlantic Highlands, N.J.: Humanities Press, 1962.

Mill, John Stuart. *Utilitarianism.* Indianapolis: Hackett, 1979; 1861.

Moore, G. E. *Principia Ethica.* Cambridge, U.K.: Cambridge University Press, 1929.

Morse, Donald. "Pragmatism and The Tragic Sense of Life." *Transactions of the Charles S. Peirce Society* 37, no. 4 (2001): 555–572.

Moyers, Bill. *A World of Ideas.* New York: Doubleday, 1989.

———. *The Language of Life.* New York: Doubleday, 1995.

Myers, Gerald E. *William James: His Life and Thought.* New Haven, Conn.: Yale University Press, 1986.

Nietzsche, Friedrich. *On the Genealogy of Morals.* Trans. W. Kaufmann. New York: Vintage, 1989.

Noddings, Nel. *Caring: A Feminine Approach to Ethics and Moral Education.* Berkeley: University of California Press, 1984.

Nussbaum, Martha. *The Fragility of Goodness: Luck and Ethics in Greek Tragedy and Philosophy.* Cambridge, U.K.: Cambridge University Press, 1986.

———. *Love's Knowledge.* Oxford: Oxford University Press, 1990.

———. *Upheavals of Thought: The Intelligence of Emotions.* Cambridge, U.K.: Cambridge University Press, 2001.

Pappas, Gregory F. "Dewey's Moral Theory: Experience as Method." *Transactions of the Charles S. Peirce Society* 33, no. 3 (1997): 520–556.

———. "Dewey's Ethics: Morality as Experience." In *Reading Dewey,* ed. Larry Hickman, 100–123. Bloomington: Indiana University Press, 1998.

———. "The Latino Character of American Pragmatism." In *Transactions of the Charles S. Peirce Society* 34, no. 1 (1998): 93–112.

Parker, Dewitt H. Review of *Ethics. Philosophical Review* 43 (1934): 525.

Peirce, Charles S. "Letters to Lady Welby." In *Charles S. Peirce: Selected Writings,* ed. Philip Weiner, 380–432. New York: Dover, 1958.

———. *The Essential Peirce: Selected Philosophical Writings.* 2 vols. Ed. Nathan Houser and Christian Kloesel. Bloomington: Indiana University Press, 1992, 1998.

Pepper, Stephen. *World Hypotheses.* Berkeley: University of California Press, 1942.

Perry, Ralph Barton. *General Theory of Value.* New York: Longman's, Green, 1926.

Petts, Jeffrey. "Aesthetic Experience and the Revelation of Value." *Journal of Aesthetics and Art Criticism* 58, no. 1 (2000): 61–71.

Pipher, Mary. *Reviving Ophelia: Saving the Selves of Adolescent Girls.* New York: Ballantine Books, 1994.

———. *Hunger Pains: The American Woman's Tragic Quest for Thinness.* New York: Ballantine Books, 1995.

Plato. *Meno.* In *Five Dialogues,* trans. G. M. A. Grube. Indianapolis: Hackett, 1981.

———. *Republic.* Trans. G. M. A. Grube. Indianapolis: Hackett, 1992.

———. *Statesman.* Trans. J. B. Skemp. Indianapolis: Hackett, 1992.

Putnam, Hilary. *The Many Faces of Realism.* Chicago: Open Court, 1987.

Quine, Willard V. *Word and Object.* Cambridge, Mass.: MIT Press, 1960.

Quinn, Naomi. "Convergent Evidence for a Cultural Model of American Marriage." In *Cultural Models In Language and Thought,* ed. Dorothy Holland and Naomi Quinn, 173–192. Cambridge, U.K.: Cambridge University Press, 1987.

Rahula, Walpola. *What the Buddha Taught.* New York: Grove Weidenfeld, 1974.

Rawls, John. *A Theory of Justice.* Cambridge, Mass.: Harvard University Press, 1971.

———. *Justice as Fairness: A Restatement.* Ed. Erin Kelly. Cambridge, Mass.: Belknap Press, 2001.

Reichling, Mary. "Dewey, Imagination, and Music: A Fugue on Three Subjects." *Journal of Aesthetic Education* 25, no. 3 (1991): 61–78.

Ricoeur, Paul. *Time and Narrative.* Trans. K. McLaughlin and D. Pellauer. Chicago: University of Chicago Press, 1984.

Rorty, Richard. *Philosophy and the Mirror of Nature.* Princeton, N.J.: Princeton University Press, 1979.

———. *Consequences of Pragmatism.* Minneapolis: University of Minnesota Press, 1982.

Sacks, Oliver. *An Anthropologist on Mars.* New York: Alfred A. Knopf, 1995.

Sagan, Carl. *The Demon-Haunted World.* New York: Random House, 1995.

Santayana, George. *Scepticism and Animal Faith.* New York: Dover, 1955.

Schlosser, Eric. *Fast Food Nation.* New York: Houghton Mifflin, 2001.

Searle, John. *Expression and Meaning.* Cambridge, U.K.: Cambridge University Press, 1979.

———. *Intentionality.* Cambridge, U.K.: Cambridge University Press, 1983.

Seigfried, Charlene Haddock. *William James's Radical Reconstruction of Philosophy.* Albany: SUNY Press, 1990.

———. *Pragmatism and Feminism.* Chicago: University of Chicago Press, 1996.

———. "Introduction." In Jane Addams, *Democracy and Social Ethics,* ix–xxxviii. Champaign: University of Illinois Press, 2002.

Shakespeare, William. *As You Like It.* In *The Riverside Shakespeare,* ed. G. Blakemore Evans. Boston: Houghton-Mifflin, 1974.

Shermer, Michael. *Why People Believe Weird Things.* New York: W. H. Freeman, 1997.

Shook, John. *Dewey's Empirical Theory of Knowledge and Reality.* Nashville: Vanderbilt University Press, 2000.

Shusterman, Richard. *Pragmatist Aesthetics: Living Beauty, Rethinking Art.* 2nd ed. Oxford: Blackwell, 2000.

Singer, Peter. *Ethics into Action.* Lanham, Md.: Rowman & Littlefield, 1998.

Sinnott-Armstrong, Walter. *Moral Dilemmas.* Oxford: Oxford University Press, 1989.

Skinner, B. F. *The Behavior of Organisms.* New York: D. Appleton-Century, 1938.

———. *Walden Two.* New York: Macmillan, 1976.

Sleeper, Ralph. *The Necessity of Pragmatism.* New Haven, Conn.: Yale University Press, 1986.

Sontag, Susan. *Illness as Metaphor* and *AIDS and Its Metaphors.* New York: Doubleday, 1990.

Stern, Daniel. *The Interpersonal World of the Infant.* New York: Basic Books, 1985.

Stevens, Wallace. *Collected Poetry and Prose.* Ed. Frank Kermode and Joan Richardson. New York: Library of America, 1997.

Stevenson, Charles L. *Ethics and Language.* New Haven, Conn.: Yale University Press, 1944.

Sullivan, Shannon. *Living Across and Through Skins: Transactional Bodies, Pragmatism, and Feminism.* Bloomington: Indiana University Press, 2001.

Taylor, Charles. "The Diversity of Goods." In *Utilitarianism and Beyond,* ed. Bernard Williams and Amartya Sen, 129–144. Cambridge, U.K.: Cambridge University Press, 1982.

———. "Overcoming Epistemology." In *Philosophical Arguments,* 1–19. Cambridge, Mass.: Harvard University Press, 1995.

Taylor, Eugene, and Robert H. Wozniak. *Pure Experience: The Response to William James.* Bristol: Thoemmes Press, 1996.

Thompson, E. *Colour Vision: A Study in Cognitive Science and the Philosophy of Perception.* London: Routledge, 1995.

Tiles, J. E. *Dewey.* London: Routledge, 1988.

Tivnan, Edward. *The Moral Imagination: Confronting the Ethical Issues of Our Day.* New York: Simon & Schuster, 1995.

Tolstoy, Leo. *The Death of Ivan Ilyich.* New York: Bantam Classics, 1981.

Trilling, Lionel. *The Liberal Imagination.* New York: Charles Scribners, 1950.

Tuan, Yi-Fu. *Morality and Imagination: Paradoxes of Progress.* Madison: University of Wisconsin Press, 1989.

Varela, Francisco, Evan Thompson, and Eleanor Rosch. *The Embodied Mind.* Cambridge, Mass.: MIT Press, 1991.

Varner, Gary E. *In Nature's Interests?* Oxford: Oxford University Press, 1998.

Warnock, Mary. *Imagination.* Berkeley: University of California Press, 1976.

———. *Imagination and Time.* Oxford: Blackwell, 1994.

———. *An Intelligent Person's Guide to Ethics.* London: Gerald Duckworth, 1998.

Watson, John B. *Psychology from the Standpoint of a Behaviorist.* 2nd ed. Philadelphia: J. B. Lippincott, 1924.

Watterson, Bill. *The Calvin and Hobbes Tenth Anniversary Book.* Kansas City, Mo.: Andrews & McMeel, 1995.

Welchman, Jennifer. *Dewey's Ethical Thought.* Ithaca, N.Y.: Cornell University Press, 1995.

Werhane, Patricia. *Moral Imagination and Management Decision-Making.* Oxford: Oxford University Press, 1999.

West, Cornel. *Race Matters.* New York: Vintage Books, 1994.

Westbrook, Robert B. *John Dewey and American Democracy.* Ithaca: Cornell University Press, 1991.

Whitehead, Alfred North. *Science and the Modern World.* New York: Macmillan, 1953.

Williams, Bernard. *Moral Luck.* Cambridge, U.K.: Cambridge University Press, 1981.

———. *Ethics and the Limits of Philosophy.* Cambridge, Mass.: Harvard University Press, 1985.

Williams, Oliver, S.J., ed., *The Moral Imagination: How Literature and Films Can Stimulate Ethical Reflection in the Business World.* Notre Dame: University of Notre Dame Press, 1997.

INDEX

logical positivism, 45
Looking Backward (Bellamy), 104
Love's Knowledge (Nussbaum), 92–93, 107
Luther, Martin, 15, 32

Machiavelli, Niccolò, 99
McCollough, Thomas, 63, 117
McDermott, John, 9, 21, 47
MacIntyre, Alasdair, 1, 38, 51, 140n2; on deliberation, 79; on rule-governed ethics, 56; stage metaphor and, 111
McKenna, Erin, 148n40
male dominance, 25
Malebranche, Nicolas de, 41
Marx, Karl, 25
masculinity, 16, 21, 34, 51, 105
mass culture, 10
Mead, George Herbert, 11, 12, 22, 50, 66; on self and other, 128; social interaction and, 81; theory of the self, 96, 146n11
means-end reasoning, 49, 80
Meldon, A. I., 56
Menand, Louis, 31, 135n14
Meno (Plato), 27
Merleau-Ponty, Maurice, 10, 44, 45, 138n22
metaethics, 4, 57
"Metaphor" (Searle), 112
metaphors, 82–91, 119, 128
Metaphors We Live By (Lakoff and Johnson), 110
The Metaphysical Club (Menand), 31
metaphysics, 39, 57
Middlemarch (Eliot), 86
Mill, John Stuart, 30, 57, 99, 114
mind, 9, 10, 11, 45–46, 66, 83
Mingus, Charles, 96
Moore, G. E., 75, 77–78, 115
moral accounting (metaphor), 109–110
moral agency, 72, 95, 110, 118
Moral Dilemmas (Sinnott-Armstrong), 121
moral education, 5, 29
"The Moral Equivalent of War" (James), 24
"moral images," 89, 108
Moral Imagination (Johnson), 63, 86
The Moral Imagination (Williams), 62
The Moral Imagination and Public Life (McCollough), 63, 117
"The Moral Philosopher and the Moral Life" (James), 101–102

morality, 27, 32, 46, 55; as art, 90; autism and, 72; intelligence and, 56; moral conduct as art, 107–19
The Morality of Pluralism (Kekes), 63, 97
multicultural society, 11
Murray, Charles, 25
music, 94–95, 107
Mussolini, Benito, 43, 137n15

Napoleon, 127
Nash equilibrium, 29, 125
naturalistic fallacy, 75
nature, 88, 89, 90; and nurture, 22–26
neopragmatism, 42, 63
Niebuhr, Reinhold, 101, 105
Nietzsche, Friedrich, 23, 24, 39, 48–49, 134n45
Noddings, Nel, 1, 56, 105
Nussbaum, Martha, 1, 49, 92–93; Aristotelian practical wisdom and, 113–14; on improvisational morality, 111–12; on jazz metaphor, 96; on moral failing, 107

objectivity, 48–49, 145n46
"On a Certain Blindness in Human Beings" (James), 102
On the Origin of Species (Darwin), 88
On the Revolution of Heavenly Bodies (Copernicus), 32
operant behavior, 14

Pappas, Gregory, 131n4, 137n13, 145–46n1
Parker, Dewitt H., 120, 121
patriarchy, 25
Peirce, Charles S., 30, 31–33, 36, 44, 50; "abductive inference" theory, 65, 76; belief-doubt-inquiry sequence and, 74, 135nn15,16, 136n24; on habits, 15–16, 31; on imagination, 64; pragmatism of, 31
Pepper, Stephen, 50–51
perceptiveness, 113–16
Pericles, 114
Perry, Ralph Barton, 102
perspectivism, 48–49
phenomenologists, 41, 43, 44
The Phenomenology of Perception (Merleau-Ponty), 10
Philosopher's Index, 2
Philosopher's Quest (Edman), 46
Philosophy in the Flesh (Lakoff and Johnson), 82, 85

Steven Fesmire teaches philosophy
and is Chair of Environmental Studies at
Green Mountain College in Vermont.